Constructing Brexit Britain

Corpus and Discourse

Series Editors: Michaela Mahlberg (University of Birmingham, UK) and Gavin Brookes (Lancaster University, UK)

Consulting Editor: Wolfgang Teubert (University of Birmingham, UK)

Editorial Board

Paul Baker, Lancaster University, UK
Frantisek Cermák, Charles University, Prague
Susan Conrad, Portland State University, USA
Matteo Fuoli, University of Birmingham, UK
Maristella Gatto, University of Bari, Italy
Dominique Maingueneau, Université de Paris XII, France
Christian Mair, University of Freiburg, Germany
Alan Partington, University of Bologna, Italy
Charlotte Taylor, University of Sussex, UK
Elena Tognini-Bonelli, University of Siena, Italy
Ruth Wodak, Lancaster University, UK
Ruihua Zhang, Tianjin University of Science and Technology, China
Feng Zhiwei, Institute of Applied Linguistics, Beijing, China

Language is ubiquitous. As never before, it is now commonly understood how crucial language is for human interaction, for negotiating and shaping our material and ideational reality. In the digital age, the speed, scale and diversity of forms of communication and language use have grown rapidly. The increasing amount of language data that influences attitudes, decision-making and relationships highlights how the methodology of corpus linguistics together with the explanatory power of discourse analysis are indispensable for deciphering the world around us.

Situated at the interface of corpus linguistics and discourse studies, the *Corpus and Discourse* series publishes innovative research where humanities and social sciences come together to understand the relationship between discourse and society in an increasingly digital world.

Titles in the Series:

Academic Vocabulary in Learner Writing, Magali Paquot
Children's Literature and Childhood Discourses, edited by Anna Cermakova and Michaela Mahlberg

Contrastive Corpus Linguistics, edited by Anna Cermakova, Hilde Hasselgård and Markéta Malá
Corpus Approaches to the Language of Sports, edited by Marcus Callies and Magnus Levin
Corpus-Based Approaches to English Language Teaching, edited by Mari Carmen Campoy, Begona Belles-Fortuno and Maria Lluisa Gea-Valor
Corpus, Discourse and Mental Health, Daniel Hunt and Gavin Brookes
Corpus Linguistics and 17th-Century Prostitution, Anthony McEnery and Helen Baker
Corpus Linguistics and World Englishes, Vivian de Klerk
Corpus Linguistics in Literary Analysis, Bettina Fischer-Starcke
Corpus Stylistics in Heart of Darkness *and its Italian Translations*, Lorenzo Mastropierro
The Discursive Construction of Economic Inequality, edited by Eva M. Gomez-Jimenez and Michael Toolan
Evaluation and Stance in War News, edited by Louann Haarman and Linda Lombardo
Historical Corpus Stylistics, Patrick Studer
Investigating Adolescent Health Communication, Kevin Harvey
Keywords in the Press, Lesley Jeffries and Brian Walker
Learner Corpus Research, Vaclav Brezina and Lynne Flowerdew
Multimodality and Active Listenership, Dawn Knight
New Trends in Corpora and Language Learning, edited by Ana Frankenberg-Garcia, Guy Aston and Lynne Flowerdew
The Prosody of Formulaic Sequences, Phoebe Lin
Representation of the British Suffrage Movement, Kat Gupta
Rethinking Idiomaticity, Stefanie Wulff
Sadness Expressions in English and Chinese, Ruihua Zhang
Web As Corpus, Maristella Gatto

Constructing Brexit Britain

A Corpus-Assisted Approach to National Identity Discourse

Tamsin Parnell

BLOOMSBURY ACADEMIC
LONDON • NEW YORK • OXFORD • NEW DELHI • SYDNEY

BLOOMSBURY ACADEMIC

Bloomsbury Publishing Plc, 50 Bedford Square, London, WC1B 3DP, UK
Bloomsbury Publishing Inc, 1359 Broadway, New York, NY 10018, USA
Bloomsbury Publishing Ireland, 29 Earlsfort Terrace, Dublin 2, D02 AY28, Ireland

BLOOMSBURY, BLOOMSBURY ACADEMIC and the Diana logo are trademarks of Bloomsbury Publishing Plc

First published in Great Britain 2024
Paperback edition published 2026

Copyright © Tasmin Parnell 2024, 2026

Tamsin Parnell has asserted her right under the Copyright, Designs and Patents Act, 1988, to be identified as Author of this work.

For legal purposes the Acknowledgements on p. xii constitute an extension of this copyright page.

Cover design: Jade Barnett
Cover image © KTSDESIGN / SCIENCE PHOTO LIBRARY / Getty Images

All rights reserved. No part of this publication may be: i) reproduced or transmitted in any form, electronic or mechanical, including photocopying, recording or by means of any information storage or retrieval system without prior permission in writing from the publishers; or ii) used or reproduced in any way for the training, development or operation of artificial intelligence (AI) technologies, including generative AI technologies. The rights holders expressly reserve this publication from the text and data mining exception as per Article 4(3) of the Digital Single Market Directive (EU) 2019/790.

Bloomsbury Publishing Plc does not have any control over, or responsibility for, any third-party websites referred to or in this book. All internet addresses given in this book were correct at the time of going to press. The author and publisher regret any inconvenience caused if addresses have changed or sites have ceased to exist, but can accept no responsibility for any such changes.

A catalogue record for this book is available from the British Library.

A catalog record for this book is available from the Library of Congress.

ISBN: HB: 978-1-3504-3694-7
PB: 978-1-3504-3725-8
ePDF: 978-1-3504-3695-4
eBook: 978-1-3504-3696-1

Series: Corpus and Discourse

Typeset by Deanta Global Publishing Services, Chennai, India

For product safety related questions contact productsafety@bloomsbury.com.

To find out more about our authors and books visit www.bloomsbury.com and sign up for our newsletters.

For mum

Contents

List of Figures	x
List of Tables	xi
Acknowledgements	xii
Transcription Conventions	xiii

1	Introduction	1
2	The Discursive Construction of Britishness and Europeanness	23
3	Researching the Language of National Identity in Times of Brexit	41
4	Pro-Brexit Newspaper Representations of the UK and EU-rope	69
5	Constructing Britain and Europe in UK Government Documents	107
6	Discursive Constructions of Britain and Britishness in Oral Interviews	133
7	Concluding Remarks	167

Notes	191
References	193
Appendix A: Media Corpora Composition	219
Appendix B: Interview Plan	221
Index	226

Figures

3.1	Distribution of articles per month	46
3.2	Methodological processes	59
4.1	British way of life theme per 100,000 words	70
4.2	Politeness as a British value theme per 100,000 words	81
4.3	Distribution of themes per 100,000 words	86
5.1	British life after Brexit and shared experience themes per 100,000 words	109
5.2	Normalized frequencies of relationship-based terms per 100,000 words	122

Tables

3.1	Breakdown of annual subcorpora into months, articles, words, and political events	47
3.2	Breakdown of text types in the government corpus	51
3.3	Breakdown of annual government subcorpora	52
3.4	Participant demographics for interviews	56
3.5	Typology of story type	65
4.1	Statistical information about the 'Alive' semantic domain	70
4.2	Statistical information about the Polite semantic domain	80
4.3	Statistical information about the No Respect semantic domain	85
4.4	The four key themes in the No Respect semantic domain	85
5.1	Statistical information about the 'Alive' semantic domain in the government subcorpora	108
5.2	Statistical information for Personal Relationship: General domain	121
A.1	Composition of overall media corpus	219
A.2	Composition of media corpus	220

Acknowledgements

This book started life as a doctoral thesis at the University of Nottingham. I received funding from Midlands4Cities for the project; without this financial support, I would not have been able to undertake a PhD. I am grateful to staff in the School of English at the University of Nottingham for creating a welcoming academic community that enabled me to thrive. Every lecture and seminar, from Old English classes to discussions of Romantic period literature, inspired me and cultivated my love for English Studies.

I could not have been blessed with a better, more understanding supervisory team during my PhD. Thanks are due to Dr Kevin Harvey, who made supervisions such a joy with his humour, warmth and kindness, and Dr Daniel Hunt, whose patience and support have guided me since my undergraduate days.

My family and my fiancé have been a source of never-wavering support throughout my career so far. I am especially grateful to my mum, Kerry, to whom this book is dedicated, for the sacrifices she has made to enable me to do what I love. I am also grateful to my fiancé, Connor, for reminding me how important it is to have a work–life balance. Finally, I would like to thank my feline companions – Daisy, Willow and Jasmine – who have powered this research through their purrs.

Transcription Conventions

( ) Paralinguistic features such as laughter
(.) Indicates a pause that is less than 1.0 second
: Marks an extension of the sound it follows
^ Marks rising (upward) intonation
<u>underlining</u> Indicates emphasis
CAPITALS Indicate speech that is louder than the surrounding talk

1

Introduction

At the time of writing (October 2023), seven years have passed since the United Kingdom (UK) voted to leave the European Union (EU). During that period, no less than five Conservative MPs have served as British prime minister (with one, Liz Truss, lasting only forty-nine days in office). The world has faced a global health crisis, and rising living costs across Britain have led to the claim that we are experiencing a cost-of-living crisis. In these turbulent times, the word 'Brexit'[1] has never been far from the minds of politicians, journalists, academics and citizens, all of whom have tried to make sense of Britain's departure from the EU. This book shares the aim of trying to make sense of Brexit. It asks how this unprecedented political process has affected discourses of British (and necessarily) European identities in the UK. To do so, it examines the language used to write and talk about the UK and Europe in pro-Brexit newspapers, government documents and interviews with citizens living in Nottinghamshire. Specifically, the book traces shifting representations of British and European identities as the Brexit process extends. It explores the relationship between identity representations and their socio-political contexts, considering their potential democratic consequences. The book argues that Brexit is a site of discursive contestation within which debates play out about who 'we' are and who 'they' are. In other words, it provides evidence that understandings of national identities in the UK are 'part of the story of Brexit' (Ashcroft and Bevir, 2016: 356). To begin, the book examines the contextual background to Brexit: Where are we now, and how did we get here? This information, which constitutes a timeline and contextual point of reference for readers, is paramount for understanding the texts and surrounding contexts that will be analysed later in the book.

The road to Brexit

In 2016, the Vote Leave campaign stated that the UK would 'lose out hugely' in the next EU treaty. It claimed that 'we will lose even more control and money and our public services like the NHS will be under even more strain. The Eurocrats are just waiting to get our referendum out of the way before pushing ahead with the new treaty to take even more money and power' (Vote Leave, 2016: n.p.). This quote presents common criticisms levelled by the official Vote Leave campaign at the EU: it was power-hungry and cost the UK too much money. It is important to recognize that these criticisms were not new. Eurosceptic[2] sentiments circulated when the UK joined the Common Market in 1973 and were present in 1975 when Labour leader Harold Wilson held the first referendum on whether the UK should stay in the then European Community. They persisted in 1988 when then British prime minister Margaret Thatcher delivered her Bruges speech, warning of a 'super-state exercising a new dominance from Brussels' (Thatcher, 1988: n.p.). In fact, as Spiering (2014: 2) notes, the UK has 'always' shown reservations about post-war European integration, such that George (1990) labelled the UK as the EU's 'awkward partner'. Nevertheless, the Brexit 'conjuncture' can be traced back to the early 2010s, a period characterized by, inter alia, 'polarization within the nation's social and political fabric, empowerment of populist and anti-immigrant voices in public discourse' and socio-economic inequalities driven by austerity policies (Mintchev, 2021: 124). In this period, there was growing public support for the Eurosceptic United Kingdom Independence Party (UKIP) which caused divisions in the Conservative Party. Among other factors, these divisions led David Cameron to announce his intention to hold a second referendum on the UK's EU membership if the Conservatives won the 2015 election.[3] After his party was re-elected, Cameron fulfilled his promise.

On 22 February 2016, Cameron announced the date for the EU referendum to the House of Commons. The public would vote on 23 June of that year. Before this announcement, he had been engaged in renegotiations with the EU to reach a more favourable deal for the UK that would allow it to remain part of the Union. The renegotiated deal was criticized for failing to secure the concessions Cameron had demanded, particularly in limiting free movement (Glencross, 2016). In the following months, political campaigns vied for public attention and support. Britain Stronger in Europe, the official Remain campaign group supported by David Cameron, sought to persuade voters to remain in the EU based largely on the claim that it would be better for the British economy (Zappettini, 2019). Meanwhile, the official Vote Leave campaign, spearheaded by Conservative MPs

Michael Gove and Boris Johnson, and Labour MP Gisela Stuart, told the public that leaving the EU would save the UK £350 million a week, ensure the country had control over its borders and allow the UK to produce and apply its own laws (Vote Leave, 2016). Those who supported remaining in the EU accused Leavers of lying about the money the UK would save by leaving. This accusation was later supported by the independent fact-checker Full Fact, which concluded that the £350 million figure was incorrect (Full Fact, 2017). Those who wanted to leave accused Remainers of embarking on 'Project Fear' by catastrophizing the effects of withdrawing the UK's membership (see, e.g., Habib, 2019; Elphicke, 2019). After weeks of intense campaigning, Britons went to the polls.

The UK voted to leave the EU by 51.89 per cent to 48.11 per cent on 23 June 2016, but these figures mask the 'deep disunity among citizens' (Wincott, 2019: 15) across the UK's constituent countries. In short, while Wales and England voted to leave, Scotland and Northern Ireland opted to remain. Remain votes were particularly prominent in London (BBC, 2021a). In terms of regions, the West Midlands had the 'highest vote share for Leave', followed closely by the East Midlands (BBC, 2021a: n.p.). As the UK began a period of negotiations to consolidate a process that had yet to be attempted by any country, then first minister of Scotland, Nicola Sturgeon, declared that Brexit could precipitate another Scottish independence referendum (BBC, 2016a).

As a result of the EU referendum, David Cameron resigned, contrary to his promise to remain in office. Standing outside 10 Downing Street, he declared that the UK needed 'fresh leadership' to guide it through its withdrawal from the EU (BBC, 2016b: n.p.). He was succeeded in July 2016 by Conservative MP and former home secretary Theresa May. May wrote to the European Council president Donald Tusk on 29 March 2017 to trigger Article 50 – the legal mechanism for leaving the EU – setting in motion the UK's withdrawal. To secure a stronger mandate for her Brexit plans, she called a general election on 18 April 2017, with the date set for 8 June. Expecting a majority, May's hopes were dashed when the election resulted in a hung Parliament (i.e. no political party won a majority) just two weeks before the first round of UK–EU negotiations began.

The first UK–EU negotiation took place on 19 June 2017. Over the next year, the UK and the EU would meet countless times to discuss the terms of Britain's withdrawal, with both sides releasing statements after each round. On 26 June 2018, the European Union (Withdrawal) Bill received Royal Assent and became an Act of Parliament. Although this gave the illusion that progress was being made, there was internal division over the UK's approach to negotiations. On 9 July 2018, Brexit secretary David Davis resigned, telling BBC journalists he felt the UK was 'giving away too much and too easily' to the EU (Walker, 2021: 32; BBC, 2018a). Conservative MP Dominic Raab took his place on the same day. However, Raab's tenure was to last only four months: he resigned in November, a day after the publication of the Withdrawal Agreement that May had negotiated and published with EU leaders. Raab stated that he opposed May's deal. Several other ministers, including the then junior Brexit minister Suella Braverman, resigned alongside him.

In January 2019, May's plans were set back further by an amendment which meant that if the government lost a meaningful vote on her Withdrawal Agreement in mid-January, she would have to present an alternative 'Plan B' deal within three days. (A meaningful vote is a unique parliamentary vote that offers Parliament a more 'proactive' role than it typically would have in ratifying international agreements (UK Parliament, 2018: n.p.).). When the meaningful vote on May's deal took place, the government suffered a substantial defeat, losing by a majority of 230. She presented her 'Plan B' Brexit deal to the House of Commons on 21 January 2019, outlining six key issues that were at the centre of cross-party talks about the UK's withdrawal. These issues included concerns about the possibility of leaving without a deal, a second referendum, the Northern Ireland backstop and the political declaration. A second meaningful vote took place on 12 March. The government once again lost; a majority of 149 voted against the deal. As Parliament did not support May's deal, an extension to the withdrawal process became inevitable.

The first extension was announced on 15 March 2019. A day later, May wrote in the *Sunday Telegraph* that it would be patriotic for MPs to vote in favour of her Brexit deal. Despite her pleas for patriotism, the prime minister wrote to request an extension to the Article 50 period until 30 June 2019. On 21 March, after 8 hours of talks, the European Council agreed to an extension until 22 May 2019 if the Withdrawal Agreement was approved by MPs in a week, or 12 April 2019 with further indications of a way forward if the agreement was rejected. As the deal was rejected, 12 April became the new exit day. The second extension to the withdrawal process came on 5 April, when May asked Donald Tusk to move the exit day to 30 June 2019. The UK and EU27 agreed that an extension of Article 50 would last until 30 October 2019, with the possibility of an earlier withdrawal if both sides ratified an agreement before then. With this extension guaranteed, Theresa May announced her resignation. In her departing speech, she told the public that it would 'always remain a matter of deep regret' to her that she had 'not been able to deliver Brexit' (Walker, 2021: 60). After winning the Conservative Party leadership race, former foreign secretary Boris

Johnson became the UK's third prime minister since the EU referendum had been announced.

Johnson faced a range of challenges on the road to delivering Brexit. One significant challenge was Labour MP Hilary Benn's Bill, presented with support from other politicians on 2 September 2019. The bill established two deadlines. It set 19 October 2019 as the date by which Johnson would have to pass a Withdrawal Agreement, convince MPs to agree to a no-deal Brexit or request yet another extension from the EU. If the latter became a reality, the proposed deadline for leaving the EU would be 31 January 2020.

On 9 September, the Benn Act became law. The same day, Boris Johnson officially prorogued Parliament. The prorogation was intended to last until the state opening of Parliament on 14 October 2019. However, just two days after Parliament prorogued, the Court of Session in Scotland ruled that the prime minister's decision to suspend Parliament was unlawful. On 17 September, the Supreme Court in London began a three-day hearing into a case brought by activist Gina Miller, who argued that the suspension of Parliament in the current uncertain climate was an 'unlawful abuse of power' (Walker, 2021: 66). A week later, the Supreme Court justices passed a unanimous judgement that the decision to advise Queen Elizabeth II to prorogue Parliament was unlawful because it frustrated Parliament's ability to 'carry out its constitutional functions without reasonable justification' (Walker, 2021: 67). Although Boris Johnson condemned the judgement, Parliament sat again the next day.

Following the prorogation controversy, Independent MP Sir Oliver Letwin filed an amendment to withhold MPs' approval of Johnson's Brexit deal until the legislation to enact it was passed. This amendment would automatically trigger the Benn Act, forcing the prime minister to request an extension of Brexit until 31 January 2020. On 19 October 2019, the deadline that the Benn Act had established, the Letwin amendment passed by 322 votes to 306. The same day, the prime minister wrote to Donald Tusk to formally ask for an extension. He made clear that his correspondence was a legal formality and that he did not want an extension. To illustrate his discontent, he did not sign the photocopy of the request he was obliged to send and included a personal letter to Tusk explaining why he did not want to extend Article 50. Nevertheless, on 28 October, the European Council announced that an extension until 31 January 2020 had been granted.

Johnson held a general election on 12 December 2019. Unlike the previous election, the Conservative Party won a significant majority (365 seats), giving Johnson a mandate for his Brexit deal. Over the next month, his deal was debated in both the House of Commons and the House of Lords. Amendments were accepted, and the European Union (Withdrawal Agreement) Bill became an Act on 23 January 2020. The act was the legislation that would implement the agreement negotiated by the UK and the EU. Accordingly, on 31 January 2020 at 11.00 pm, Britain officially left the EU and entered a transition phase, which ended on 1 January 2021. The effects of Brexit did not end there; since exit day, there have been stumbling blocks between the UK and the EU in negotiating a trade deal (BBC, 2020) and in making Coronavirus vaccines available (BBC, 2021b). There will undoubtedly be further challenges and transitions as the UK and the EU navigate their new relationship. However, it is important to recognize that some challenges facing the UK–EU relationship appear to be dissipating: former Scottish first minister Nicola Sturgeon has resigned, backgrounding the case for Scottish independence, and the UK has, as of January 2024, rejoined the EU Horizon programme.

Discourse

Rooted in the context outlined above, this book is concerned with representations of British and European identities as they feature in *discourse*. The term 'discourse' is conceptually fuzzy (van Dijk, 1997) and can be confusing, largely because it is used to refer to different ideas across disciplines. Burr (2015: 74–75) offers an accessible definition of discourse which I follow: 'a set of meanings, metaphors, representations, images, stories, statements and so on that in some way together produce a particular version of events'. As Fairclough (2003, 2011) argues, producers of discourse depict the material, mental and social worlds from a particular ideological perspective. Each discourse constitutes only one 'particular version' of the world; competing discourses produce divergent representations of processes, objects and identities (Burr, 2015: 32). Brexit is one example of a process subjected to various representations: it is a site of discursive contestation whereby discourse producers within and outside of the UK construct different images of Britain and its withdrawal from the EU (Adler-Nissen et al., 2017).[4]

In discourse analytical studies, 'discourse' has a secondary meaning; it refers to the language associated with a particular text genre, such as newspaper articles or political speeches (Fairclough, 2011; Partington et al., 2013). Newspaper articles are a type of media discourse, which is a manufactured interaction that is broadcast and oriented to typically non-present readers or viewers on a mass scale (O'Keeffe, 2012). Political speeches are part of political discourse. A broad definition of political discourse would include the text and talk of all people involved in political processes when their talk relates to political actions, such as legislating, protesting or voting (van Dijk, 1997). As this definition highlights, context is integral to identifying discourses: the text and talk of politicians only constitute political discourse if they relate to the domain of politics. The definition also recognizes that discourses are language-in-action (Gee, 2001). That is, discourses go beyond the language as a static element of a text, to incorporate the ways in which 'semiotic instruments are actually deployed' and work together to produce meaning in society (Blommaert, 2005: 3). In this book, both the primary and secondary meanings of 'discourse' are applied; context differentiates between the two uses.

Discourse is inextricably linked to power (Fairclough, 2015). Fairclough (2015) distinguishes between power *in* discourse and power *behind* discourse. Power in discourse refers to the 'exercise of power in unequal encounters', whereas power behind discourse is the ability to 'shape and constitute "orders of discourse" or what discourses and genres are available' (Fairclough, 2015: 27). Power relations in discourse are not always explicit; in fact, they are very often hidden and naturalized (Fairclough, 2010). For example, media discourse producers, including journalists and editors of newspaper articles, exercise power over their readers by deciding what should be included in or excluded from news articles, how events and people should be represented and which ideological position should be presupposed for the audience (Fairclough, 1989). In the case of editors excluding news, their power corresponds to a disproportionate access to information that, if presented to readers, could lead them to take a different view of current affairs. Given this dialectic of discourse and power, critical studies of discourse are concerned with deconstructing how language is used, either explicitly or implicitly, by socially powerful institutions to influence the beliefs and behaviours of individuals and groups (Fairclough, 2015; Partington et al., 2013). In this book, I am interested in critically deconstructing how people and institutions use language to create specific versions of (supra)national identities and who they include in or exclude from these collectives.

An important concept in studies of discourse and power is recontextualization. Producing discourse often involves recontextualizing an argument, discursive practice or social practice by extracting it from its original context ('decontextualizing' it) and placing it in a new context (van Leeuwen and Wodak, 1999). Recontextualization is an intrinsically ideological process, as one group appropriates a particular discourse from another group whose ideologies and intentions are often different (Fairclough, 2011). As Krzyżanowski (2016: 314) notes, 'some discourses not only recontextualize parts of the other, but also become tools in the process of creating and sustaining the hegemony of certain discursive frames'. In other words, recontextualization can be understood as 'the semiotic relation of hegemony between discourses' as well as 'a tool whereby some social actors can achieve hegemony through the reordering of discourses, the resemioticization of meanings, the colonization of practices, and the closure of voices' (Zappettini and Unerman, 2016: 524). Linell (2009) acknowledges that recontextualization can occur within the same text or conversation (intratextuality). Texts can also reuse elements from other texts or discourses (Semino et al., 2013), a practice referred to as intertextuality.

Corpus linguistics, critical discourse analysis (CDA) and narratives

To examine how powerful institutions imagine (supra)national identities in the Brexit context, including their recontextualization patterns, I employ a combination of corpus linguistics and CDA. Corpus linguistics is the study of naturally occurring language use; it involves analysing texts that are stored in a large, electronic database called a 'corpus' (Baker, 2006). As the texts in a corpus are electronically encoded, they can be subjected to complex calculations that reveal patterns in language use within and across different documents (Baker, 2006). In contrast, CDA is an analytical practice that investigates how social inequality is represented, constructed and legitimized both explicitly and implicitly in discourse (Wodak, 2001; van Dijk, 2015). It is concerned with the interplay between relationships of power, discrimination, history and ideology[5] as they are constructed in language and social practice (Wodak, 2001). CDA is 'committed to political intervention and social change' (Machin and Mayr, 2012: 4). The adjective 'critical' alludes to the intention to denaturalize language to reveal taken-for-granted assumptions (Machin and Mayr, 2012), and to take an explicitly political stance on the data (Wodak, 2001). It also reflects the role of CDA in asking *how* and *why* discourse works in a particular way (Fairclough, 2015).

CDA studies share three underlying assertions: that 'discourse is structured by dominance', that every discourse is 'situated in time and space' and that powerful groups, such as politicians and news organizations, legitimate dominance structures through their ideologies (Wodak, 2001: 3). At the core of these three principles is an interest in the roles of context and power. Given the interest in power and dominance that underpins CDA, the analytical focus is typically on institutional discourses or language produced by people with socio-political power, such as political and media actors.

Although different CDA scholars take distinct approaches (e.g. Faircloughian CDA and Wodak's Discourse-Historical Approach), they often share tools for microanalysis. This is because CDA grew out of Critical Linguistics, which itself drew upon Halliday's Systemic Functional Linguistics (SFL) (Jahedi et al., 2014; Halliday, 1985). SFL is a complex system which identifies three types of meaning: the experiential, where language is used to talk about the world; the interpersonal, where language is used to interact with others; and the textual, where language is organized to fit its context (Thompson, 2013). As CDA studies are interested in representations of the world and social relationships, they often draw on the experiential meta-function, commonly examining transitivity patterns (Thompson, 2013). CDA studies also frequently draw upon frameworks of social actor and social action representation, which provide socio-semantic resources to examine how people and processes are constructed in discourse (van Leeuwen, 1995, 2008). One example of an effective corpus-based critical discourse analytical study that adopts van Leeuwen's (1995, 2008) frameworks is Mulderrig's (2011) work on New Labour's educational governance.

The combination of corpus linguistics and CDA is commonly referred to as corpus-assisted critical discourse analysis (CA-CDA). CA-CDA is an increasingly popular way of conducting critical analysis (Kennedy, 2022) that is praised for its 'methodological synergy' (Brookes and Baker, 2021: 33; Baker et al., 2008). The combination of approaches allows for a 'systematic and thus *replicable* form' of critical analysis (Mulderrig, 2011: 564, original emphasis). In other words, corpus linguistic methods enable researchers to illustrate that the patterns of representation they identify in qualitative analysis 'occur frequently enough to be significant' (Hart and Kelsey, 2019: 44).

CA-CDA has been employed to examine identity representations in a variety of studies, from representations of bisexual people (Wilkinson, 2019) to media portrayals of people experiencing homelessness (Parnell, 2023). CA-CDA studies of identity representation tend to employ common corpus linguistic methods such as keyword analysis and collocation analysis. Keyword analysis involves comparing relative word frequencies from the corpus of interest (the 'target' corpus) with frequencies from another, discursively related corpus (the 'reference' corpus). Words which occur statistically significantly more frequently in the target corpus than the reference corpus are called positive keywords;

they are considered to indicate the 'aboutness' of the corpus texts (Scott, 1999). Positive keywords shift depending on the reference corpus and so the keyword list that is generated always belongs to a particular comparison rather than to the target corpus (Pojanapunya and Watson Todd, 2018).

In contrast, collocation analysis examines the phenomenon of words consistently occurring next to or near each other, typically in a narrow span of four or five words on either side of the node word (Kang, 2018). Put another way, it is 'the above-chance frequent co-occurrence of two words' (Baker et al., 2008: 278). Analysing collocations can reveal semantic preferences, which are the semantic fields with which a word co-occurs (Stubbs, 2001). It can also uncover discourse prosodies – the evaluative patterns surrounding a word or phrase (Baker, 2006). Collocation analysis is one of the most widely used methods in CA-CDA for identifying discourses and semantic prosodies because it is a principled process. The statistical measures of collocational association provide objective evidence for the interrelationships between words and hence the existence of certain discourses, offering a counter to the argument that CDA is often based on 'cherry-picking' data to suit a particular agenda.

Recently, researchers such as Kennedy (2022) and Gillings and Mautner (2023) have sought to strengthen another key method used in CA-CDA: concordance analysis. Concordance analysis, as the name suggests, examines 'concordances' – lines of text from a corpus which include a particular search term (Baker, 2006). Concordance lines help to contextualize search terms by revealing the co-text surrounding them; it is this role which gives concordance lines their alternative name, 'keywords-in-context' or KWIC (Baker, 2006).

As Gillings and Mautner (2023) argue, in CA-CDA research, concordances can bring language patterns (which reflect patterns in social attitudes, values and behaviours) into sharp relief. These language patterns are built up incrementally and thereby form discourses (Gillings and Mautner, 2023). The process by which researchers analyse concordance lines can sometimes be opaque; Gillings and Mautner (2023) highlight issues linguists might face in examining concordance lines (such as lines unrelated to the research question) and then offer ten recommendations for future research. The two main principles underpinning these recommendations are transparency and self-reflective critique. I have tried to follow these principles in my methodological reflections on the CA-CDA approach taken in this book – diachronic key semantic domain analysis – which I introduce and describe in detail in Chapter 3.

In addition to the CA-CDA of media and government texts, this book employs a discourse analysis of narratives produced by members of the public with ties to Nottinghamshire. Narratives are 'texts that recount events in a sequential order' (De Fina, 2003: 11). This book analyses *personal* narratives, or narratives of personal experience: stories through which speakers construe and perform identities for themselves and others. Personal narratives have captured the interest of researchers across a variety of disciplines. As a result, there are many definitions and conceptualizations of what constitutes a personal narrative (De Fina and Georgakopoulou, 2012). For instance, Ochs and Capp (2001: 2) define personal narratives as 'a way of using language or other symbolic systems to imbue life events with a temporal and logical order, to demystify them and establish coherence across past, present, and as yet unrealized experience'. This definition interprets narrative as a sense-making device that helps narrators to reinterpret real-life experiences. A similar, more recent definition is provided by Cinque et al. (2021: 1759), who argue that narratives are 'devices through which individuals interpret and understand themselves and the social world as they temporally organize different life experiences and events into a story'. In this book, I follow Lawler's (2002: 2) broader reading of narratives as 'interpretive devices, through which people represent themselves, both to themselves and others', as this definition demonstrates the role that narratives play in identity construction.

Narrative analytical research has examined both elicited narratives of personal experience (e.g. Labov, 1972; De Fina, 2003) and storytelling in everyday conversations (e.g. Ochs and Capp, 2001; Georgakopoulou, 2007). Within these studies, the focus has often been on the construction and performance of different types of identities. This is unsurprising given that narrative is a 'prime vehicle for expressing identity' (De Fina, 2015: 351). Early biographical narrative research treated identity in narrative 'as something revealed through the process of people telling their stories' (Evans, 2019: 28). However, later analysts have problematized approaches that view narratives as 'transparent and unmediated records' for identity (De Fina and Georgakopoulou, 2012: 161), preferring to view identity construction as emergent in discourse (see below, alongside De Fina, 2003; De Fina and Georgakopoulou, 2012).

In the context of Brexit, very little narrative analytical work has taken place, especially of lay texts. Three exceptions are Agnisola, Weir and Johnson's (2019) important study of the views of Scottish Fishers; Patel and Connelly's (2019) work on post-race racisms; and Gawlewicz's (2020) examination of narratives of Scotland's distinctiveness in the post-Brexit era. While the authors of these studies claim to offer a narrative approach, there is a notable lack of linguistic analysis of the stories in the examples. The method adopted in this book aims to build on these studies by offering a finer-grained analysis of lay narratives that attends to the language used to construct (supra)national identities in the Brexit context.

Discourse and identities

Attempting to provide the broadest possible understanding of identity, Benwell and Stokoe (2006: 6) offer the definition of 'who people are to each other'. However, identity is not solely about external perception: it is also a conceptual understanding of oneself in relation to the social world (Greenfeld and Eastwood, 2009). Perhaps, then, a more precise definition of identity would be who people construct and understand themselves to be, in relation to how they construct and understand others. This definition indicates that identities emerge out of a process of negotiation between a sense of self and other. Each version of a constructed self is context-dependent; as identities are multiple and multifaceted, different aspects of an individual's sense of self can become significant in different contexts (Smith, 1991). For example, a person might construct gender identities, professional identities and national identities for themselves at different stages of their lives. Which identities become salient at any given moment depends on the context: professional identities might be most relevant at work, while national identities might be more relevant during an international sporting event or when recounting experiences of war.

In sociolinguistic studies, language is a part of a range of resources for identity work (Preece, 2016: 5). Indeed, studying language as interactional discourse reveals that categories such as gender and class are 'not constants that can be taken for granted but are communicatively produced' (Gumperz and Cook-Gumperz, 1982: 1). Drummond and Schleef (2016) divide sociolinguistic approaches to language and identity into three waves. First-wave work, such as Labov (1966) and Trudgill (1974), linked social categories to linguistic features, an approach which has been criticized for 'reductive theorising around identity, in simplistic purposive accounts of identity-as-motive' (Coupland, 2008: 268). Second-wave research also considered language variation and change, but rather than focusing on macro-level sociological categories such as age and gender, it focused on 'locally relevant groupings' (Drummond and Schleef, 2016: 52). Third-wave work moves from interpreting linguistic features as indexing social categories to indexing social meanings (Drummond and Schleef, 2016). The underlying idea of third-wave projects is that 'exploring the social meaning of a feature can help us understand the role language plays in identity construction' (Drummond and Schleef, 2016: 53).

Bucholtz and Hall (2005) sits within third-wave variationist sociolinguistics. Conceiving of identity as relational, Bucholtz and Hall propose a sociolinguistic framework for analysing identity as 'constituted in linguistic interaction' (2005: 585–586). The authors outline five principles for identity construction in interaction. The first principle is emergence, which positions identity not as pre-existing discourse but as the 'emergent product' (2005: 588). The second principle, positionality, holds that, in addition to sociological identity categories at the macro-level, such as age and gender, identity emerges discursively through temporary roles and orientations assumed by participants in interaction. The third principle is indexicality. An index refers to a linguistic form that depends on interactional context for its meaning; broadly speaking, indexicality 'involves the creation of semiotic links between linguistic forms and social meanings' (2005: 594). Indexicality operates on all levels of linguistic structure, including overt category labels, implicature and presupposition. Principle four, relationality, contends that identity is relational and intersubjectively constructed not just along the lines of similarity/difference, but also along the dimensions of genuineness/artifice and authority/delegitimacy. The final principle, partialness, argues that identity is a partial account; it constantly shifts in different contexts and through interaction.

Identities are not only constructed by individuals for themselves: they are often construed by institutions and people with socio-political power for those who lack socio-political power. These are 'ascribed identities' (Blommaert, 2005: 251). Ascribed identities are not ideologically neutral: labels are chosen for their connotations (O'Doherty and Le Couteur, 2007), and lexical choices can be politically motivated (Goodman and Speer, 2007). Given the socio-political power of public institutions like the media and the government, identity representations in discourse produced by journalists or politicians are often projected as 'common sense' (Fairclough, 1989). This introduces a problematic dynamic: people whose identities are associated with a lack of socio-political power, such as immigrants and asylum seekers, often lack the resources to construct their own identities publicly in the way that they would wish to be understood. As a result, in the absence of close encounters with people from these social groups, public knowledge about these identities hinges upon universal discourses of 'common sense' projected by more powerful people in their discursive representations of others (Fairclough, 1989). Identity thus becomes an area of discursive contestation, as people and institutions with different socio-political agendas compete to establish universal, 'common sense' identities.

Discourse, nations and nationalism

Related to the concept of identity is that of *national* identity, which relies on the naturalization of the nation. Speaking of the nation, Valluvan (2019: 29) argues that it remains 'not only the most entrenched imaginative form but also the most concrete institutional arrangement' through which people 'enact their sociopolitical lives'. He contends that 'to deal with politics in the contemporary is therefore also to deal with claims to the nation' (Valluvan, 2019: 29). Defining the nation is notoriously difficult (Anderson, 2006). While acknowledging this difficulty, Anderson (2006) refers to the nation as an imagined political community; 'imagined' because it is impossible for each person in a national territory to know one another and yet they believe there are many others with whom they share land and fundamental values. The imagined national community is constructed, negotiated and renegotiated through discourse; language reifies an otherwise abstract idea (Billig, 1995). The discourse of the nation is often one of territory – 'the homeland', 'our soil' – which naturalizes the relationship between people and place and provides a tangible referent for the concept of nationhood (Malkki, 1992). National discourse is also underpinned by a sense of timelessness, based on the retelling of a shared history, the elaboration of a shared present and the vision of a collective future (Anderson, 2006). As nation-building is, in part, a discursive act, there is no single, undisputed national frame: there are multiple, sometimes competing, constructions of the nation that differ depending on the discourse producer and the production context (Billig, 1995). Some have more cultural reach and weight than others, but it is nevertheless the case that though constructions of a nation share a focus on time and place, there are subtle differences in the way that the government, the media and citizens talk about and evaluate their country.

The ideology that posits that the world is naturally split into nations that demarcate different groups is called nationalism (Billig, 1995). Nationalism can be defined as an 'ideological movement for attaining and maintaining autonomy, unity and identity on behalf of a population deemed by some of its members to constitute an actual or potential nation' (Smith, 1991: 73). The nationalist perspective holds that (a) the world is divided into nations, each of which has its own unique culture and history, (b) individuals belong to a nation and their loyalty to the nation overrides all other allegiances and (c) nations must be 'united, autonomous, and free to pursue their goals' (Triandafyllidou, 1998: 595). There are several strands of nationalism, all of which conceptualize national membership in different terms. Civic nationalism, for example, assigns membership to an individual based on citizenship and shared institutions (Greenfeld and Eastwood, 2009). That is, it conceives of belonging to a nation as dependent on adherence to a nation's political institutions and laws (Filsinger et al., 2021). In contrast, ethnic nationalism allocates membership to people based on characteristics that derive from an imagined shared descent (Greenfeld and Eastwood, 2009). On the one hand, nationalist sentiment can be flagged implicitly through deictic words – pronouns such as 'we' and adverbs such as 'here' – which construct an in-group with the homeland at the centre. On the other, it can be marked through explicit discursive constructions of nationhood. The former is labelled banal nationalism, while the latter is 'hot' (Billig, 1995). In the context of Brexit, Virdee and McGeever (2023: 1) argue that the politics and language of nationalism constitute a way of expressing 'the deleterious effects of deindustrialization, the defeat of the labour movement and the erosion of the welfare state' in Britain. In short, then, the language of nationalism can elucidate conceptualizations of the state of the nation.

There is some debate over whether nationalism is an elite phenomenon or one which is diffused through the masses. Providing an overview of different understandings of nationalism, Mann and Fenton (2017: 5) cite Breuilly (1993) who thought that 'the success of nationalism as a political project . . . relates to the connection between elite portrayals of the nation and the way this appeals to and resonates with popular beliefs and grievances held by large sections of the population'. This book aligns with this multi-pronged understanding of contemporary nationalism, and therefore seeks to examine some of the connections between elite portrayals and popular constructions of the nation by individual citizens.

A successful nation relies on its members sharing a sense of national identity (Schlesinger, 1991). National identity is 'a broad tradition comprised of multiple and competing strands upon which political actors draw selectively to suit their particular purposes' (Ashcroft and Bevir, 2021: 119). de Cillia et al. (1999: 153) draw on Bourdieu to argue that national identities are a form of *habitus*, 'a common complex of ideas, concepts or perception schemes'. The collective conception of national identities is strengthened by a belief in united ideals, values and goals which differentiate one nation from all others and add emotional weight to group belonging (Henderson and McEwan, 2005; Bellucci et al., 2012).

Building a collective sense of national identities involves delineating what a nation is not as well as what it is (Benhabib, 1998; Triandafyllidou, 1998). This process involves demarcating a national Other – an out-group – based on the political concept of borders (Wodak et al., 2009; Nortio et al., 2022). The Other usually appears as one of three types: friendly, non-radical or radical (Gibbins, 2014). A friendly Other is constructed in terms of solidarity and partnership, while a non-radical Other is depicted through mild differentiation (Gibbins, 2014). The radical Other, in contrast, is subjected to a clear dichotomization that reveals a nexus of superiority versus inferiority (Gibbins, 2014). As collective national identities are fluid and context-dependent, Others are never fixed identities; the construction of a particular nation as a type of Other depends on socio-political context. National identities 'have political implications' and are often used in 'political mobilisation' (Wincott, 2019: 22). The political implications of national identities in the context of Brexit are the focus of this book.

Brexit, discourse and identity

The tumultuous period of political activity surrounding Brexit that I explored above has been widely documented in national newspapers. Each political event has also been duly recorded by the government on its website. At each stage of the process, discussions about national identities have been omnipresent. Within these discussions, the government has set out its vision for a 'truly Global Britain' (Raab, 2019), Scottish politicians have promoted a second independence referendum (Carrell, 2019), and national and regional news outlets have written about the need to address national identities in the UK context (e.g. Cockburn, 2018; Winder, 2018; ITV Central, 2020). Questions of identity and belonging have also arisen at an individual level, as migrants and minority ethnic social groups have faced discrimination and calls to 'go home' (Home Office, 2019; Keith, 2019). Through these discussions of nationhood and belonging, an already emotive political process has drawn greater significance for national identities in the UK.

Koegler et al. (2020) argue that no recent political event has had as much influence on British narratives of national and transnational identities as Brexit. Browne (2017: 89) agrees, claiming that the 'underlying causes of the Leave vote' can be 'found in the issue of identity – national identity, regional identity and in the individual sense of self worth [sic] and identity'. Part of the discussion about identity and Brexit has been taken up by researchers who have sought to characterize who was more likely to vote Leave or Remain and why the nation, when taken as a whole, opted to leave the EU. Studies have found that geography and education were key factors influencing the way that a person voted in the referendum (e.g. Green, 2017; Hobolt, 2016; Jump and Michell, 2021). According to YouGov (2016), 70 per cent of voters whose educational attainment is GCSE or lower voted Leave, while 68 per cent of degree holders voted Remain. Age was also an important factor: 64 per cent of voters over the age of sixty-five voted Leave (YouGov, 2016). For those aged under twenty-five, the pattern was reversed: 71 per cent of voters from this age group voted to remain in the EU (YouGov, 2016). In sum, there were clear educational, geographical and age-related divisions in the way British people voted in the EU membership referendum.

An identity-related interpretation of the Leave vote is that it was an expression of national discontent. According to this view, voters wanted Britain 'to be Great again', albeit with English dominance (Calhoun, 2017: 57). The vote, Calhoun (2017: 59) argues, symbolized anger and resentment in addition to 'hope' that 'a proud national identity' could be celebrated once more (2017: 58). In this vein, Calhoun (2017: 59) posits that Brexit was a particularly English nationalist phenomenon, specifically among 'the England of the vanished industry in the North' and 'rural poverty in the Southwest'. In this narrative, England is divided between cosmopolitan centres with high investment such as London, and areas which have been left behind economically and politically (Calhoun, 2017; Jennings and Stoker, 2016; Hobolt, 2016). The referendum reflected these socio-economic divisions – with London voting Remain and most English counties voting Leave (YouGov, 2016) – but also cemented them. As Gifford (2016: 15) recognizes, 'Europe was used to reinforce and essentialize those divisions and to create new ones'. That is, following the referendum, attitudes towards Europe became the basis for supposedly new divisions in the UK. With those 'new' divisions came new nouns to describe people based on their attitudes towards the referendum: 'Brexiteer', 'Remainer' and even 'Remoaner' (Charteris-Black, 2019).

In 2019, Kelley argued that the categories of Remainer and Leaver have developed into a political cleavage in the UK, with Britons expressing greater allegiance to these identity labels than traditional political parties. However, the labels of Remainer and Leaver can be 'profoundly unhelpful' because they perpetuate a view of people as coherent political subjects when multiple, contradictory selves are at play (Clarke and Newman, 2019: 68). Indeed, divisions surrounding Brexit did not just exist between Leave and Remain voters; the referendum also 'amplified deep-seated fissures – of class, of gender, of race, of age, [and] of place' within the UK (Clarke and Newman, 2019: 68). Despite this, support for Leave and Remain cut across the left/right-wing political divide, drawing together citizens whose experiences and backgrounds were different (Kennedy, forthcoming).

While the interpretation of Brexit as an expression of *national* discontent has weight, it is also true that campaigners and members of the public communicated concrete concerns about the inner workings of the EU and the effect these had on British identity (Calhoun, 2017). For example, immigration was such a key concern in the referendum campaign that Geddes (2017: 18) asserted in an early analysis of the referendum that 'if about one thing, the 2016 referendum was about immigration'. In the year before the referendum campaign, British newspapers had been reporting consistently on a 'migrant crisis' in Europe. Thousands of refugees, asylum seekers and immigrants had been arriving in EU countries, and for the year ending June 2015, the net migration of EU citizens and non-EU citizens to the UK had increased by a statistically significant amount (ONS, 2015). The long-term international migration figure for the UK in the year ending 2015 was +336,000, an increase of 82,000 on the previous year (ONS, 2015). The Vote Leave campaign drew on the rising immigration figures in 2016, asserting that a vote to leave the EU would mean 'we can control immigration' (Vote Leave, 2016: n.p.). Such assertions represented rising immigration as a problem with EU membership, and a Leave vote was pitched as the means through which Britain could avoid increasing its net migration further. As the Vote Leave campaign motto implied, then, Brexit was partly a vote for the UK to 'Take Back Control' of immigration from the EU (Vote Leave, 2016: n.p.).

The motto 'Take Back Control' pointed to a second, related concern about the EU that was voiced during the referendum campaign: that the EU compromised Britain's sovereignty, a central tenet of its national identity narrative (Vote Leave, 2016: n.p.; Mautner, 2001). Sovereignty refers to Parliament's position as the 'supreme legal authority in the UK' and its power to 'create or end any law' (UK Parliament, 2020: n.p.). The pro-Leave argument was that the UK's EU membership jeopardized its parliamentary sovereignty because the European Court of Justice could supersede British law when it contradicted European laws (Ringeisen-Biardeaud, 2017). The only way to regain British sovereignty, campaigners argued, was to leave the EU. This proposition was made both by journalists and politicians. For example, the Business Editor of *The Telegraph* claimed that 'the Brexit vote is about the supremacy of Parliament' (Pritchard, 2016: n.p.), while

Conservative MP Boris Johnson stated that voting to Remain would cause the 'erosion of parliamentary democracy in this country' (Johnson, 2016: n.p.). The Vote Leave campaign reiterated the sovereignty argument in its online briefing, where it labelled as 'fact' the declaration that 'EU law is supreme over UK law' and that this situation 'stops the British public from being able to vote out those who make our laws' (Vote Leave: 2016: n.p.).[6]

Claims about political sovereignty were closely tied to a third concern voiced in the EU referendum: that the EU is bureaucratic, which runs counter to the popular construction of the UK as a democracy. A month before the referendum, *The Telegraph* published an opinion piece with the headline, 'The EU bureaucrats cannot cope with democracy' (Telegraph, 2016: n.p.). Around the same time, the Leave campaign referred to the EU model as '1950s bureaucratic centralism' and 'this bureaucracy over which we have so little influence' (Vote Leave, 2016: n.p.). When talking about EU bureaucrats, politicians were largely referring to the European Commission, whose officials are not directly elected but are proposed by national governments (BBC, 2016c). Accusations regarding the EU's undemocratic bureaucracy intensified concerns for sovereignty, as it was not just European laws taking precedence over British laws, but also unelected European officials making decisions for Britain. Through these acts, the EU allegedly undermined the UK's position as a democracy.

Together, the three related concerns of immigration, sovereignty and bureaucracy reveal that in addition to expressing national discontent, the Leave vote reflected concerns about the power dynamic in the UK–EU relationship. In other words, at the heart of Brexit were contested representations of Britain and Britishness and Europe and Europeanness, as well as concerns over how the two pairs of identities related to one another both at the level of international relations and at the local level of individual encounters.

Although identity has been a core concern throughout the Brexit process – and has been dissected by scholars to determine who voted for which outcome – the (re)production and performance of *Britishness* has surprisingly not been the subject of many qualitative studies. Among the plethora of existing Brexit-related projects, there *has* been some linguistic work considering national identity within the domains of political debate (Wenzl, 2019), nation branding (Wenzl, 2020) and political cartoons (Lennon and Kilby, 2020). For example, Wenzl (2019) reveals that the construction of national identity between Leave and Remain supporters in the Conservative Party did not vary substantially, as Remain-voting Conservatives depicted Britain as culturally distinct from the EU. Similarly, her analysis of nation branding uncovers that Remain voters' representations of Britishness perpetuated the 'same cultural narratives about Britishness as the Leave side' (Wenzl, 2020: 73). Meanwhile, Lennon and Kilby (2020) find that in political cartoons, Brexit is repeatedly framed as a domestic issue rather than one which the UK and the EU must work together to address.

A smaller number of geographical and sociological studies have interviewed Britons to examine their intersectional performance of identities during discussions about Brexit (e.g. Bromley-Davenport et al., 2018; Davies, 2021). In their study of older, working-class white men in Sunderland, for example, Bromley-Davenport et al. (2018: 808) rightly conclude that 'we need to unpack how different types of voters are borne from individual lived experiences and perceptions' and not assume that 'the country is comprised of just two types of people – Leavers and Remainers'. Until this book, however, there has been no single study that considers the diachronic representation of British and European identities and their interrelations within the press, politics and public opinion during the time of Brexit. There is a great need for such a panoptic study, given that the EU referendum result was largely based on whether voters took a 'cosmopolitan' or 'relatively insular' view of the UK's place in Europe (UCL, 2021: n.p.), a personal perspective which is undoubtedly influenced by media outlets and politicians who have long communicated the inner workings of the EU system to British citizens (Oberhuber et al., 2005).

Book outline

To examine the discursive construction of British and European identities, this book analyses pro-Brexit newspaper articles, government texts and interviews with members of the public. It is the first of its kind to consider how politicians, journalists at pro-Brexit newspapers and fifteen citizens discursively construct Britishness and Europeanness in relation to Brexit and how their representations of these identities converge or diverge. In doing so, it aims to chart the negotiation of British and European identities across three salient sites of political discourse over time and to understand the relationships between them. It seeks to uncover how Britain and Europe are discursively constructed and positioned in relation to one another, to identify British national identity narratives and to consider the democratic implications of these identity constructions. To this end, Chapter 2 defines the theoretical concepts of Britishness and Europeanness and surveys the existing literature on the representation of Britain and Europe in the British press, politics and public opinion. Chapter 3 considers the collection of the three data sets and outlines the methodological frameworks through which the data are analysed: diachronic key semantic domain analysis and a discourse analysis of narratives. Chapter 4 is the first analytical chapter. It investigates the discursive construction of British and European identities in five pro-Brexit national newspapers using CA-CDA. Chapter 5 complements Chapter 4 methodologically, as it offers a CA-CDA of the construction of (supra)national identities in UK government documents. In Chapter 6, a discourse analysis of narratives produced in semi-structured interviews provides a view of individual constructions of Britishness. The book draws to a close in Chapter 7 with a discussion of the findings across the data sets and some concluding remarks on possible democratic implications of the findings.

2

The Discursive Construction of Britishness and Europeanness

Introduction

On the morning of 24 June 2016, I was in a hairdressing salon. The results of the EU membership referendum had just been announced over the radio and the hairdresser said, 'well, it's best for the country that we voted to Leave'. This was not the first time I had heard claims being made about what would be best for 'the country' or 'for us' from people on both sides of the debate. Every time, I would think, 'which country?' or 'who are "we"'? To members of my family from Scotland, who decided after the vote that they would rather have Scottish independence than leave the EU, leaving was not best for *their* country, which they understood to be Scotland, not the UK. It occurred to me that 'our country' and 'we' could mean very different things to people living on the same street, never mind people from two different constituent parts of the UK. Despite this, Leave and Remain campaigners seemed to be mobilizing national identities such as 'British' (often expressed through the pronouns 'we' and 'our' and the noun phrase 'the country') as though they were categories that we all agreed on. For instance, the Vote Leave campaign website, since the day of the referendum result, has claimed that 'it's because of everyone involved, all across *the country*, that we achieved this magnificent result' (Vote Leave, 2016: n.p., italics mine). From that moment in the hairdressing salon, I became eager to understand what role language like this – the language of national identities – would play in the construction of a post-Brexit Britain.

This chapter sets out to provide an understanding of Britishness and Europeanness, and to consider how these identities have been discursively constructed in British politics, press and public opinion over the past thirty years. I am interested in the interplay between politics, press and the public because discourses of (supra)national identities are presented to the public through the mass media and the government, both of which disseminate narratives about the nation with which citizens identify (Hall, 1996).[1] These narratives include memories which connect the past with the present and national symbols and rituals which represent shared experiences (Hall, 1996). As discourse and social practice are dialectical, the media and the government do not just discursively construct international relationships and national identities – they reify them through law and social practice (De Cillia et al., 1999; Diez Medrano, 2003). For example, the Home Office defines the boundaries of a national homeland through its discourses and practices, while the Foreign Office institutionally and legally, as well as discursively, delineates international Others (Law, 2001). Through the immigration laws produced in these departments, both internal and external borders are defined which 'maintain Britain as a racially and colonially configured space' (El-Enany, 2021: 3). In other words, the legal documents produced by these ministerial departments formally delimit the categories of (intra)national self and other and provide the framework within which Britain interacts with other nations. Without engaging with citizens, it is not possible to measure the extent to which government and media representations of national identity enter and relate to individuals' conceptualizations. Nevertheless, the representations of nations and international relationships in media and political discourses reveal how a national community is encouraged to conceptualize itself by nation-building institutions.

Politicians' institutional power, representative status and expert knowledge have been said to furnish them with privileged access to the media to such an extent that they act as primary definers of news (Eldridge et al., 1997). However, the primary definers model has been widely criticized; the relationship between politicians and journalists is much more complex than mere regurgitation, as government sources frequently speak in disparate voices and journalists have access to other sources of information that contradict official political lines (Eldridge et al., 1997). That politicians act as sources for journalists about national and supranational issues, then, does not mean that politicians' versions of events dominate media representations. Indeed, the different linguistic strategies available to journalists when they report speech enable them to offer varying degrees of commitment to the claims politicians make (Bednarek, 2016). Similarly, news articles that include quotes from politicians are often accompanied by comment and analysis which frame the news according to a newspaper's socio-political agenda (Kuhn, 2017). Through this practice of recontextualization, official views can be bolstered or undermined at the same time as they are presented to the public. Just as politics is mediatized, the media is politicized: politics and the press are intertwined.

In addition to providing the public with political information, the press sets the agenda for public debate: the visibility of an issue in the media influences the public's perception of its importance (Dearing and Rogers, 1996). The salience of an issue in the press is determined by the media's selection processes, which are based on the news values of, inter alia, negativity, proximity and follow-up: more negative news and local stories are likely to be prioritized, and once a story appears in the media it is likely to be followed up (Bednarek and Caple, 2017; Harcup and O'Neill, 2017). Articles in British newspapers also present dominant social norms, values and attitudes to citizens through framing devices; by socializing readers into these structures, journalists contribute to the legitimation of a political system (Kuhn, 2017). For example, the repeated presupposition of consensus that a policy is bad or good for the public might lead to public acceptance of this attitude.

Although the press has the potential to influence a vast number of people, readers do not always passively accept media discourses (Schrøder, 2018). As texts are polysemic, they are open to various readings; audiences might adopt different positions towards, or readings of, a text (Hall, 1973). A reader might accept the frame in which a message is encoded, adopting a dominant-hegemonic position, or they might accept the dominant framework but negotiate its application at a local level, adopting a negotiated position (Hall, 1973). Alternatively, a reader might challenge a discourse wholesale, taking an oppositional position (Hall, 1973). These decoding options illustrate that members of the public are active readers; meaning is not confined solely to a text but is partially constructed by a reader, whose interpretation is influenced by personal experience and identity (Eldridge et al., 1997).

Relating these communication processes back to Britain and Europe, Zappettini (2019: 3), citing Delanty and Rumford (2005), notes that 'no single institutional or civic actor is exclusively capable of controlling the process of identification with European referents'. As a result, he argues, 'while normative aspects must be taken into account in the construction of Europe(anness), a wider variety of actors has also to be acknowledged' because 'an emerging European identity is best interpreted as a dynamic interplay between structural and agentive forces made up of institutions, citizens and global actors' (Zappettini, 2019: 3). Similarly, Krzyżanowski's (2010) research on European identities demonstrates that 'identities emerge discursively as a combination of the individual, the social, the agentive and the structural dimensions of society' and so are driven by both individual experiences and collective visions (Zappettini, 2019: 3). This is arguably as much the case for Britishness, which is an overarching supranational identity (McCrone, 1997), as for Europeanness. The idea that European and British identities emerge through a combination of top-down and bottom-up constructions provides the rationale for considering media, political and individual constructions of identity and their commonalities and differences in this book. The approach recognizes that in the networked public sphere (Friedland et al., 2006), there is a non-linear interplay between media, institutions and the public rather than simply a top-down impingement on individual self-identification. In other words, as Hall's (1973) various readings of a text demonstrate, there is no simple one-to-one relationship between media and political discourses and individual identification. As a result, to provide a holistic understanding of the discursive construction of national and supranational identities in Brexit Britain, it is necessary to account for both top-down and bottom-up constructions. Before I can consider this, however, it is crucial to understand which dominant (supra)national identities exist in Brexit Britain and how they have developed.

Forging Britishness

According to Lennon and Kilby (2020: 117), Britishness is 'an overarching identity of civic and political status' that subsumes regions and nations and is 'set against a backdrop of Protestant culture, recurrent war and an increasingly multicultural empire'. In this historical reading, a collective British identity was forged between the Act of Union in 1707, which joined Scotland to England and Wales, and the beginning of the Victorian age in 1837 (Colley, 1992). During this period of 130 years, Britain was engaged in a series of wars with France; English, Welsh and Scottish people united first against this continental Other and later against the people they colonized, as opposed to through cultural or political consensus (Colley, 1992). Alongside a new British identity, the older national identities of English, Welsh and Scottish continued to exist; rather than overwriting its national components, British identity sat above them as a supranational identity (Colley, 1992; McCrone, 1997). In 1800, the Acts of Union joined Britain with Ireland, a configuration which was modified by the 1922 Irish Free State Constitution to produce the United Kingdom of Britain and Northern Ireland (Marshall, 1996). As the Irish secession demonstrates, Irish identities persisted despite the creation of a supranational UK identity. As a result, there are two levels to British identity: four separate nations with individual customs and histories, and a common British political identity that provides the framework within which the nations interact (Parekh, 2009).

Public narratives of Britishness are typically rooted in history and place Britain in opposition to Europe. First, the Reformation, the Industrial Revolution and Victorian values helped to shape Britain as liberal, democratic, globally influential and detached from the continent (Maccaferri, 2019). Then the Suez crisis of 1956 precipitated a post-imperial narrative of national decline (Maccaferri, 2019). In contemporary Britain, the number of UK citizens who identify as 'British only' or British in combination with another national identity is in decline (Manners, 2018). Nevertheless, the UK government's post-Brexit national identity narrative of Global Britain – a plan to demonstrate that 'the UK is open, outward-looking and confident on the world stage' (UK Government, 2019: n.p.) – continues to position Britain as the core national unit in the UK. Although it is *English* nationalism that is most closely associated with Euroscepticism, then, the nationalist sentiment is couched in the language of Britishness (Wellings, 2010; Leith and Sim, 2022). Indeed, as Beaumont (2017) notes, it is English nationalism that conveys pride in the *British* Empire and *British* victory in the Second World War. It is partly for this reason that I examine British identity construction in relation to Brexit in this book, rather than English identity (see Henderson et al. (2016) for a consideration of Brexit and Englishness).

Although Britishness is often conceptualized as a single identity, it is 'inherently fractured, contested and unstable' (Ashcroft and Bevir, 2021: 1). Competing discourses of nationhood have always existed in the UK because of the complex dynamic between the constituent countries. In fact, over the past hundred years, Britishness has been 'endlessly debated, constructed and deconstructed' (Julios, 2008: 160). As regions can be resources of identity for the nation (Aughey, 2007), constructions of Britishness can be contested in different places and spaces within the UK. As Wincott (2019) highlights, British identity seemingly operates differently in England compared to Wales and Scotland. Which discourses of Britishness carry the most cultural weight at any given time therefore depends on socio-political context. While politicians speak of a shared British character – 'an island nation: independent, forthright, passionate in defence of our sovereignty' (Cameron, 2013: n.p.) – devolution, an appetite for Scottish independence, and divergent attitudes towards EU membership produce discourses that contradict and even reject a homogenous British identity.

As the case of Britishness reveals, a person can identify simultaneously with a nation and a supranational entity (Duchesne and Frognier, 2008). However, the relationship between these levels of identification is complex and depends, among other factors, on the nation and supranational identity involved (Duchesne and Frognier, 2008). In the case of identification with Europe, Eurobarometer surveys reveal that while a member of the EU, the UK was the only state in which most respondents who felt proud of their country did not feel proud of being European (Duchesne and Frognier, 2008). Indeed, Carl, Dennison and Evans (2019) go as far as to state that Euroscepticism was stronger in the UK than most other EU countries. As the UK consists of four countries, homogenizing attitudes towards the EU conceals nuances between the different countries. In fact, English people expressed less support for the EU than their Scottish, Welsh and Northern Irish counterparts, conceiving of it as a threat to their national identity (Carey, 2002). Given the different levels of identification with the EU among UK countries, the interplay between national and supranational identifications seemingly produced scepticism towards the EU in some parts of the UK. This scepticism and a 'weak sense of European identity' in Britain were, according to Carl et al. (2019: 282), 'key contributor[s] to the Brexit vote'.

Constructing Britishness in press, politics and public opinion

As historians argue that a united British identity was forged during historical conflict (Colley, 1992), it is perhaps unsurprising that history plays a key role in political constructions of Britishness. During parliamentary debates, politicians retell select episodes from British history to support their construction of Britain as an independent and democratic nation. In parliamentary debates on Brexit, for example, intertextual links to the Churchillian discourse of 'Britain-as-an-island-nation' were used to justify a British predilection for freedom and sovereignty and to distinguish the nation spatially, temporally and ethically from the EU. For instance, Cap (2019: 72) quotes right-wing politician Nigel Farage who argued that 'Britain is different; our geography puts us apart. . . . The roots go back seven, eight, nine hundred years with the Common Law' (Farage, 2013). Similarly, Wodak (2018) reveals that a geographical discourse of difference was woven into David Cameron's (2013: n.p.) so-called Bloomberg speech, in which he announced his intention to hold an in–out referendum on Britain's EU membership: 'our geography has shaped our psychology; we have the character of an island nation – independent, forthright, passionate in defence of our sovereignty'. In these examples, Britain's geographical separateness from mainland Europe is evoked by politicians to symbolize its fundamentally different values. The intertwined themes of history and geography are used to personify Britain and imbue its identity with morality and democratic ideals, constructing a homogenous, stable Britishness that has endured for centuries (Wenzl, 2019). Using history to characterize Britain as a long-standing democracy allows Eurosceptic politicians to conceptualize deeper European integration as weakening Britain's independent identity and its withdrawal from the EU as preserving the nation's sovereignty.

Two periods of British history recur in political constructions of the nation: the British Empire (McCrone, 1997) and the Second World War (Cap, 2019; Beaumont, 2017). These periods are often ideologically intertwined: an imperial attitude of British superiority underpinned post-war thinking and continues to pervade British self-perception today despite the loss of empire (Marquand, 1995). Although Britain's historical actions are morally problematic, politicians often frame its history positively; they ignore its exclusion of outsiders and erase its racism from public memory, feeding a myth of the British value of decency (Bennett, 2018). For example, Zappettini (2019: 146) identifies a document from the Department for International Trade which evoked a favourable historical reading when it claimed that Britain has 'a long and proud history as a great trading nation' (Department for International Trade, 2017: 5). This document alluded to the nation's identity during its empire and, by stating that 'we want to maximize our trade opportunities globally . . . by boosting our trading relationships with old friends and new allies', hinted that the UK would return to this role after Brexit (Department for International Trade, 2017: 5; Zappettini, 2019: 146). The positive recontextualization of British imperial history demonstrates that it matters less that a nation's values are accurate than that the members of the national community believe that they are (Henderson and McEwen, 2005).

Boris Johnson's construction of the 2016 EU membership referendum as 'our country's Independence Day' similarly drew on colonial discourses to position Britain as a victim of EU tyranny while ignoring the nation's history of perpetuating colonial violence (Charteris-Black, 2019: 77). By representing the UK as a colonized nation in need of freedom rather than as a colonizer, Johnson subverted the narrative of British imperial power and hailed a return to Britain's so-called independence (see Koller, 2020 for Conservative Party constructions of EU membership as restraint). Positioning Britain as a victim of EU bureaucracy contradicts its representation as a powerful nation, creating a conflicting narrative between its influential past (and potential future) and its alleged current subjugation by the EU (Wenzl, 2019). Koegler,

Malreddy and Tronicke (2020: 588) interpret this 'reverse-colonization' rhetoric as 'symptomatic of repressed anxieties surrounding empire nostalgia and narcissistic shame'. Although nostalgia for empire has been linked to the Leave campaign, it is important to acknowledge that it is not just Leave-supporting political discourses that are shaped by 'imperial modes of thought' (Saunders, 2020: 1143). Similarly, although accusations of racism have been levelled at Leave voters, in the Brexit context, the 'concept' of racism has become 'entangled in a cycle of contestations, denials and affirmations' between Leave and Remain voters (Mintchev, 2021: 123).

In the national identity discourses of Eurosceptic politicians prior to the EU referendum, two predominant national frames were used to represent the UK: the Sovereign Nation and the Invaded Nation (Charteris-Black, 2019). In the Sovereign Nation scenario, Britain symbolized freedom, democracy and autonomy, and national identity was conceptualized in terms of citizenship (Charteris-Black, 2019). In the Invaded Nation frame, sacred entities were under attack and needed defending, typically from the EU's open border policies (Charteris-Black, 2019). Both representations of Britain foregrounded the NHS as a sacred national institution that must be defended, and constructed the British Army as threatened by the inevitable creation of an EU-wide force (Charteris-Black, 2019). In discursive constructions of contemporary Britain, then, national institutions metonymically symbolize the nation; a threat to an institution is a threat to the country. Indeed, 'institutions are a recurring topos in the rhetoric of Britishness', and, within that, the NHS is commonly linked to British values (Atkins, 2022: 221).

During Brexit negotiations, the need to navigate the shifting relationship between Britain and the EU led to tensions between discourses of British exceptionalism and European collaboration in policy documents. By British exceptionalism, I mean the 'self-perception' that the UK is 'a unique, special nation' (Islentyeva and Dunkel, 2022: 1). Theresa May drew on discourses of British exceptionalism in her Brexit-related speeches, positioning a narrow national audience of Leave voters as constituting the British people while framing Remain voters as citizens of nowhere (Atkins, 2022). In contrast, other policymakers depicted Britain as continuing a European tradition of democracy and wanting to maintain a special relationship with the continent. This was visible, for example, in the claim that 'the UK has a deep, historic belief in the same values that Europe stands for: peace, democracy' (Zappettini, 2019: 150). While retelling British history is central to political constructions of the nation, then, the values that differentiate Britain from other countries are somewhat text- and context-specific.

Defining Britain by its history is not just a discursive practice that characterizes political discourses – British tabloid newspapers are constantly engaged in a reinterpretation of national history (Conboy, 2006). The tabloid history of Britain is framed in terms of conflict with continental Europe; through a narrative of British martial victory at Trafalgar and in the Second World War, Europe is implicitly constructed as an enemy that is no match for Britain's military prowess (Daddow, 2006). History is not only pervasive in tabloid news – it played an equally important role in British broadsheet and middle-market newspapers in the build-up to the EU referendum, leading Maccaferri (2019: 19) to conclude that in 'Brexit discourse, historical arguments and historical categories played a focal role'.

The construction of Britain in terms of its relationship with Europe also pervades contemporary representations of the nation. In the *Daily Mail* and the *Daily Mirror*, Britain has been characterized by its irreverence and its ridiculing of EU regulations (Henkel, 2018). These actions symbolize Britain's refusal to accept European bureaucracy, as the *Daily Mail* exemplifies in its Euromythic claim that 'we laughed when they tried to ban prawn-flavoured crisps' (Henkel, 2018: 88). While the EU is framed as severe and obsessively interfering, Britain is defiant in its humour. The prevalence of food in Eurosceptic discourse is, as Mautner (2001) argues, significant: it is a familiar aspect of daily life to which all British readers can relate. By selecting the example of prawn-flavoured crisps, the *Daily Mail* ensures that its construction of a national in-group ('we') unites the broadest possible cross-section of readers.

Constructing British values is an important part of the representation of Britishness. Bolt (2022) argues that in David Cameron's speeches between 2006 and 2015, the discursive construction of British values rested on generosity, tolerance, openness and open-mindedness. Cameron's rhetoric about Britain and Britishness – in which the nation was framed as exceptional – 'compromised his stewardship of the Remain campaign' and encouraged the country on a path towards Euroscepticism, according to Bolt (2022: 129).

The Eurosceptic press offers a vision of British values that centres on three recurring themes: sovereignty, pragmatism and global trade (Mautner, 2001). A belief in the importance of sovereignty is a key symbol of British national identity (Mautner, 2001). The nation's aversion to pooled sovereignty can be explained by the significance of this characteristic to its identity: for Britain, losing sovereignty means losing the national essence entirely. Pragmatism, as a further characteristic of the British national character according to the Eurosceptic British press, is the basis upon which Britain distinguishes itself from Europe

(Mautner, 2001). In 2001, for instance, the *Daily Telegraph* argued that Britain's 'limited view of the EC's future is more practical than the grand schemes of some of our partners' (Mautner, 2001: 14). In this Eurosceptic narrative of Britishness, practicality protected the nation from delusions about the potential of the EC. Finally, Britain has been constructed as a 'truly global nation' with 'huge trading links' (Teubert, 2001: 74). This international outlook is contrasted with a Eurocentric EU that 'is not global' but 'regional' (Teubert, 2001: 74). That these three British characteristics are so often evoked as the antithesis to European attributes suggests that national values are drawn upon by the press to emphasize why Britain should not be grouped with other European nations: it is and always has been, Eurosceptic journalists claim, fundamentally different.

Smith (2016) postulates that the UK's vote to leave the EU destabilized a sense of Britishness. However, several interview studies with British participants about their sense of national identity conducted prior to the EU referendum suggest that a single homogenous 'Britishness' was not felt at a personal level even before the vote. When asked about what they thought was typically British, white English participants reproduced a stereotype of the typical Briton as 'tea-drinking' and 'monarchy-loving' but argued that they did not fit this profile (Condor, 2000). Focus group participants across East Anglia identified individual freedom and mutual respect as British political values, and politeness, moderation and self-deprecation as cultural values (Jarvis et al., 2020). However, some participants problematized the idea of 'British values' by labelling it an elusive, context-dependent and ideologically driven phrase, often tied to a xenophobic discourse of difference (Jarvis et al., 2020). When the discussion of British national identity was explicitly grounded in the context of devolution, as in Skey's (2011) study, English participants expressed a tension between feeling uncomfortable with xenophobic English attitudes and wanting to reassert an English identity amid what they perceived to be growing Welsh and Scottish nationalism. These studies suggest that while Britons are aware of national cultural stereotypes, they are sometimes uncomfortable with the characteristics they include and reject the idea that there is a single, homogenous Britishness.

History and legend also have a place in citizens' discussions of national identities, demonstrating that the retelling of select episodes of national history is not just a discursive practice employed by journalists and politicians. Leave-voting Britons on Twitter likened Leave advocate and right-wing politician Nigel Farage to King Arthur 'risen from his slumber at the time of greatest need' (Charteris-Black, 2019: 73). By drawing on the national legend of King Arthur, tweeters imbued Farage with the values of chivalry and power and positioned him as a symbol of a very narrow version of national identity. In this case, Farage's Eurosceptic, anti-immigration, right-wing ideologies were made to symbolize a chivalrous, powerful, masculine national culture. This discursive practice indicates that contemporary political figures can symbolize a specific type of national identity for some citizens (Tranter and Donoghue, 2021).

Although existing studies of citizens' conceptualizations of Britishness are illuminating, more recent sociological research highlights an ongoing deficit in this area: a failure to consider how racial hierarchies of Britishness affect feelings of belonging (Thomas and Antony, 2015). Two separate studies examining attitudes towards Brexit among British people of colour living in EU member states and white English people living in the UK reveal a difference in interpretation. Benson and Lewis's (2019) interviews with British people of colour revealed that participants conceived of the Leave vote and surrounding discourse as evidence of British racism and understood this as part of an ongoing xenophobia problem in the nation. As one participant claimed, 'it was so obvious that [the referendum] was going to unleash all kinds of awful xenophobia that had just been simmering for years and of course it did' (Benson and Lewis, 2019: 9). Meanwhile, Higgins's (2018: 281) white English participants agreed that the Leave vote revealed racist attitudes in Britain, but they viewed this as a new phenomenon in a country that they no longer recognized; one participant stated that they found it 'difficult to recognise [their] own country now ... the attitude and the racism is so difficult to comprehend'. Although these studies do not explicitly address national identity, they illustrate the implications of recruiting only white English participants when examining national identity ideologies at the level of the individual. Experiences of living in Britain differ between white people and people of colour; any research that involves only white English participants must acknowledge that the findings only reflect a specific experience of Britishness (Benson and Lewis, 2019).

Constructing Brexit-related political identities in Britain

Related to the construction of national identities is that of *political* identities. Political identities are a specific form of social identity (Murray et al., 2017). They are not static but are socially constructed (Saurugger, 2013; Fabbrini, 2019), ideological and based on presupposed in-groups and out-groups (van Dijk, 2010). The Brexit-related identities of Remainer and Leaver (or Brexiteer) are forms of political and social identity. They are situated in a 'paired relationship'

(Meredith and Richardson, 2019: n.p.). The identities of Leaver and Remainer are 'not coherent and stable subject-positions' (Mintchev, 2021: 124; Clarke and Newman, 2019).

Brusenbauch Meislová's (2022) work on the discursive construction of affective polarization in Brexit Britain theorizes that Brexit-related identities are 'just like national identities' in that they are discursively (re)produced through language (Brusenbauch Meislová, 2022: 100). Tyler, Degnen and Blamire (2022) outline the discursive depictions of Leavers and Remainers that are pervasive in Remain-oriented public discourse. Leave voters are associated with Euroscepticism, being white, working class and older, and having lower levels of education (Tyler et al., 2022). They are also thought to be traditional and nostalgic, expressing dissatisfaction with multiculturalism (Tyler et al., 2022). In contrast, Remainers are discursively constructed as financially better off, ethnically diverse, younger and having higher educational levels. Remainers are depicted as 'anywheres' – not rooted in place – in contrast to Leavers, who are 'somewheres' (Tyler et al., 2022).

Within the discursive construction of Leaver identities in Remainers' comments on news websites, Brexiteers are often associated with gullibility, ignorance and a lack of intelligence (Meredith and Richardson, 2019). They are framed as older people who are nostalgic and backwards-thinking (Meredith and Richardson, 2019), despite research which shows that Remainers are nostalgic too, albeit expressing an egalitarian nostalgia (Hanel and Wolf, 2020). Remainers are constructed by Leavers in comments as scaremongers who are out of touch with reality (Meredith and Richardson, 2019). These studies demonstrate that the discursive construction of a divided nation is (re)produced not only by Leave-supporting narratives but also by Remainers (Browning, 2018).

The political identities of Remainer and Leaver are intimately intertwined with (supra)national identities. Browning (2018) claims that for many Remainers, Brexit destabilized narratives of self-identity and led to anxieties about Britishness – the identity which Leave campaigners were supposedly reclaiming. Throughout his paper, Browning (2018: 345) argues that there is a rupture of relationships within Britain that has led to ontological dissonance caused by 'clashing and apparently irreconcilable narratives'. He goes on to state that there is a breakdown of social trust: 'With the securitisation and reduction of political life down to two caricatured and mutually opposed identities, there is even a question as to whether the very notion that Remainers and Leavers inhabit the same polity is breaking down' (Browning, 2018: 345). Ashcroft and Bevir (2021) make the same point, arguing that it is important to decentre the imagined national community in Brexit Britain to prevent the breakdown of the polity.

Constructing a European identity

Although this book is concerned primarily with the construction of Britishness, given the relational nature of identity construction and the fact that Britain is often defined in opposition to Europe (Spiering, 2014), it is important to also consider the construction of Europeanness. Both the acronym 'EU' and the noun 'Europe' are 'poorly defined' terms with various meanings (Risse, 2004: 7). It is not surprising, then, that in the media discourses of European nations, the noun 'Europe' is used vaguely without a clear distinction between its geographical (Europe as a continent) and political (European Union) referents (Williams and Piazza, 2012). In fact, the terms 'Europe' and 'EU' are often conflated, not only in media discourses but in political language and citizens' speech (Koller et al., 2019). Given the blurred lines between Europe as a geographical unit and Europe as a constellation of political alliances, there is little clarity about what European identity is and indeed whether one exists both within and outside of the UK (Smith, 1992).

The Treaty on European Union, the first to delineate EU citizenship, declares that every person holding a Member State nationality is an EU citizen (Carey, 2002). This definition of EU citizenship constructs European identity as the sum of several national identities which are aggregated based on geographical closeness and membership of a political union (Smith, 1992). Although the EU claims that there are shared values among EU nations that lend themselves to an overarching, supranational identity – 'inclusion, tolerance, justice, solidarity and non-discrimination' (European Commission, 2021: n.p.) – there seems to be no shared understanding of what it means to be European or even how to talk about European history across EU member states. For example, the Italian print media consistently describes European history in terms of post-Second World War events; it focuses on the creation of an institutional Europe and its present and future much more frequently than the UK press (Marchi and Partington, 2012). Conversely, European history is constructed in terms of conflict in the UK press, even in pro-EU newspapers like *The Guardian* (Marchi and Partington, 2012). Discourses of European identity also diverge in early evening television news across the UK, France and Italy: while French broadcasters, and, to a lesser degree, Italian broadcasters, express a common

European 'we', the BBC and ITV consistently place Europe outside of British identity (Thornborrow et al., 2012).

The British press occupies a unique role of mediator between politicians and the public: it recontextualizes the EU's political processes for and to its readers (Oberhuber et al., 2005). Given that newspaper discourse is not ideologically neutral, the information newspapers disseminate about the EU reflects their attitudes towards the Union. As a large section of the British mass media has been on a trajectory towards Euroscepticism for many years, the proportion of readers consuming Eurosceptic discourse outweighs those consuming neutral or positive messages (Daddow, 2012). That is not to say that all British newspapers are Eurosceptic – *The Guardian*, for example, is openly pro-EU. Nevertheless, as the Reuters Institute demonstrates in its study of 2,378 referendum-focused articles, there was a 'dominant pro-Brexit bias' in the British national press prior to the 2016 EU membership referendum (Levy et al., 2016: 16). Pro-Leave articles constituted 41 per cent of the Reuters Institute's sample compared to 27 per cent with a pro-Remain stance; six out of the nine national newspapers in the study expressed a dominant pro-Leave position (Levy et al., 2016). As such, although newspapers are no longer the only source of information about the EU for citizens (social media also plays a key role), what most newspaper-reading Britons know about the EU and its institutions is likely to be bound up in Eurosceptic arguments (Diez Medrano, 2003; Daddow, 2012).

Several qualitative studies have examined the representation of the EU in British print media. For example, Hawkins (2012: 565) finds that in coverage of the negotiation of the Lisbon Treaty, the EU was framed as a 'hostile, quasi-imperial power which pose[d] an existential threat to the United Kingdom' or as a bargaining forum from which the UK was excluded. Similarly, in a diachronic corpus study of newspaper editorials about the EU, Hardt-Mautner (1995) identifies a narrow set of keywords around which the discourse was structured, including the nouns 'bureaucracy', 'federalism' and 'sovereignty'. As the data set includes articles from the pro-EU *Guardian* and *Daily Mirror*, as well as the more Eurosceptic *Daily Telegraph* and *The Sun*, these keywords seemingly cut across positive and negative discourses about the EU. That said, Räikkönen (2022) finds that in left-wing newspapers such as *The Guardian* and *Daily Mirror* between 2005 and 2015, EU-related issues were more often reported from a European perspective than in right-wing newspapers.

Taking a more manual approach to analysing Eurosceptic media constructions of the EU, Daddow (2012) identifies the repetition of the nouns 'independence', 'super-state', 'subsidiarity' and 'Eurocrats'. These salient words point to a discursive differentiation between Britain and the EU along the axes of democracy/bureaucracy and independence/integration. The words are enmeshed in two recurrent representations of the EU: 'Brussels' as a collection of European elites who are remote and bureaucratic, and European interests as at odds with national interests (Oberhuber et al., 2005). European institutions, such as the European Commission and the European Court of Justice, are frequently depicted as overbearing and as interfering in British political and legal issues (Dugalès and Tucker, 2012; Zappettini, 2019). By positioning EU institutions and elites in 'Brussels', the British press foregrounded the EU's geographical distance from the UK (Dugalès and Tucker, 2012). This geographical focus enabled Eurosceptic journalists to present the application of EU regulations in the UK as an unwelcome encroachment on national sovereignty from a geographically, culturally and politically remote group of elites (Dugalès and Tucker, 2012).

Often, the EU is portrayed as undemocratic and overbearing in Eurosceptic British political discourses, too. During parliamentary debates about Europe, Eurosceptic politicians represented the EU as an economic failure that was suffering from 'high unemployment [and] taxes', and as an undemocratic superstate that could not succeed because 'there is no European public opinion; no European national identity' (Ichijo, 2008: 54). In Brexit-related parliamentary debates, an undemocratic EU was depicted as an oppressive force (Wenzl, 2019). As Wenzl (2019: 41) shows, politicians rendered this identity linguistically through passive constructions, claiming that 'we are being told to sign up' to an unfavourable deal, 'we are told that we have a lot of influence in the EU' and 'we are driven in the EU vehicle towards ever-closer union'. These constructions implied that the EU controlled Britain's future and stripped the nation of its power. By obscuring the agent that drives 'us' in the 'EU vehicle' (Wenzl, 2019: 41), for example, politicians avoided acknowledging that the UK participated in EU decision-making processes and instead suggested that the nation had no part in directing the Union's trajectory. Even David Cameron, who stated in his speech on Europe that he 'want[ed] a relationship between Britain and the EU that keeps us in it', characterized the EU as undemocratic with a growing 'gap between the EU and its citizens' (Cameron, 2013, n.p.; Wodak, 2018: 18). Negative representations of the EU thus appeared even in the discourse of (Conservative) politicians who were pro-EU and supported the UK's EU membership (Wenzl, 2019).

British political discourse also includes representations of European citizens, typically as immigrants coming to settle in the UK. Eastern European nationals are often foregrounded in this narrative and constructed negatively as a threat to

Britain (see, e.g., Radziwinowiczówna and Galasińska (2021) on the vile Eastern European trope in the pro-Leave press). For example, Cap (2019: 75) shows that right-wing politician Nigel Farage depicted Bulgarians and Romanians negatively as descending on Britain after EU policies granted them entry. Farage labelled Bulgaria 'the EU's poorest country', emphasizing an economic divide between EU member states, and constructed a scenario in which Britain would lose control of its 'borders, identity [and] also the welfare state' if the nation continued to follow EU immigration rules (Farage, 2014a; Cap, 2019: 75). Farage argued that the EU threatened British national identity by allowing non-British people, namely Eastern Europeans, into the UK to settle. The implication is that rather than expanding the category of 'Britishness' to account for socio-political change, the presence of non-British people in Britain weakens a homogenous national identity. The negative representation of specific European nationalities is, however, text specific; in contrast to Farage's political speeches, UK administration texts about immigration did not foreground specific nationalities and avoided overtly hostile arguments about immigrants coming to the UK (Pérez-Paredes et al., 2016). The government's need to manage international relationships presumably led to an ostensibly more neutral depiction of European countries and citizens than could be found in individual politicians' speeches.

Politicians and journalists use metaphors to make the nuances and fluctuations of international relationships more accessible to the public (Musolff, 2017). In the build-up to the EU membership referendum in the UK, Vote Leave campaigners repeatedly employed metaphors to conceptualize the UK–EU relationship. Boris Johnson depicted the relationship between the nation and the Union in terms of a competitive race, arguing that 'our nation [is] racing ahead economically' with 'no need of the failing European Union' (Charteris-Black, 2019: 187). Through this metaphor, Johnson represented the UK as self-sufficient and prosperous and the EU as preventing the country from progressing. Johnson also drew on the conceptual metaphor of THE NATION AS A PERSON to depict the EU as 'surgically severing' part of the UK and 'amputat[ing] Northern Ireland' during backstop negotiations (Charteris-Black, 2019: 191). Through this image of extreme physical violence, Johnson positioned the EU as the UK's murderer and conceptualized the UK's constituent countries as parts of the national body.

Personifying the nation is a versatile discursive strategy that also underpins positive metaphorical representations of the UK–EU relationship. David Cameron used the NATION AS A PERSON metaphor to frame the UK and the EU as friends in a 2013 speech (Yang, 2018), for example. After the referendum, when the British government began Brexit negotiations with EU leaders, Leave-backing politicians also referred to European nations as Britain's 'friends' and 'neighbours' (Charteris-Black, 2019: 213–221). Similarly, this metaphor was adopted by British newspapers, which frequently conceptualized European countries as Britain's 'partners' and 'neighbours' after the referendum (Charteris-Black, 2019: 221–224). Although these relationship metaphors expressed more distance than the European Commission's metaphor of the 'European family', they represented a desire to foster a positive relationship with the EU during Brexit negotiations (Charteris-Black, 2019). Seemingly, then, metaphors can be used to conceptualize the UK–EU relationship positively or negatively depending on the socio-political agenda of the discourse producer; the need to establish a mutually beneficial Withdrawal Agreement led to more positive representations than could largely be found in pre-referendum discourse, even among Eurosceptics.

There are remarkably few qualitative projects that address British citizens' perceptions of Europe and the EU. One exception is Diez Medrano's (2003) interview study, in which British participants suggested there was a uniqueness to their culture which rendered it distinct from a homogenous European culture. In the words of one of Diez Medrano's participants, 'we feel that the Europeans are so different from us' (Diez Medrano, 2003: 214). Although responses like these reflect a discourse of difference, participants in Diez Medrano's (2003) study did not express an attitude of superiority towards a distinct European culture. Given the belief in Britain being culturally distinct from Europe, it is perhaps not surprising that some British participants expressed fear towards seemingly unstoppable EU integration and discussed feelings of powerlessness against an undemocratic bureaucracy (Ichijo, 2008). One participant in Ichijo's (2008: 117) study of attitudes towards the EU, for example, stated that they 'have picked up the view that the EU is an overly bureaucratic . . . institution'. The verb phrase 'picked up' intimates that there is a relationship between personal interpretations of the UK–EU relationship and broader discourses circulating in the public sphere.

Conclusion

In this chapter, I elucidated the collective identities of Britishness and Europeanness, before exploring existing empirical research that has examined the discursive construction of Britain and Europe in the British press, politics and public opinion over the past thirty years.

3

Researching the Language of National Identity in Times of Brexit

Introduction

As I explained at the beginning of Chapter 2, this research began in embryonic form in a hairdressing salon the day after the EU membership referendum vote. I knew I wanted to explore how institutions and people used language to construct national identities in the context of Brexit. The next steps were to identify research methods, gain ethical approval, collect data and then analyse data. In this chapter, I outline those processes. Rooted in the mediatization of political discourses and the politicization of media discourses – processes explored in Chapter 2 – I provide a rationale for the collection of three data sets: pro-Brexit newspaper articles, government documents and interviews with members of the public. I describe the creation of the corpora and the downsampling methods used to compile them. Following this, I explain the methods for collecting the fifteen interviews with members of the public. I go on to introduce the analytical framework developed and adopted in the first two chapters: a diachronic key semantic domain analysis performed in conjunction with a micro-linguistic analysis of textual examples. Finally, I elucidate the method used to examine the interview data – a discourse analysis of narratives.

Collection of the media corpora

The diffusion of Brexit discourse means that there are several types of media data that could have been analysed in this book. The sheer diversity of genres available to analyse is evident in the variety of existing Brexit-related discourse studies, which range from analyses of Wikipedia pages (Kopf, 2019), through citizens' Twitter accounts (Bouko and Garcia, 2019), to vox pops on news programmes

(Miglbauer and Koller, 2019). Newspaper data has not been neglected either; there have been entire books dedicated to Brexit-related themes across the UK national media (Buckledee, 2018) and book chapters addressing discourse in specific newspapers, such as *The Guardian* (Lutzky and Kehoe, 2019). However, there has been no sustained study of how newspapers constructed British and European identities in the periods between the EU referendum and Britain's withdrawal from the EU in January 2020. This absence was one factor that influenced the decision to focus on national newspaper data rather than other text types.

The intention to interview members of the public about their interactions with institutional discourses of national identity was a second factor that informed the decision to analyse traditional media data. It was important to select a text type that would be familiar across age groups. News consumption on the internet via social media is much lower among those over sixty-five than it is for those aged sixteen to twenty-four (Ofcom, 2017), making social media data an inappropriate data type for a project interested in the opinions of older members of the public. While younger people are more likely to consume news via social media, they also use the websites or apps of traditional media outlets and so will be familiar with the genre conventions of a written news article (Ofcom, 2017).

I considered television and radio broadcasts to be less ideologically insightful than newspaper data because there is no regulation against partisan reporting in newspapers, whereas the broadcasting industry has strict regulations that demand impartiality (Ofcom, 2021). As a result of their greater editorial freedom, newspapers were able to conduct their own campaigns in the lead-up to the EU referendum, intending to influence their readers at a time of democratic decision-making. Some pro-Brexit newspapers also explicitly took credit for the referendum result the day after the vote. For example, the *Daily Express* openly labelled its pro-Leave campaign as a victory. The newspapers' persuasive discourses and the way in which they drew on (supra)national identities are worthy of sustained analysis, not least because they highlight how certain identities are mobilized to support a specific socio-political agenda.

Reach and readership figures for national newspapers provide their own case for examining newspaper data. Each year, Ofcom produces a report on news consumption in the UK. The 2016 report contains figures for the combined print and digital monthly readership of newspapers, while the annual reports covering 2017/18 and 2018/19 offer weekly figures. Readership levels, though diminishing, remain strikingly high for most national newspapers and, in fact, Maccaferri (2019: 10) notes that '3 million more national newspapers were sold during the last month of the referendum campaign'. Maccaferri (2019) interprets this figure as evidence that the British public turns to newspapers at times of national crisis, such as Brexit.

The decision only to focus on pro-Brexit newspapers in this book needs some explanation, especially as Hearn (2017: 20) argues that 'both sides of the Brexit debate were mobilizing nationalist ideas'. Ultimately, I wanted to capture the most dominant, widely accessible and widely accessed representations of Britishness and Europeanness. A Reuters Institute study found that two-thirds of British national newspapers had a pro-Leave dominance in their articles around the time of the referendum (Levy et al., 2016). This research clearly shows that Leave discourses were in the majority in the media: they were the dominant voice. Equally, Swales (2016) found that five pro-Brexit newspapers – those that I analyse in this book – had the highest number of Leave-supporting readers, pointing to a possible echo chamber effect whereby readers' beliefs were likely reinforced by media representations. Of course, analysing Leave discourses only provides a *partial* overview of media constructions of Britain between the periods of the EU referendum and Brexit. As such, I acknowledge that this book necessarily only provides *part* of the story of (supra)national identity construction in Brexit Britain and cannot claim to capture the entire tapestry of constructions of Britishness in contemporary Britain. Future research must consider Remain-backing constructions of national and political identities, building on the work of, for example, Alkhammash (2020) and Thommessen (2017). Nevertheless, the comparison with government data provided in this book can illustrate the ways in which ministers drew upon Leave-backing discourses in their constructions of post-Brexit Britain. This is especially interesting given that one of the leaders of the Vote Leave campaign, Boris Johnson, eventually presided over the UK–EU deal that was approved by Parliament and used to enact the UK's withdrawal. Equally, the analysis of narratives produced by Remain voters in Chapter 6 also demonstrates the extent to which discourses identified in Leave-backing newspapers were more widespread than just these media outlets.

After the decision was made to focus on pro-Brexit national newspapers, specific newspapers were selected based on their editorial stance towards Brexit. *The Express* was unequivocal in its attitude towards the EU referendum; after the result was announced, it claimed that '[the] world's most successful newspaper crusade [had] end[ed] in victory for your *Daily Express*' (*Daily Express*, 2016: 1). *The Sun* was equally transparent, urging its readers to 'BeLEAVE in Britain' and 'Vote to quit EU on June 23' (*The Sun*, 2016: 1). Meanwhile, the *Daily Mail* demanded, 'If you believe in Britain, vote Leave' (*Daily Mail*, 2016: 1). The

Daily Telegraph pitched a Leave vote as an expression of hope for the future of the country: 'In supporting a vote to leave the EU, we are not harking back to some Britannic golden age lost in the mists of time but looking forward to a new beginning for our country' (*The Telegraph*, 2016: 1). Finally, the *Daily Star* covered its front page with a bulldog wearing a Union Jack hat alongside the headline: 'Now let's make Britain great again' (*Daily Star*, 2016: 1).

Articles from the five national newspapers (*The Sun*, *Daily Express*, *Daily Mail*, *Daily Telegraph* and *Daily Star*) and their online counterparts were downloaded from the online news repository Nexis. News and comment articles, alongside letters to the editor, were selected for analysis because they contribute to the newspapers' overall constructions of UK and European identities. Although letters are written by readers and submitted to the newspaper, they are subjected to editorial processes in much the same way as commissioned pieces. That is, they are selected for inclusion in the publication and headlines are added by editors to establish a sense of coherence between the different submissions. These processes mean that the letters become part of the editorial product of the newspapers and are unlikely to represent opinions that are oppositional to the publications' ideological positions.

During the data collection process, the decision was made not to collect live blogs from the newspapers' websites. This was because each time a live blog was updated, it appeared as a separate article in Nexis. Collecting each iteration of a live blog would skew any type of linguistic analysis focused on collocations or phraseology, as repetitions could be from different versions of the same article. Each article was manually checked to ensure it was not a live blog before downloading (e.g. by searching for time stamps or evidence of updates in the body of the article). Any live blogs that slipped through were deleted after the initial data collection.

The search criteria for selecting articles stipulated that each piece had to include 'Britain' or 'British', 'Europe' or 'European' and 'Brexit', 'nation' and 'people' somewhere in the text. The decision to focus on 'Britain' and 'British' was made due to interest in discourses of (supra)national identity that transcended the constituent countries of the UK. As explained in previous chapters, although *English* nationalism is associated with greater Euroscepticism, often this is framed through the language of Britishness (Wellings, 2010; Leith and Sim, 2022). For an understanding of the role of Englishness in the Brexit process, it would be prudent to read Henderson and Wyn Jones (2021).

The decision to include 'Europe' and not 'EU' was made on two grounds. First, a preliminary search revealed that only having 'EU' as a search term excluded discourses about Europe as a continent, which are central to identity discussions because they are closely tied to ideas of culture. Second, 'Europe' is often used to refer to the EU in political, press and individual discourses (Koller et al., 2019), so talk about the 'EU' would undoubtedly surface in articles that also mention 'Europe'. The noun 'Brexit' ensured that the political context was consistent with the government data (see below) and that the data were relevant to the research questions. The decision to include the nouns 'nation' and 'people' was based on the need to limit the texts to those that focused on national identities amid broader discourses about political agreements, negotiations and politicians. 'Nation' was a specific choice based on the unique, supranational identity of Britishness (McCrone, 1997). As there are four constituent countries in the UK, the noun 'country' with its geographical connotations could have presented articles that focused on individual countries. Given the tendency towards Anglocentrism in political discourses about the UK (Mycock and Hayton, 2012), that country would likely be England. This would be problematic as, of course, the EU referendum had ramifications for all UK countries.

The articles that were collected had been published between 22 February 2016, when the EU referendum date was first announced in Parliament, and 12 December 2019, the date of the general election organized by Boris Johnson (see Chapter 1 for political context). Beginning with the parliamentary announcement ensured that articles published during the referendum campaigns, both political and newspaper-led, were included in the data sets, which made it possible to track shifts in the discourses of national identity pre- and post-referendum. Concluding with the general election in December 2019 seemed reasonable as it shaped the context of interview responses by participants.

When the data were collected, the entire media corpus amounted to seven million words. After a preliminary key semantic domain analysis of this corpus, I realized that it was extremely difficult to consider how political events might relate to changes in the salience of semantic domains across the Brexit timeline without segmenting the data. To be able to map the relationship between political events and discursive shifts, a top-down diachronic segmentation into months and years would be necessary (Marchi, 2018). At the same time, I decided that I wanted to reduce the size of the corpus so that I could say something concrete about identity construction around several politically significant events in the Brexit timeline. To reduce the corpus size while maintaining its representativeness, the number of relevant articles published each month across the years was counted and the two months from each year that had the greatest

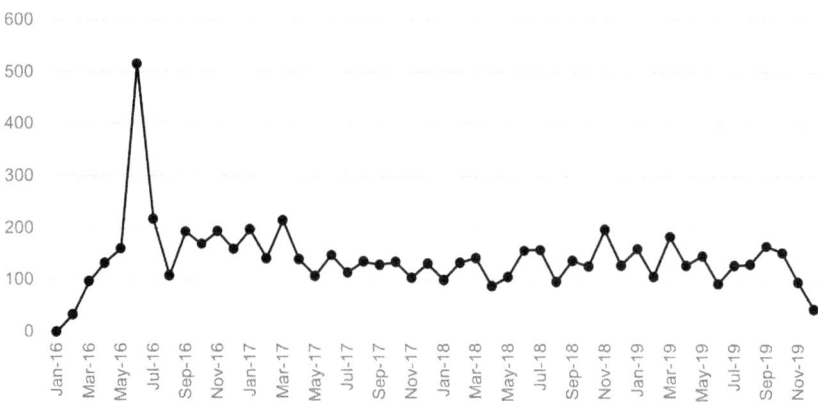

Figure 3.1 Distribution of articles per month.

number of published articles were selected. Figure 3.1 illustrates the publication output of the articles across the data collection period.

When the two peak months from each year were identified, I created four annual subcorpora, with each subcorpus including the two months of peak output data from that year. When the peak months were mapped onto events in the Brexit timeline, it revealed, unsurprisingly, that months with the highest output of data corresponded to key political events. Table 3.1 shows the months included in each annual subcorpus, alongside the number of articles and words, and the political events that occurred during each month. While the number of words in the 2017, 2018 and 2019 subcorpora is remarkably balanced, the 2016 subcorpus is twice the size. This is not surprising: the EU referendum took place in June 2016 and the higher number of articles and words reflects increased reporting around the referendum. In total, across the four annual subcorpora, 2,205 articles and 1,647,707 words of media data were analysed.

Composition of the media corpora

The decision to exclude live blogs from the newspapers' websites slightly affected the representativeness of the data because the *Telegraph Online* and *MailOnline* frequently used live blogs in their Brexit-related reporting. Excluding live blogs meant that the contributions these two publications made to the corpora were smaller than their actual output during the data collection period. In turn, this made the contribution of *Express Online* seem greater than it would be if live blogs from the *Telegraph Online* and *MailOnline* were considered.

Table 3.1 Breakdown of annual subcorpora into months, articles, words, and political events

Annual Subcorpus	Peak Months	Number of Articles	Number of Words	(Key) Political Events
2016	June, July	733	666,734	The EU referendum and the immediate aftermath
2017	January, March	609	332,140	Jan: Supreme Court says government needs primary legislation to trigger Article 50; government publishes Withdrawal Bill draft. Mar: Article 50 is triggered.
2018	July, November	513	332,262	July: government publishes White Paper on relationship with EU; David Davis resigns. Nov: Dominic Raab resigns.
2019	March, September	350	316,571	Mar: Extension to withdrawal process announced and approved. Sept: Benn Act is presented and becomes law; Boris Johnson prorogues Parliament; Supreme Court judges that Boris Johnson's decision to prorogue Parliament is unlawful.

Although the decision to exclude live blogs somewhat affects the representativeness of the data, in that it amplifies the voices of some publications while diminishing others, it is less detrimental to the validity of the analysis than skewing the statistical results by including terms that only achieve keyness because of duplication in the corpus compilation. It is possible to account for the effect of excluding live blogs by explaining that the analysis herein is representative of media output during peak months rather than the entire period, adding the caveat that the *Telegraph Online* and *MailOnline* are underrepresented. However, it would be difficult to account for the effect on the statistical analyses if live blogs had been included.

The decision to exclude live blogs is not the only factor that affected the representativeness of the data. As mentioned above and revealed in Table A.1, compiling separate subcorpora comprising two peak months from each year means that some publications make a greater contribution to the downsampled corpora relative to the original, seven-million-word data set. However, this provides a revealing insight into the Brexit-related publishing patterns of the newspapers. Several of the publications whose articles made the smallest contributions to the overall media corpus are overrepresented in the annual subcorpora. This overrepresentation demonstrates that the publications which focused less on Britain, Europe and Brexit in general tended to write more about these topics around key events in the Brexit timeline, whereas other publications with higher outputs appeared to publish a steady stream of articles over the three-year period. The publications that are consistently overrepresented are *Daily Star*, *Daily Star Online* and *The Sun*. The *Daily Star* and the *Daily Star Online* constitute 0.18 per cent and 1.11 per cent of the overall media corpus, respectively. However, their contribution to the annual subcorpora ranges from zero per cent to 0.52 per cent in the case of the *Daily Star* and 0.56 per cent to 4.23 per cent in the *Daily Star Online*. While the overrepresentation of the *Daily Star* is marginal, it is much more significant in the *Daily Star Online*'s contribution to the 2016 corpus. *The Sun* is overrepresented in all the subcorpora by at least 0.23 per cent, although this is only a very minor difference. The *Daily Mail* is also overrepresented marginally in the 2018 and 2019 subcorpora but is representative of overall output in the two earlier years.

The Sun Online is a unique case because it is not present at all in the subcorpora in 2016 and 2017, yet it contributes around 10 per cent in 2018 and 6 per cent in 2019. Based on its contribution to the overall media corpus (3.55 per cent), these subcorpora figures look like stark underrepresentations in the early years and clear overrepresentations in later years. However, the single figure for the overall media corpus is misleading. As there are no instances of articles from *The Sun Online* at all in the larger 2016 data set and only thirty-five in 2017, the publication's contribution to the 2016 subcorpus is faithful, and its figure for 2017 is only a slight underrepresentation. The 3.55 per cent figure for the entire corpus masks the fact that it is weighted more towards the later subcorpora; that the two later subcorpora show higher figures is not surprising. However, there is still a slight discrepancy. To contribute 10 per cent to the entire media corpus for 2018, there would have to be 148 articles from *The Sun Online* in 2018. There are only 119, which represents around 8 per cent contribution. This means that *The Sun Online* is slightly overrepresented in the 2018 subcorpus. Similarly, the 2019 figure for *The Sun Online* overrepresents its contribution to that year's discourse by around 0.5 per cent – again, a minor effect.

Not all publications are over- or underrepresented. The distributions of *The Express*, *Daily Telegraph*, *Telegraph Online*, *MailOnline* and *Express Online* are largely faithful reflections of their contribution to the overall media corpus of seven million words. As *Express Online, Telegraph Online* and *MailOnline* contribute the most to the overall corpus, representing around 76 per cent of the overall data when taken together, this means most of the articles and examples are likely to be representative of the general output. Despite their potential limitations, then, the subcorpora offer the most representative images available to date of the discourses of (supra)national identities that appeared in Leave-backing newspapers between February 2016 and December 2019. They are worthy of examination because they can provide new insights into the way that these newspapers mobilized (supra) national identities to influence the public's political decision-making at key points in the Brexit timeline. The diachronic data segmentation and downsampling methods enable the discourses to be clearly mapped onto political events, allowing the analysis to go beyond the texts to their socio-political ramifications.

Collection of the government subcorpora

Data from the UK government were collected from three ministerial departments involved in Britain's withdrawal from the EU: the Home Office, the Foreign Office and the Department for Exiting the European Union (henceforth DExEU). The Home Office was chosen because, as its name implies, it is responsible for delimiting a national homeland and outlining who belongs in it (Law, 2001). Similarly, the Foreign Office was selected as it legally and politically defines which nations and people are different from the national in-group. As both departments are responsible for representing the UK to national and international audiences, their documents frequently include discourses of nationhood and belonging. In other words, the documents represent the government's public-directed discourse about Britishness and foreignness. The Home Office and the Foreign Office were also involved, alongside the DExEU, in negotiating Brexit deal points and reporting these negotiation details back to the public, so they were partly responsible for constructing a post-Brexit Britain. Given their focus on discourses of nationhood, the documents produced by these departments are likely to reveal the identities being constructed by the government for post-Brexit Britain.

Each of the government's twenty-four ministerial departments has its own webpage on the UK government website. On each webpage, information is organized into roughly six sections: 'Services', 'Guidance and Regulation', 'News and Communications', 'Research and Statistics', 'Policy Papers and Consultations' and 'Transparency and Freedom of Information Releases'. Two sections were collected from each of the three respective ministerial department webpages: 'News and Communications Documents' and 'Policy Papers and Consultations'. The former category included government-written news articles, press releases and speeches. These documents were selected because they represent the government's construction of events that are also likely to be reported on by the media. This allows for a comparison between the governmental and media representations of national, Brexit-related events as well as an analysis of recontextualization patterns between the two government text types. The policy papers and consultations were also selected because they represent the government's public-directed discourse about Britishness, offering an opportunity to examine the government's perspective without additional media framing.

Data were selected for inclusion in the government corpus if they had been tagged as related to 'Brexit' on the government's website, and if they had been published by one of the three ministerial departments in either their 'News and Communications' or 'Policy Papers and Consultations' sections between 22 February 2016 and 12 December 2019. All documents were copied from the website and pasted into a plain text document, except for documents which consisted solely of tables. These documents were excluded from the corpus because they do not constitute uninterrupted prose and so were unlikely to be processed accurately by the concordance software. As all available government data were collected aside from the tables, the corpus is representative of spoken and written government-produced discourse about Brexit and national identity during the data collection period.

The two sections from which the data were collected contain a wide variety of documents. Each document has its own format and style which are outlined in a style guide published on the UK government website. The result of these different formats is a complex web of editorial and publishing processes of which the public is not necessarily aware. Table 3.2 offers a breakdown of the different document types that contribute to the overall government corpus.

As Table 3.2 shows, press releases are by far the most frequent document type published in the 'News and Communications' sections of the Home Office, Foreign Office and DExEU's pages. Press releases are 'relatively short texts resembling news stories and containing what is considered by the issuer to be newsworthy information' (Catenaccio, 2008: 11). As Catenaccio (2008: 11) notes, press releases 'display a typical mix of informative and promotional' writing. According to the government website, press releases are published 'unedited' as they were sent to the media (Government Digital Service, 2020: n.p.). In addition to providing transparency for the public, publishing unedited press releases

Table 3.2 Breakdown of text types in the government corpus

Document Type	Frequency	Document Type	Frequency
News and communications (NC): Press release	140	Policy papers and Consultations (PC): White Papers, Position Papers and 'future framework' presentations	38
NC: Statement	56	PC: Legal texts and impact assessments	33
NC: Speech/editorial	55	PC: Draft agreements and Bill overviews	30
NC: News story	31	PC: Communiques and memoranda	27
NC: Letter	30	PC: Technical information	26
NC: Explainer/factsheet	5	PC: Explainer/factsheet	21
		PC: Report on negotiations and committees	7
		Policy papers and consultations (PC): Skeleton argument	1
		PC: Government response to White Paper	1
	Total: 317		Total: 184

allows those who are interested to identify the ways in which official government information is recontextualized by the media for public consumption. All official statements by an organizational spokesperson or minister on a newsworthy topic are counted as press releases, except for parliamentary statements, which have their own format and publishing procedure (Government Digital Service, 2020). Within the press release genre, then, several voices are represented, including those of civil servants, organizational representatives and government ministers. These voices may not reach the public in equal measure, however, because press releases are intended for journalists (Catenaccio, 2008), who will publish the information in a story that fits their publication's editorial position.

Statements, speeches and editorials are also frequently published in the 'News and Communications' sections of the departmental websites. These documents are even more complex than press releases: speeches and statements are written by professional speech writers, performed by ministers and then, in some cases, published on the government's website. Not all speeches are published online; the government's style guide states that speeches should only be published where there is an expectation that there will be a high level of public interest in everything that was said, rather than an interest in segments of the speech (Government Digital Service, 2020). The speeches on the government website, then, reflect civil servants' perceptions of what is newsworthy to the national audience. In other words, because of the selection processes, these texts can be viewed as curated for the purposes of an audience and so selected because they express what the government would like the public to know.

In the 'Policy Papers and Consultations' section, the most frequent document type is the policy paper, which exists to make a persuasive case in favour of the government's position. The government's policy papers are aimed at 'high-level specialists' and 'people who hold the government to account' (Government Digital Service, 2020: n.p.). It is reasonable to expect, then, that these texts will include more legal and political jargon than the 'News and Communications' documents. This is certainly also true for the other frequent text types in this section: legal texts and impact assessments, and draft agreements and bills. These texts are more likely to be descriptive than persuasive and are less likely to have a public audience. In total, 501 government documents were collected and analysed, amounting to 1,481,439 words. Table 3.3 outlines the number of documents and tokens in each subcorpus.

The decision to analyse both government and media data was made because of the interrelatedness of government and media discourses: the media facilitates access to political news. For as long as the media covers political events, there is less need for citizens to trawl through the government's website to learn about what each ministerial department is doing. Although no data that measures public consumption of government-produced documents is available, given the extra effort required to locate the information on the government website, it is unlikely that members of the public consistently engage with political news via the government's communication channels. In short, government documents are unlikely to have the same reach and weight as the media coverage of them. This dynamic is termed the mediatization of politics, a phrase which recognizes that government discourses are likely to be reported on by the media and are often presented directly to the public through media channels (Moffitt and Tormey, 2014). The awareness of media interest in political stories means that

Table 3.3 Breakdown of annual government subcorpora

Annual Subcorpus	Number of Documents	Number of Words (Tokens)
2016	30	71,169
2017	178	308,262
2018	194	699,569
2019	99	402,439

political discourse producers must consider how best to discursively package the main points of their messages so that they reach the public despite media framing. Of course, the relationship between the media and politicians is not one way but bidirectional, with media discourses also influencing political stories (Bennett, 2019).

Analysing institutional representations of (supra)national identities without considering both political and media discourses would mean considering only part of the production and consumption process. That is, examining only one would result in an incomplete representation of the dynamics between institutional and individual discourses of (supra)national identities at a critical juncture in British nation-building (Capoccia, 2016). This is especially true in the context of the UK–EU relationship, where politicians 'often respond to Eurosceptic portrayals of the EU in the media, rather than formulating their own' (Rowinski, 2017: 2). Analysing both media and government discourse enables a consideration of whether there is a clear institutional line on what it means to be British or European across the UK press and politics, or whether the different institutions construct these identities in divergent ways.

A further consideration in favour of analysing government data is that any institutional data collected for the project would be used as the basis for interviews that would probe public opinion. Collecting this data and presenting it to members of the public offers them the opportunity to engage explicitly in sustained critical reflection on longer government documents in a way that they might not usually do due to the tendency of the media to report political news in short sound bites.

Collecting public opinion data

In addition to considering media and governmental constructions of Britain, this book investigates how (supra)national identities are constructed in interviews about Brexit with members of the public. I chose to look at personal perspectives towards Brexit and (supra)national identity alongside media and political texts because, as Lennon and Kilby (2020: 116) note, 'regardless of how national identity is socially engineered or politically reworked in elite discourse, it always requires the emotional endorsement of its citizenry'. Equally, as highlighted earlier, Krzyżanowski's (2010) study demonstrates that identity construction exists at the intersection between individual experiences (bottom-up processes) and collective visions (top-down processes). To understand (supra)national identity construction in Brexit Britain, then, it is necessary to consider both institutional and individual discourses.

Ethical approval for the project was awarded by the University of Nottingham Faculty of Arts ethics committee in February 2020. As part of the ethics approval process, I was required to produce a set of interview questions which became the basis of my semi-structured interview plan (see Appendix B). Given that discussions around national identity and potential marginalization are emotional and could lead to distress, I committed to explaining the topics of the interview beforehand to the participants and reminding them that they had the right to stop the interview at any point and withdraw their data. I felt that these reassurances would mitigate any risks associated with the research.

Interviews were split into five topics that corresponded to different levels of identification and influences on (supra)national identity construction in the Brexit context: the locality, the nation, EU-rope, the EU referendum and a stimulus exercise. The first section, the locality, explored participants' connections to the area in which they live to ascertain the discursive construction of regional and local identities and emotional connections to place (see Di Masso et al. (2013) for more on people-in-places discourses). The second section examined participants' expressions of nationality and the degree to which their national identity figures in the way they understand and present themselves. The third section surveyed identification with EU-rope, both as a continent and a political community. The fourth section considered the motivations for voting the way the participant did in the EU referendum and the materials the participants consulted to make their decisions.

The fifth section, the stimulus task, examined the way that interviewees position themselves in relation to media and government discourses. I selected one text from the government corpus that represented the early optimism of Theresa May's cabinet (see Chapter 5 for an analysis of this text). This was a speech by Theresa May, delivered in 2017, which outlined her vision for post-Brexit Britain. I also selected one text from the media corpus (from *The Telegraph*) which reflected the dominant narrative of division in the newspapers in the later years (see Chapter 4 for an analysis of this excerpt). The extracts were chosen to be representative of the narratives at different points in the Brexit process but were also carefully selected so that they could be simultaneously interpreted as two sides to the same argument *or* two completely different constructions of Britain. (That is, they could represent unity and division respectively, or both reflect the need for unity because of division.) The texts acted as a stimulus for discussions of the kind of nation in which participants lived and would like to live.

Initially, I had planned to recruit interviewees by visiting areas within the East Midlands that had voted overwhelmingly to Leave. I had intended to leave leaflets on public information boards and in locations where people were likely to meet, such as churches and town halls. I also had intended to contact people through local groups and societies. Unfortunately, less than a month after ethics approval was awarded, the UK went into lockdown due to the Covid-19 pandemic. As a result, travel was restricted, and face-to-face research became impossible, necessitating a change to online recruitment and online interviews. To make the recruitment process easier, I focused on the smaller localities of Nottingham and Nottinghamshire, places that, in some constituencies, voted very firmly to leave the EU (see, e.g., Mansfield, where 70.9 per cent of voters opted for Leave).[1]

As an initial stage of online recruitment, I asked admins of locality-based Facebook groups if I could share my call for participants with their members and posted information about the project when that permission was granted. Two people expressed an interest through this recruitment strategy, and only one of the two went ahead with the interview. Recruitment online was challenging, not just because Brexit became a less important topic for discussion than the pandemic (Davies and Carter, 2021), but also because there was an underlying suspicion among potential Leave-voting participants about the intentions of the project. One potential participant displayed hostility and concern towards the project, accusing me of trying to frame Leave voters as racist and xenophobic. These suspicions and the articulation of them on public Facebook posts made recruitment for interviews doubly difficult.

As I live in Nottinghamshire, I decided to post a call for participants on my personal Facebook page. This yielded nine interviewees who were my acquaintances (e.g. people I had previously known at university, and former neighbours). All but one of these interviewees had voted to Remain. While I had a former connection with these participants – which may have encouraged them to participate in the study and be more open in their answers – except in the case of two participants, these former relationships were minimal. The two participants with whom I had a closer relationship tended to be more reserved in expressing their views about other voters, although I anticipate that this did not unduly affect the interviews given that both participants still (re)produced discriminatory discourses and their interviews lasted as long as the participants with whom I did not have much of a relationship (around an hour and a half). I recruited five further participants through informal networks, such as friends of friends, all of whom I did not already know. In total, I interviewed fifteen participants. I chose to cap the interviews at fifteen due to limitations on the amount of time I had to collect the data and the difficulties I had recruiting participants online due to the Covid-19 pandemic. Given that the uptake for participating was so low, it took months just to recruit a single participant, and I required sufficient time to analyse the data. The semi-structured interviews were conducted between March 2020 and June 2021. All participants signed informed consent forms and had the opportunity to ask questions about the project before they participated. They were told that they could leave the project at any time.

As Table 3.4 demonstrates, I interviewed five Leave voters and ten Remain voters. While I had initially intended to speak only to Leave voters to reflect the focus on the pro-Leave press in Chapter 4, problems with access to Leave voters necessitated a broader recruitment strategy. Six of my interviewees were female-identifying and nine were male-identifying. All the Leave-voting participants aligned themselves with the Conservatives, while the Remain-voting participants supported a mix of Labour, the Liberal Democrats and the Green Party. (It is worth noting that this is *not* a representative sample of the complex intersection between Remainer and Leaver identities and political affiliation across the UK –

Table 3.4 Participant demographics for interviews

Participant ID	Vote in the EU Referendum	Age	Gender	Political Affiliation	National News Outlets
Participant A	Remain	35–54	Female	Labour	BBC, Sky
Participant B	Remain	35–54	Female	Labour	*Telegraph*, BBC, Sky
Participant C	Leave	75+	Female	Conservative	BBC, Sky, *The Sun*
Participant D	Leave	75+	Male	Conservative	*Telegraph*
Participant E	Leave	75+	Female	Conservative	*Telegraph*
Participant F	Remain	35–54	Male	Labour	BBC
Participant G	Remain	25–34	Male	Labour	*Guardian*
Participant H	Remain	25–34	Male	Greens, Lib Dems, Labour	*Guardian, Independent, Times, Telegraph*
Participant I	Remain	18–24	Female	Labour, Green	*Mirror, Guardian*
Participant J	Remain	25–34	Male	None	BBC
Participant K	Remain	25–34	Male	Liberal Democrats	*Telegraph, Guardian*
Participant L	Remain	18–24	Female	Labour	BBC, *Guardian*
Participant M	Remain	25–34	Male	Labour	*Independent, Guardian*, BBC
Participant N	Leave	35–54	Male	Conservative	BBC, *Times, Guardian*
Participant O	Leave	35–54	Male	Conservative	*Daily Mail*

'preferences to leave or remain do not fit neatly onto the traditional Left/Right' dimension (Woollen, 2022: 98)). Participant IDs were allocated in the order in which the respondents were interviewed.

Due to the Covid-19 pandemic, face-to-face interviewing was not possible throughout 2020 and the first half of 2021. As a result, all fifteen interviews were conducted online. All but three of the interviews were conducted over video conferencing software (a mix of Facebook Messenger calls, Skype, Microsoft Teams and FaceTime). The other three were conducted via audio call due to the participants' lack of familiarity with video conferencing software. There were at least three negative effects of having to conduct interviews online. The first is that older Leave voters, who were less familiar with video conferencing software and the social media site (Facebook) I used for recruitment, were unlikely to either see or self-select to participate in the study. As Jones (2020) notes, some groups of potential participants become invisible to us as researchers because they do not have access to the equipment they need to participate; this, in turn, limits the perspectives and voices captured by the research. The second effect is that I was only able to note paralinguistic features in the interviews that were conducted over video. As a result, I cannot consistently comment on paralinguistic features, such as facial expressions, in my analysis. A final negative effect is that it can be difficult to pick up on 'subtle contextualization cues over Zoom' (Jones, 2020: 187).

Following the interview, my participants filled in a post-interview survey which provided information about their age, political affiliation, consumption of news and use of social media websites as news sources. Collecting this information allowed me to see whether my participants regularly encountered the pro-Leave discourses I analyse in Chapter 4, either directly or through social media posts. It also enabled me to compare and corroborate patterns with broader quantitative studies which found that older voters were more likely to vote to leave the EU in the referendum (Ashcroft, 2016).

Key semantic domain analysis

Having explored the data collection processes, I turn now to the analytical method applied in the first two analysis chapters of this book: key semantic domain analysis, which is conducted through the web-based programme suite, Wmatrix (Rayson, 2008). Wmatrix itself is well-established software, and key semantic domain analysis has been employed by some discourse analysts in recent years (e.g. Prentice, 2010; Potts, 2015; Hayes and Poole, 2022). Nevertheless, in comparison to other popular corpus tools, such as keyword analysis and collocation analysis, it remains relatively underused.

Key semantic domain analysis works by establishing statistically significant, key semantic fields by comparing the relative frequencies of words automatically tagged as belonging to a semantic domain in the target corpus with those in a reference corpus (Rayson, 2008). The semantic domain tool on Wmatrix first tags all the words in a data set according to their part of speech using the CLAWS tagger developed at Lancaster University (Garside and Smith, 1997). It then uses a tagger called the UCREL Semantic Analysis System (USAS) to assign every word or multiword expression to a semantic field (Rayson et al., 2004). There are 21 categories of semantic domains and 232 subcategories, all of which are used by Wmatrix to classify words into different semantic fields (Rayson et al., 2004). As Hayes and Poole (2022) note, examples of semantic domains include, but are not limited to, government and the public domain, and psychological actions, states and processes. USAS has an accuracy rate of 91 per cent according to its developers (Rayson et al., 2004).

As words are grouped into semantic fields, the key semantic domain tool reveals instances where several words with similar semantic meanings are used consistently. Although in some cases the words in key semantic domains can be key by themselves, semantic domain analysis can also highlight domains comprised of lexical items that may not be sufficiently frequent individually to constitute keywords, but which are cumulatively frequent in the whole corpus. The Wmatrix approach to keyness in semantic domain analysis is two-pronged. It allows researchers to set a cut-off for the log-likelihood value, which is a measure of the confidence that a difference in relative frequencies is not due to error or chance (Gabrielatos, 2018). It also allows users to select an effect size measure, which examines the size of the relative frequency difference between the target and reference corpora (Gabrielatos, 2018). Using the two measures means that the results show a tangible difference between instances of the semantic domains in each corpus – a difference which is highly unlikely to be due to error or chance (Pojanapunya and Watson Todd, 2018).

To date (and to my knowledge), only one study of national identity construction has employed semantic tagging: an examination of Scottish nationalist discourse about Scottish independence (Prentice, 2010). This study analysed concordance lines that belonged to key semantic domains to produce a replicable CDA of many texts. The author drew on the Discourse-Historical Approach to CDA, specifically in terms of macro-strategies of argumentation, to reveal how posters to a nationalist forum discursively differentiated between Scotland and England (Prentice, 2010). The study demonstrated that key semantic domain analysis, concordance analysis and CDA frameworks can be usefully combined to identify discourses of nationhood. Despite the obvious success of semantic tagging in this project, it did not examine discursive shifts over time. Given the diachronic focus in this book, it was necessary to develop a method that accounted for semantic change (and consistency) over the years. As a result, the method used in this book expands on existing CA-CDA studies that employ key semantic domain analysis by offering an innovative diachronic element, providing an alternative to the approach taken in Hayes and Poole (2022).

Diachronic key semantic domain analysis

The method developed and used in the CA-CDA sections of this book draws on Bednarek's (2009) three-pronged approach to analysing discourse. That is, it has three levels: a macro-level analysis, a meso-level analysis and a micro-level analysis. The method is intended as a framework for conducting a diachronic study across multiple, temporally organized data sets by combining semantic domain analysis with a micro-linguistic analysis that adheres to the principles of CDA. The three levels can be visualized as a process, with each level providing greater linguistic detail than the previous section, as indicated in Figure 3.2.

The macro-level key semantic domain analysis reveals which semantic fields are consistently key across the majority of the annual subcorpora (similar to

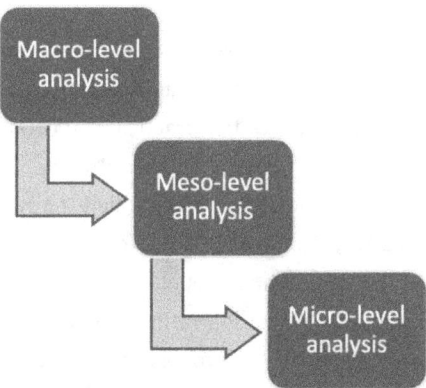

Figure 3.2 Methodological processes.

c-collocates, introduced by Gabrielatos and Baker (2008)). The identification of semantic fields is based on keyness, as indicated by the effect size measure of log ratio, and statistical significance, as reflected in the log-likelihood value.

In the media analysis, two months of data from each year were collected and compiled into four separate (annual) text files. For the government data analysis, all the available texts were divided according to the year of publication and assembled in four separate text files. Each text file was loaded onto the web-based programme Wmatrix separately, producing four annual subcorpora per data set (Rayson, 2008). Working chronologically, each subcorpus was compared to the reference corpus, which was the BNC Written Informative Sampler. The Written Informative Sampler is taken from the larger BNC sampler corpus, which contains two million words (UCREL, 1998). It is the only pre-loaded corpus on Wmatrix that is similar to the target corpora in terms of genre; it consists of 779,027 words, just over a third of which is about public affairs (UCREL, 1998). The written texts in the Written Informative Sampler are taken from a range of sources, including books, newspapers and magazines (BNC, 2008). I selected the Informative Sampler instead of the BE06, which is also available on Wmatrix, because it includes only informative language. By comparing the media and government corpora to informative writing, I could identify rhetorical or evaluative language. As the BE06 includes fiction, where evaluative language is more frequent, a comparison with this corpus could obscure more evaluative uses of language in my corpora – uses which go beyond the task of providing objective information.

When each subcorpus was compared to the reference corpus, a log-likelihood cut-off of 6.63 was imposed and the resulting key domains were sorted according to the effect size – the log ratio score. A frequency cut-off of five was also imposed to prevent the analysis from focusing on infrequent semantic domains. Both log-likelihood and log ratio measures were considered as they are complementary, offering different perspectives on the data (Pojanapunya and Watson Todd, 2018). The log ratio score indicates the practical importance of the difference between the two normalized frequency values (Brezina, 2018), while the log-likelihood value reflects the confidence with which the null hypothesis can be rejected (Gabrielatos, 2018). Combining the two measures results in key terms that are reliably characteristic of the target corpus.

All the semantic domains with a log ratio score above 1.0 were copied into an Excel spreadsheet; the semantic domains for each annual subcorpus were presented in adjacent columns. Semantic domains which only appeared in one or two of the keyness lists were immediately deleted, as the focus was on domains which were consistently key across the data collection period. Once the consistently key domains were identified, a second manual filtering process was undertaken to remove those domains that did not relate to discourses of national identity. This process involved manually examining the concordance lines for each domain to search for nationality-related words; if the concordance lines did not discuss 'Britain', relationships between Britain and Europe or relationships between Britons, then the domain was removed from the lists. For example, the semantic domain Seen was consistently key across the four media subcorpora. However, examining the concordance lines revealed that they referred to discourses about 'noticing', typically with first-person subjects. For example, in the 2017 subcorpus, there was a letter to the editor which stated, 'SIR – I have just received my first new 1 coin [sic]. However, I **notice** that it is dated 2016.' I judged examples like this to be irrelevant to representations of national identity and so removed the semantic domain from the list. I went back over the semantic domains several times to ensure that I had not missed or miscategorized anything, as is also recommended by Gillings and Mautner (2023). The manual examination process was crucial for identifying semantic domains which had a title that intuitively seemed unrelated to national identity but which, upon inspection, revealed many national identity-related discourses. For instance, the No Respect semantic domain does not, by name alone, appear to be related to discourses of nationhood, but many concordance lines within the semantic domain discussed (inter)national relationships in the media data (see Chapter 4). The semantic domains identified through this process were then organized according to log ratio scores, and the semantic domains with the highest log ratio scores were taken forward to the meso-level analysis.

'Meso-level' is used in this book to refer to a level of analysis that provides connections between the macro-level identification of semantic domains and the micro-level analysis of examples from the corpus texts (Bednarek, 2009). The manual, meso-level analysis is an inductive process that involves examining the concordance lines from consistently key semantic domains and organizing them into discursive themes. All the concordance lines from the semantic domain are copied into the Excel spreadsheet. Each individual concordance line is read through and linguistic patterns surrounding the tagged word(s) are noted. For example, if the words are a series of related verbs, such as 'deride' and 'scorn', all the subjects of the verbs and all the objects of the verbs are noted. If the tagged words are nominalizations or nouns, such as 'life', pre-modification and post-modification are examined to identify whose 'life' is being described. Sometimes several words from the same semantic domain form part of a single pattern: the construction of the EU as viewing the UK with contempt could, for example, involve lemmas such as 'disdain', 'contempt' and 'disrespect'. In other cases, a particular word might form the crux of a discourse. For instance, the lemma 'humiliate' might point to a representation of Britain as humiliated because it is consistently the object of the verb. Examining the subjects represented as perpetrating the humiliation can then reveal sub-discourses within the humiliation theme.

Once the social actor and action patterns are identified, the concordance lines are colour-coded and sorted in Excel so that all examples from a particular theme appear together. The metadata for each concordance line are then added: the year and month of publication, in addition to the newspaper from which the article derives. The normalized frequencies of a pattern, or theme, in each subcorpus are plotted to identify diachronic patterns in the salience of the themes within a semantic domain. For example, within a semantic domain of 'Evaluation: Good', a country could be evaluated as 'great' fifty times one year and only four the next when normalized to account for differences in the sizes of the annual subcorpora. This quantitative information can be mapped onto key contextual events that influenced the perception of the country to provide an interpretation of the diachronic change.

As outlined above, a manual, meso-level analysis was conducted by organizing the concordance lines into themes. The themes identified at this level were not predetermined but were judged to emerge out of the data. For instance, the most key semantic domain in the media data – No Respect – was deemed to have four themes based on who was positioned as the object of contempt and who was identified as the subject of contempt (see Chapter 4). (In other words, the themes were identified through a combination of data-driven (i.e. object and subject positions) and author interpretation approaches.) Each concordance line was colour-coded according to the theme to which it belonged. Once identified, normalized instances of the theme (per 100,000 words) in each subcorpus were put into a line graph to identify patterns in their frequency over the years. Plotting the data in this way revealed shifts in discourses that were not perceptible when the subcorpora were examined individually. Once the diachronic patterns were identified, I examined each concordance line from the themes with the greatest number of instances to reveal how representations of national actors were borne out linguistically.

Concordance lines that belong to themes with the greatest number of instances are considered in the micro-level analysis. At this final level, the examples from the texts are subjected to a detailed linguistic analysis of transitivity and socio-semantic patterns. The micro-linguistic patterns are considered in terms of their potential socio-political, democratic consequences. Together, the three levels of analysis provide an overview of how discourse patterns in discussions of national identity shift diachronically; they provide both breadth and depth while maintaining a qualitative, linguistic focus.

The micro-linguistic analysis of individual concordance lines was based predominantly on van Leeuwen's (1995; 2008) socio-semantic models for social actor and social action representation, and Halliday's (1985) transitivity framework. These models allow for a diverse range of lexical strategies to be involved in the construction of (supra)national identities. In my analysis of the linguistic data, I particularly drew on parts of van Leeuwen's (1995) framework that refer to the construction of groups (*assimilation*) and individuals (*individualization*). For example, I employed analytical categories such as *collectivization*, which involves homogenizing groups of social actors, and *functionalization*, which means representing social actors in terms of an activity, occupation or role (van Leeuwen, 1995). I also examined linguistic exclusion, in terms of *suppression* and *backgrounding* (van Leeuwen, 1995). Suppression refers to instances where there is no mention of the social actor anywhere in the text, whereas backgrounding refers to instances where the social actor is not included in a specific representation of action but is mentioned elsewhere in the text and so can be inferred by readers (van Leeuwen, 1995). In these cases, it is often necessary to consult the entire text rather than just the concordance line. In terms of transitivity, I often identified material and mental processes. Material processes are those which involve physical actions such as kicking or throwing (Thompson, 2013); the 'doer' of the action is the Actor and the object or person having something done to them is the Goal. Mental processes, in contrast, refer to 'something that goes on in the internal world of the mind' (Thompson, 2013: 97).[2]

I recognize that this method of diachronic key semantic domain analysis is time consuming and probably only possible for projects with the capacity to spend extended time with the data. However, I believe that for those projects, the time spent with the data in this way is highly rewarding – it provides a level of familiarity with the texts that counters the – admittedly now quite old – criticism that corpus linguistics deals with decontextualized examples (see, e.g., Charles et al. (2009: 1) who say that 'corpus linguistics tends to use techniques that decontextualize individual texts and focuses on recurrent patternings of small-scale items such as words and phrases'). Equally, it accounts for both consistency in the higher-level semantic domains and subtle differences in the discourses that emerge from an analysis of those domains. In this way, it allows for a nuanced picture of the data to emerge.

An approach to narrative: Story genres

In combination with the key semantic domain analysis of media and government texts, this book offers a discourse analysis of narratives told in oral interviews. To analyse the stories, I draw on Martin and Plum's (1997) framework of three story genres that recur in narratives of personal experience: the Recount, the Anecdote and the Exemplum. These approaches are deemed to be agnate with the traditional Labovian narrative. The Recount is a story in which a sequence of events is presented by the teller as 'unfolding unproblematically', while the Anecdote is an account 'of a remarkable event, the point of which is to invite a listener or reader to share' (Martin and Plum, 1997: 301). The Exemplum, in contrast, shares 'a judgement about a noteworthy incident' (Martin and Plum, 1997: 301). Martin and Rose (2008) adopt these three story genres alongside a fourth: the Observation, the purpose of which is 'to share a personal response to things or events' (Martin and Rose, 2008: 65).

Although they are now around twenty-five years old, the four story genres outlined by Martin and Plum (1997) and Martin and Rose (2008) are more applicable to the spoken data I have collected than, for example, the traditional Labovian narrative or what Georgakopoulou (2007) terms 'small stories'. That is, they are somewhat more flexible in terms of what constitutes a story than Labov (1972) – in that they allow for different components of a story – while allowing for a more monologic approach than Georgakopoulou's (2007) small stories framework. As a result, I have drawn on the typology of the 'story family' used by both Martin and Plum (1997) and Martin and Rose (2008) for the first step of my discourse analysis of narratives: determining what constitutes a story in my data. The story genres are reproduced in Table 3.5.

As Table 3.5 shows, there are four principal story genres used in the analysis of stories in my interview data: Recount, Anecdote, Exemplum and Observation. (It should be noted that these are not the only story genres that exist: 'storytellers continuously creatively construct and negotiate (new) narrative genres' (Van de Mieroop, 2021: 6) and so choosing this story genre family necessarily limits the stories I am able to analyse in Chapter 6.) The four story genres I have drawn upon have slightly different structural elements and purposes. The Recount, as outlined above, is used to narrate a past experience. It differs from the Labovian

Table 3.5 Typology of story type

Type of Story	Definition	Function	Structure
Recount	'A retelling of a sequence of events presented by the teller as unfolding unproblematically in a Record of Events' (Martin and Plum, 1997: 301). It does not have 'a suspension of action through evaluation' as evaluation is typically prosodic (Martin and Plum, 1997: 301). The ending is 'not about restoring a disturbed equilibrium' (Martin and Plum, 1997: 301).	To narrate past experience	Orientation → Record of Events → Reorientation
Anecdote	A retelling of a remarkable event/disruption to usuality intended to invite the listener to share a reaction (Martin and Plum, 1997). It is typically used to negotiate solidarity by inducing an affectual response from the listener (Martin and Plum, 1997).	To share a reaction with the audience	Orientation → Remarkable Event → Reaction → Coda The reaction is often recorded by the narrator through reiteration of a key aspect of the Remarkable Event.
Exemplum	A retelling of a disruptive event which is interpreted rather than reacted to or resolved (Rose and Martin, 2008). An exemplum is 'intended to share/induce a judgement about a noteworthy incident rather than an emotional response to an event' (Martin and Plum, 1997: 301). 'The listener is positioned to approve or disapprove of the conduct of a story's protagonists and their behaviour' and 'tellable events of the story are downgraded to an incident whose only function is to make a point about an event that lies outside of the text' (Martin and Plum, 1997: 301).	To share a moral judgement	Orientation → Incident → Interpretation → Coda

(Continued)

Table 3.5 (Continued)

Type of Story	Definition	Function	Structure
Observation	A retelling that 'states what happened as a single event (collapsing a series of sequenced events into one)' and describes how the event affected the narrator (Martin and Plum, 1997: 304).	To share a personal response to things or events	Orientation → Event Description → Comment

story in that it does not have a Resolution. While it contains the Labovian Orientation, used to set the scene of the story, it has a Record of Events through which the action of the story takes place, and a Reorientation, during which the story's main point is recapitulated.

The Anecdote differs from the Recount in that there is a Remarkable Event which does not unfold unproblematically. The Remarkable Event is typically narrated as a disruption to usuality and is intended to negotiate solidarity through a shared reaction. The Anecdote contains a traditional Labovian Coda. The Exemplum differs further, in that the Remarkable Event is interpreted rather than resolved. A single Incident is described and then interpreted morally to share a judgement about a character or an event. Often, Exempla make a moral point outside of the story world. They too have a Coda. Finally, the Observation collapses several events into a single Event Description and is followed by a Comment which articulates how the event affected the narrator. These story genres are useful because they illustrate that stories are told to 'do something' (De Fina, 2009: 235), whether that is to express solidarity or to convey moral judgements about social actors.

Martin and Plum (1997) and Martin and Rose's (2008) frameworks were used to identify stories in my interview data. If the data did not align with one of the four story genres outlined above, they were considered not to be a story for the purposes of this project. Comparing segments of the interview data to the story genres led to the identification of 128 stories as candidates for analysis. Of course, identity construction also took place outside of the stories. While the analysis of lay narratives in this book – constituting only a single chapter – is novel and important, then, it is only a partial account of citizens' constructions of Britishness in the context of Brexit. I hope to produce further research in this area, looking not only at other types of stories but also identity performances that take place outside of stories (see, e.g., Parnell, forthcoming).

The next step of the analysis involved thematically categorizing the stories to identify common identity constructions. Using NVivo to assist with data management, I categorized each story into thematic groups, such as 'remembering a great British past', 'narrating inequality', 'reporting discrimination' and 'emphasizing British division'. The most common thematic representations were selected for close linguistic analysis. The discourse analytical approach I take to narratives is perhaps closest to what Riessman (2008) labels the thematic approach to narratives, which focuses on the content of stories. However, I have combined this focus on story content, where relevant, with what De Fina and Georgakopoulou (2012: 24) would call 'dialogic-performance analysis', which is a consideration of the performance of identities in interaction. In other words, my approach to narrative in this book is eclectic.

There are many frameworks for the micro-linguistic analysis of identity construction in stories. In this book, I have largely followed Wortham (2001), who recommends analysing reference and predication strategies, alongside metapragmatic descriptors (verbs of saying or nominalizations that describe speech patterns), quotations, evaluations and epistemic modality. These strategies focus primarily on identity representations in the story world. While useful, they are less helpful for considering the interactive elements of the story. To redress this limitation, Wortham (2001) usefully employs Bakhtin's (1981) concept of ventriloquation (the voicing of others' speech) to address the *performance* of identities in stories; this concept proved to be useful to some extent in my analysis, too, as Remain-supporting participants tended to voice Leave-voting ideologies in a different pitch or tone of voice, thereby performing a Leaver identity. Beyond Wortham's (2001) recommendations, to ensure consistency across the three analytical chapters, I also applied van Leeuwen's (1995; 2008) socio-semantic categories of social actor and action to help analyse how people and their behaviours were construed in the stories.

Within the micro-linguistic analysis, I have made use of the concept of indexicality. As outlined briefly in Chapter 1, indexicality focuses on how 'linguistic forms are used to construct identity positions' (Bucholtz and Hall, 2010: 21). Indexical meanings are 'meanings that connect discourses to contexts and induce categories, similarities and differences within frames, and thus suggest identities, tones, styles and genres' (Blommaert, 2007: 115). In other words, an index is a linguistic form that points, either directly or indirectly, to a particular identity construction. Indexical processes, according to Bucholtz and Hall (2010: 21), include overt mentions of identity labels, implicatures and presuppositions, and the use of linguistic structures 'that are ideologically associated with specific personas and groups'. As Ochs (1992) points out, most of the time the connection between a linguistic form and a social identity is indirect; words are linked to a particular stance, which is in turn associated with a particular social category. Indexicality has often, although not exclusively, been applied to constructing gender identities (see Ochs, 1992). In this book, however, I apply indexicality to political and national identity construction (see Llamas et al. (2009) for more on indexicality as applied to national identities).

Conclusion

In this chapter, I have outlined the processes through which I collected the data analysed in this book. I have provided a rationale for why I chose to analyse media, government and interview data which is rooted in existing scholarly research. I have explained how I will analyse my three data sets, drawing on a substantial body of literature about research methods.

4

Pro-Brexit Newspaper Representations of the UK and EU-rope

Introduction

In this chapter, I examine the discursive representation of Britain and Europe in the pro-Brexit press at various points between 2016 and 2019. Through key semantic domain analysis, I illustrate how the pro-Brexit press narrates Britain's journey from unity to disunity. I elucidate the EU's discursive role as a scapegoat for British problems and demonstrate how this representation positions Brexit as the solution to public discontent. Taking a diachronic approach, I uncover an argumentative shift in late 2018, prompted by Theresa May's Brexit deal and parliamentary indecision. The construction of a UK with a cohesive, civic national identity transforms into a depiction of a nation torn apart by social inequality and political incompetence. The nouns 'Remainer' and 'Brexiteer' persist in linking socio-political divisions to the EU, even in 2019; the terms foster resentment between a so-called metropolitan elite and 'ordinary Britons' in the UK, threatening to destabilize a collective British identity that will prove increasingly important in the post-Brexit period.

Constructing Britain and Europe in the early post-referendum years (2016–17)

The Alive semantic domain

Each year, the Alive semantic domain appears among the ten most key domains. As shown in Table 4.1, the log ratio values indicate that the normalized frequencies in the target subcorpora are consistently over four times higher than those in the reference corpus.

Table 4.1 Statistical information about the 'Alive' semantic domain

Year	Relative Frequency in C1 per 100,000 Words (Media)	Percentage of C1 (Media)	Relative Frequency in C2 per 100,000 Words (ref)	Percentage of C2 (ref)	Log-Likelihood	Log Ratio
2016	40.3	0.05	7.1	0.01	216.70	2.67
2017	33.7	0.04	7.1	0.01	107.07	2.36
2018	33.4	0.04	7.1	0.01	124.41	2.55
2019	44.5	0.05	7.1	0.01	170.14	2.78

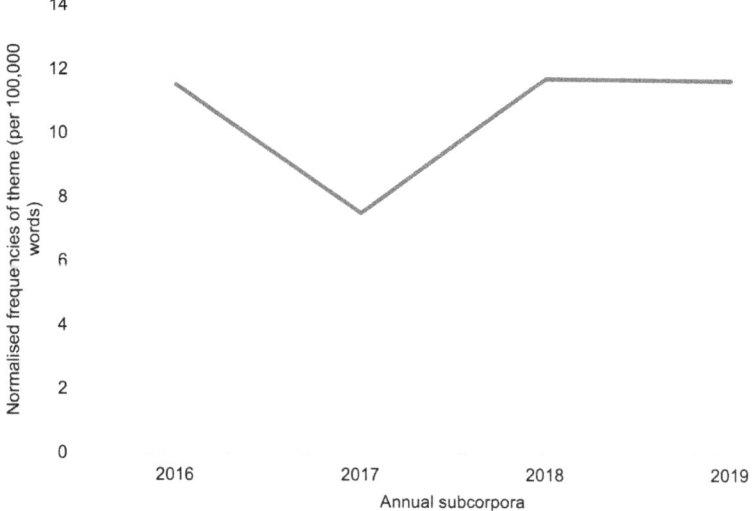

Figure 4.1 British way of life theme per 100,000 words.

Through a manual reading of concordance lines, I identified that a construction of a common British way of life is the main national identity-related representation realized by the Alive semantic domain. Instances of the theme remain stable over the years, with only a small decrease in 2017, as shown in Figure 4.1. The diachronic consistency demonstrates that a national lifestyle is integral to the depiction of a collective British identity throughout the withdrawal period.

There are two principal constructions of a British way of life: the EU's interference in British life (thirteen examples) and the characteristics of a British lifestyle (fourteen instances). The first theme features only in the two earlier subcorpora, where it appears nine and four times, respectively. The representation reflects the interrelated construction of Britain and Europe in the early post-referendum years; depicting Britishness, in these articles, involves making value judgements about the EU's social actions (see Spiering (2014) on the opposition between the UK and the EU). The theme's absence from the later subcorpora suggests that following the Leave vote, the EU's social actions become less salient in the data.

The second theme, the characteristics of a British lifestyle, features in all four annual subcorpora. The most consistent representation of British life appears in 2017, in the context of calls for a second Scottish independence referendum. Journalists foreground British unity in these examples to undermine nationalist arguments about Scotland's cultural and territorial distinctiveness. The remaining concordance lines presuppose common experiences across Britain but the circumstances they describe differ, from technological advancements to the mutable nature of human existence. Only two concordance lines narrate multiple versions of British life based on socio-economic inequalities. Overall, then, the emphasis of the domain is predominantly on British unity.

The EU's interference in British national life

Nine of the thirteen concordances from this theme acknowledge the diversity of British life through the plural noun 'lives'. Extracts (1)–(3), which constitute a representative sample across different newspapers in the corpus, presuppose that there is a plethora of lived experiences in the UK:

(1) Miss [Priti] Patel said: 'The EU is undemocratic and interferes too much in our daily **lives**. We have seen that with the scale of migration, and the impact this has had on local communities – and key public services such as the NHS, housing and schools'. (*MailOnline*, June 2016)

(2) The British people never voted for endless directives and EU rulings which invade and restrict their **lives** day in, day out. Political sovereignty is owned by every elector in this country and it was never a gift our politicians had a right to hand over to Brussels and those fat cats in the Commission. (*The Express*, June 2016)

(3) For almost half a century, Brussels has tightened its bureaucratic grip over every nook and cranny of our daily **lives**. Once power is seized by the centre, it is never handed back. (*The Sun*, January 2017)

Four additional concordance lines assume greater homogeneity in the lifestyles of Britons through the singular noun 'life'. One representative example is shown in Extract (4).

(4) And with thousands of individual pieces of legislation (which speaks volumes about how Brussels has insinuated itself into the minutiae of British **life**), two years is a tight schedule. (*Daily Mail*, March 2017)

The presumption of diversity and the presupposition of homogeneity are not as contradictory as they first appear. Homogenizing a British lifestyle through the singular noun 'life' allows the journalist to assert that the EU affects every person in the UK while ignoring how experiences differ between countries and socio-economic backgrounds. Conservative MP Priti Patel achieves the same effect by emphasizing the unifying experiences of public services in Extract (1). As a member of the government, Patel could be considered responsible for policies that have negatively affected the national health, housing and education systems. To shift the blame towards the EU, she creates a common enemy against which all members of the nation can unite. Patel realizes this by positioning a rhetorical tripartite list of core elements of national infrastructure, 'the NHS, housing and schools', as casualties of EU interference. Including herself among those affected by the EU through the possessive determiner 'our', Patel recontextualizes British politicians as powerless victims rather than the agents responsible for funding public amenities. Although Patel implies that 'key public services' are crucial for 'local' communities to function, the NHS, for example, is regulated at the (devolved) national level and so underpins communities whether they live in small, rural areas or larger towns and cities (Morrison, 2019). This universal applicability is fundamental to Patel's argument that no matter how they live day-to-day, all readers will be affected by the breakdown of the healthcare, housing and education systems.

The argument that national services are under attack and need defending is part of an Invaded Nation frame (Charteris-Black, 2019); it constitutes a national call to action to protect sacred infrastructure from collapsing. Patel's use of grammar indicates that the fundamental problem for the nation to resolve is EU intervention in British culture: 'interferes' is the only dynamic material process (Halliday, 1985) assigned to the out-group's actions in the extract and so is more grammatically salient than the backgrounded action of the nominalization 'migration'. The connotations of external action surrounding 'interferes' place the EU at a geographical and political distance, marking it as a radical Other – an invader of the UK (Gibbins, 2014). The verb's linguistic salience accentuates the overtones of outside meddling and delegitimizes the EU's right to insert itself into British life. From this representation, Patel's primary exhortation emerges: the public should vote to leave the EU so that Britain can regain control of its immigration policies and protect its public services. Valluvan (2019: 6) states that 'solutions that project a nationalist tenor increasingly obtain a panacean value in the popular imagination, suggesting that various significant challenges – be they economic, security, social or cultural – will be magicked away through the emasculation of the significant Others in the nation's midst'. Patel's argument undoubtedly subscribes to this 'panacean value': she implies that leaving the EU will reduce immigration, which will be a panacea for problems with the 'NHS, housing and schools'.

Although Patel's central call to action is focused on the EU, her choice to frame migration as the consequence of EU interference encourages division between British citizens and EU migrants. The pejorative semantic prosody of the noun 'impact' (Cook, 2011) depicts EU migrants as draining the public services Britons use every day, even if this is not the grammatical or argumentative focal point of the sentence (see Zappettini (2019) for more on the construction of EU migrants as a drain on British services). The claim that migration affects 'local communities' places migrants who live in the UK outside of the spatial imaginary of the nation, a common strategy in the British government's discourse about immigration (Bennett, 2018). The discursive exclusion of migrants creates a neoliberal hierarchy among the public that positions 'native' Britons' economic needs above the needs of migrants. The underlying presupposition is that migrants threaten to overpower British services simply by using them; there are not enough resources available for Britons *and* migrants. This neoliberal argument shifts attention away from the fact that there are already insufficient resources by employing the common Eurosceptic British media trope of securitizing immigrants; that is, transforming immigrants into matters of security (Chernobrov, 2019).

Conceptualizing EU migrants' use of public services as a threat asserts that protecting Britain's amenities involves preventing migrants from accessing British infrastructure. On a political level, this may be achieved by leaving the EU and creating a national migration policy. This is, arguably, what Patel is advocating for, albeit implicitly. However, for readers, whose only immediate control is over their lives, this argument could inspire intolerance towards EU migrants and bolster support for policies that prohibit migrants' access to primary public services. Overall, the example can be seen as underpinned by the ideology of welfare chauvinism – a concept introduced by Andersen and Bjørklund (1990: 212) as 'welfare state chauvinism' to refer to the belief that 'welfare services should be restricted to our own' (see Donoghue and Kuisma (2022) for more on Brexit and welfare chauvinism).

The overriding account of how the EU interferes in British national life is through legislation and regulations, as Extracts (2)–(4) illustrate. As rules and regulations are more abstract for readers than the public services they encounter daily, the effect that these entities have on the daily lives of the British people is perhaps less clear. To persuade readers that regulations do impinge upon their lives, the journalist personifies the actors 'endless directives' and 'EU rulings' and positions them as the perpetrators of the metaphorical material processes 'invade' and 'restrict' in Extract (2) (Halliday, 1985). The personification and material processes combine in a metaphor of violation to reinforce the Invaded Nation frame (Charteris-Black, 2019), arguing that EU legislation poses an immediate, tangible threat to the lived experiences of people in the UK. Positioning British 'lives' as the goal of the material processes (Halliday, 1985) 'invade' and 'restrict' frames the European threat as one which targets individuals in addition to the entire nation; readers are encouraged to feel personally victimized by EU law. Through the belligerent connotations of the material processes, the journalists solidify the EU's role as a radical Other, positioning it against the UK in dichotomies of enemy and victim, invader and invaded (Gibbins, 2014).

Despite the effect of the grammatical and lexical choices in creating a sense of tangible impact, the extracts do not articulate how British life is affected or which regulations restrict Britain. These omissions are arguably intentional. The lexical choices in the extracts situate the discourse in the semantic field of bureaucracy; journalists cite 'directives' and 'rulings' in Extract (2) and the nominal group 'bureaucratic grip' in Extract (3). A central tenet of Eurosceptic discourse is the construction of the EU as faceless, bureaucratic and untransparent (Oberhuber et al., 2005); by referring to vague, political manoeuvres, the journalists strengthen the EU's reputation as a complex and opaque institution that meddles in British life. Commentators argue that the perceived complexity of EU practices influenced the vote to Leave; in the face of incomprehensible legalese and institutional jargon, it was easier for voters to defer to emotional instincts (Toynbee and Walker, 2020). That these articles place an opaque EU within a discourse of threat suggests that the pro-Leave press contributed to this phenomenon – the extracts draw out an instinctual desire for self-protection while failing to delineate the exact nature of the threat. The adjective 'endless' and the nominal group 'thousands of individual pieces' form a numerical argumentation strategy (Wodak et al., 2009); they imply EU legislation is churned out on a whim without direction. Through the construction of the EU as a power-hungry, faceless institution, journalists shift the responsibility for unfavourable policies towards Brussels, diverting the blame away from the national government.

An Invaded Nation frame consistently encases the depiction of a British way of life in the earlier subcorpora; it encourages the public to vote to leave the EU to protect national infrastructure (Charteris-Black, 2019). Identity construction in this representation is relational: journalists repeatedly dichotomize Britain and the EU and demonize the Union as an intruder and an enemy. The newspapers do not delineate the official workings of the EU; a semantic field of bureaucracy frames the Union as overly complex and too far removed from the lives it regulates. Although the intended call to action is a Leave vote, Patel's use of migration to disparage the EU reduces migrants to 'political rivalry discourse' (Baker et al., 2008). In this frame, EU migrants become the unspoken perpetrators of the collapse of the national infrastructure; such a depiction makes migrants vulnerable to intolerance and sows the seeds of discord in British society. Ultimately, the representation shifts the blame for problems in Britain away from the national government and towards Europe.

Characterizing British national life

Only 14 of the 179 concordance lines from the Alive semantic domain depict what a British lifestyle involves. Of those fourteen extracts, four constitute nationalist responses to calls for a second Scottish independence referendum. To represent the consistency of this discourse, three of the four selected extracts below are from March 2017, when then Scottish first minister Nicola Sturgeon sought approval from the Scottish Parliament to lay the groundwork for a second independence referendum (Scottish Government, 2017). Examples (5) and (6) are direct quotations from a speech by Theresa May, which *Express Online* and *Daily Mail* both published without editorial intervention. Extract (7) is from a lifestyle feature while Example (8) is from an editorial, which accounts for its more explicit bias and personal tone.

(5) As Britain leaves the EU and we forge a new role for ourselves in the world, the strength and stability of our union will become even more important. This proud shared heritage provides the bedrock of our **lives** in the UK. As we face this great national moment together I hope you will continue to play your part to build a stronger Britain, a more united Britain that I'm determined we shall be once we emerge from this period of national change. (*Express Online*, March 2017)

(6) And the great institutions which we have built together, the pillars of our national **life**, are the result of common endeavour. The National Health Service, the BBC, our armed forces, our Parliamentary democracy, our constitutional monarchy, our commitment to the rule of law, our respect for fundamental human rights. (*MailOnline*, March 2017)

(7) Practical and character building the humble potato crisp is at the heart of national **life**. Imagine a childhood without licking the salt and vinegar flavour off your fingers. Impossible. (*Express Online*, March 2017)

(8) I wonder if they will be happy with what they reap, and what astounding damage they have done not just to our political settlement but to the famous civility and fair mindedness of British **life**. (*Telegraph Online*, March 2019)

In contrast to the plurality of lifestyles acknowledged in the EU-related version of this theme, most extracts above use the singular noun 'life'. Selecting the singular noun instead of the plural is significant because it constructs a shared lifestyle which denies the existence of cultural diversity between Scotland, England, Wales and Northern Ireland. In the context of calls for Scottish independence, this denial is especially key; Scottish nationalism is primarily civic and posits that Scotland has a unique territorial and institutional identity (Leith and Soule, 2011). Using the singular noun to refer to a homogenous Britain, then, undermines the nationalist argument that Scotland is institutionally autonomous and territorially and politically distinct (Leith and Soule, 2011). During this period, Theresa May and Nicola Sturgeon were embroiled in a public dispute over Scottish independence; that Extracts (5) and (6) are examples of direct speech from Theresa May is significant. The pro-Leave text producers give extended, unedited space to May's full speech because her arguments match the newspapers' pro-domestic Union editorial position. In contrast, Nicola Sturgeon's assertions are only alluded to implicitly by May's call for unity. Through this omission, the journalists lead readers to believe that Scottish independence is merely Sturgeon's desire, rather than a genuine threat to the existence of the UK. This is important when considering Virdee and McGeever's (2023: 3) claim that 'Scotland, and more specifically, Scottish independence, is now the weak point of the British state'. By alluding only implicitly to Sturgeon's desires, the newspapers underplay the significance of Scottish independence to Britain's continued existence, but the fact that they recognize a need to emphasize unity highlights the very real consequences of Brexit on Anglo-Scottish relations.

Nationalist discourse exhibits a sense of timelessness as a country's history is retold, its present elaborated and its future envisioned (Anderson, 2006). This temporal unity seeps through in Extract (5), which draws on a narrative of national history through the nominal group 'proud shared heritage' to argue that a national way of life has developed out of a long-term union between the four countries. The construction of the union as 'heritage' locates unity in the past, evoking nostalgia for a period of 'strength' and 'stability' that will 'become even more important' in coming years. Through this example, May exploits the public's desire, expressed through the Leave vote, to return to a British golden era (Calhoun, 2017); she feeds into an interpretation of British hegemony as a relic of a bygone age that must be reclaimed. In this way, her vision of Britain is retrotopian (Beaumont, 2017). The call to 'continue' the union, represented through the metaphorical material process (Halliday, 1985) 'build [a stronger Britain]', is based on a conservative plea to respect a long-established tradition, rather than on present ideological cohesion between the UK's constituent countries. Foregrounding the past and positioning it as the road map to the future obscures the dwindling ideological unity between the UK's countries after the referendum. More importantly, it undermines the Scottish nationalist argument that Scotland is fiscally and politically peripheral to an English core by positioning Scotland at the shared centre of British institutional innovation (Whigham, 2019). Given Scotland's desire to remain in the EU, shoring up support for the UK and presenting Brexit as inevitable through the present tense verb 'leaves' dispels Sturgeon's hopes that Scotland could become an independent member state (Macnab, 2019).

The retrospective focus continues in Example (6) in the present perfect tense of the material process 'we have built'. Again, collective British achievements are situated in history. This extract goes beyond a vague reference to historical 'union' by presenting concrete examples of what can be achieved through UK collaboration in an asyndetic list: 'The National Health Service, the BBC, our armed forces, our Parliamentary democracy, our constitutional monarchy, our commitment to the rule of law, our respect for fundamental human rights'. Through its open-ended nature, the asyndetic list suggests that the potential for UK collaboration is infinite and what has already been achieved is too great to enumerate, hence the lack of conjunction signalling a final example. The ideological work performed by the list is noteworthy: it begins with an institution that is specific to the UK (the NHS), but by degrees introduces institutions and ideologies that characterize any democratic country. Many nations have armed forces, for example, and respect for human rights is enshrined in the

European Convention on Human Rights, in addition to national legislation. What this genericity suggests is that rather than constructing an image of a uniquely British way of life, then prime minister Theresa May emphasizes the fundamental democratic principles that underpin the UK's institutions. This strategy encourages readers who might sympathize with Scottish secession to consider the UK's democratic values as transcending any cultural distinctiveness that Scotland may possess. The focus on general democratic principles in place of more specific British attributes offers an important insight into national identity construction: generic qualities can be framed as unique to a particular nation to obscure areas of socio-political discord and give the illusion of cultural affinity.

Rowinski (2017) argues that in recent years, Britain has experienced a shift from patriotism to ethnic nationalism in the British press. In their expressions of civic nationalism, Extracts (5)–(8) somewhat challenge his claim. May bases her calls for unity on shared institutions and military history, rather than specifically on British lineage. Britons are united by 'licking the salt and vinegar flavour off [their] fingers' and by their 'Parliamentary democracy' and 'constitutional monarchy', rather than thousands of years of shared ancestry. Although a nation is typically defined by its historical territory (Smith, 1992), there is no reference to British geography in any of the constructions of British life. Rather, each example draws on abstract elements of nationhood: a culture united by food and a legal framework rooted in democracy. That the list in Example (6) becomes increasingly generic rather than nation specific indicates a preference for civic belonging over ethnic ties; the marked lack of specificity does not fit with the biological and geographical distinctiveness so important to ethnic nationalism. Arguably, the distinct histories of the UK's nations render civic nationalism the only option; no majority ethnic lineage exists to unite the English and Scottish peoples, for example, as Scots historically separated their national identities from their loyalty to the British state (McCrone and Kiely, 2000; Morton, 2001). As a result of the supranational nature of Britain, the only feasible legacy that can be drawn upon to claim shared 'heritage' is the creation of the domestic Union, a civic act. While ethnic nationalism might be a persuasive tool for journalists when distinguishing a homogenous UK identity from an international Other, it is not fruitful for a prime minister addressing the UK's constituent countries and their relationships through the media (Rowinski, 2017).

In addition to calls for national unity based on shared history, the newspapers draw on childhood experiences and alleged personal attributes to construct a distinctly British personality. For example, the adjective 'character-building' premodifies 'the humble potato crisp' in Example (7), positioning the act of eating crisps as a process of initiation into the national character. Using food as a symbol for British 'childhood' is significant because it transcends national divisions in the UK and unites people from different socio-economic backgrounds in a single, recognizable experience (Mautner, 2001). The crisp is likely a deliberate choice because of its interdiscursivity and cultural salience; it has appeared several times in Eurosceptic discourse. In 1993, for example, the UK press claimed that the European Commission was going to ban prawn cocktail crisps, an allegation the institution later denied. A decade later, the *Sunday Times* alleged that the EU would outlaw smoky bacon-flavoured crisps, a point again refuted by the European Commission. In Eurosceptic discourse, then, the crisp has long been a symbol of a national culture under threat. By positioning the crisp in the context of national childhood experiences, the newspaper elicits a protective instinct to prevent UK children from losing the opportunity to participate in this unifying, national experience. At the same time, it relies on interdiscursivity to evoke a European threat to British culture, creating an in-group based on a common enemy.

In Example (8), two national personality traits, 'civility and fair-mindedness', underpin the national character and make Britons culturally distinct. The two abstract nouns contribute to the positioning of tolerance as a uniquely British quality, a representation which has underpinned British media discourse on national values for at least a decade and was prominent in David Cameron's rhetoric about the nation (Bennett, 2018; Bolt, 2022). The nouns are positioned as the Goals of the material process 'damage' (Halliday, 1985), suggesting a second threat to British national culture. UK politicians, rather than an international enemy, pose this threat. The shift in the perpetrator of UK distress marks a broader move towards domestic division in the newspaper discourse, a phenomenon explored later in the chapter. Nevertheless, the examples illustrate that just as British identity was born out of conflict and a common enemy (Colley, 1992), so too is the call for the preservation of that identity at a time of perceived national crisis. The interrelated key semantic domain Polite, which is instantiated by nouns such as 'civility' and 'decency', extends the depiction of Britishness as performative civility and will be deconstructed in the next section.

Descriptions of the EU's interference in British life enact division between Britons and EU migrants, while enumerations of British characteristics write into being a unified UK history, personality and childhood. Taken together, the two representations obscure potential discord among Britons and redirect anger towards two common enemies: the EU and migrants. Throughout the examples, journalists and politicians shift the blame for the breakdown of British public services towards the EU and diminish the threat of Scottish independence by suppressing calls for secession. The extracts reveal that the unique supranational nature of the UK renders civic nationalism a more pertinent framework for a collective British identity than the ethnic nationalism that has previously been identified in British media discourse (Rowinski, 2017).

Constructing Britain and Europe in the later post-referendum years (2018–19)

The Polite semantic domain

The Polite semantic domain expands on the discourse of a British way of life by revealing the characteristics of a presupposed British public character. It is slightly less key than the Alive domain, placing twenty-second in 2016 and rising to eighteenth in 2019. Nevertheless, the log ratio scores in Table 4.2 reveal that the domain consistently occupies over twice as much space in the target corpus as in the reference corpus.

As Figure 4.2 reveals, articles that cite politeness as a British value are most frequent in 2019, after two years of comparatively low frequency. The semantic domain centres on many recurrent words, the most frequent of which are 'courtesy', 'decency' and 'civility'. Extracts (9)–(13) illustrate how journalists employ the latter two nouns.

(9) Finally, the Remainers are now desperately trying to suggest that anyone who wants to Leave is somehow against the spirit of modern Britain; against openness, tolerance, **decency**. (*Telegraph Online*, June 2016)

Table 4.2 Statistical information about the Polite semantic domain

Year	Relative Frequency in C1 per 100,000 Words (Media)	Percentage of C1 (Media)	Relative Frequency in C2 per 100,000 Words (ref)	Percentage of C2 (ref)	Log-Likelihood	Log Ratio
2016	20.7	0.02	6.8	0.01	65.19	1.76
2017	15.7	0.02	6.8	0.01	20.78	1.31
2018	15.0	0.02	6.8	0.01	24.99	1.46
2019	23.0	0.03	6.8	0.01	52.57	1.89

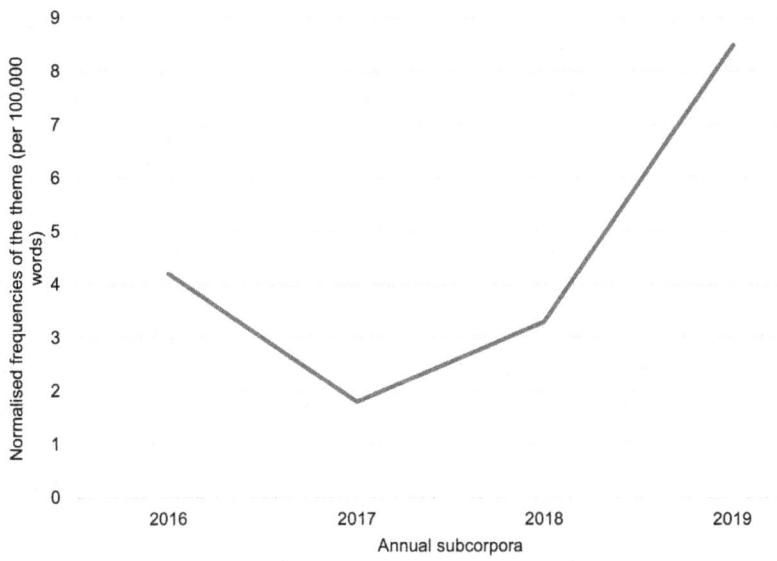

Figure 4.2 Politeness as a British value theme per 100,000 words.

(10) The **civility** of the people waiting patiently in line at the bank. The daily miracle of seeing queues of traffic next to empty bus lanes a sight so incomprehensible to my inner Italian it still makes me smile in amazement. (*Daily Mail*, June 2016)

(11) I wonder if they will be happy with what they reap, and what astounding damage they have done not just to our political settlement but to the famous **civility** and fair mindedness of British life. (*Telegraph Online*, March 2019)

(12) And what is worst, the people have learnt something they will not forget about how much they are despised by those who actually run the country. God help us. The great national virtues of reason and **decency** are about to be tested to their limits. (*Telegraph Online*, March 2019)

(13) Speaking a [*sic*] People's Vote rally last week, Ms Soubry said: 'There is a profound danger of the country being seized by a minority who don't share basic British values of **decency**'. (*Express Online*, September 2019)

The Polite semantic domain complements the Alive domain in more than just its thematic coherence: it includes several words which share connotations with 'life', revealing a second linguistic strategy used to construct a particular way of being British. The abstract nouns 'spirit' (9), 'virtues' (12) and 'values' (13) imply a British essence that evades concrete description; their positive semantic prosody and selection over neutral alternatives such as 'norms' indicate a framing of Britishness as imitable.

There is a remarkable continuity to these extracts in their construction of the British national character as grounded in 'decency'. Consistency is important when ascribing qualities to collective national identities because the cohesion of a nation depends primarily on a strong consensus about national values (Hroch, 2019). Equally, the persuasiveness of discourses about national values depends partly upon their repetition. That the different newspapers share a vision of British values appears promising for the generation of a cohesive pro-Brexit British identity. The extracts expand upon the moral Briton characterization by identifying the qualities of 'openness, tolerance, decency' (9). The asyndetic tripartite list creates an open-ended selection of values, suggesting that these three examples are just a sample of many positive qualities attached to Britishness. The nouns share connotations of acceptance and equality, envisioning Britain as a country that champions difference and debate. The noun 'openness' is particularly striking as it encapsulates the 'dual voice of a modernist democratic nationalism' (Leith and Soule: 73). That is, it positions 'openness' as a symbol of a unique British 'spirit' even though an open nation would necessarily be diverse. As diversity would dilute the supposed singularity of Britishness, this construction of Britain exhibits a tension between British exceptionalism and the liberal-democratic values of civic nationalism (Tabachnik, 2019).

Constructing a collective national character has a specific function in Extract (9), where an innate, transcendental 'decency' counters alleged criticisms of the Brexit vote as xenophobic. *Telegraph Online* presupposes that the 'spirit of modern Britain' is 'openness, tolerance [and] decency'. As Leavers are Britons, they are imbued with these values and so cannot be xenophobic, according to the newspaper. Following this logic, readers must question *Remainers'* claims to Britishness because, in their allegations, they do not exhibit the tolerance that characterizes modern Britons. This discursive technique reveals that in addition to constructing a collective identity, national values can be drawn upon to ostracize social groups by implying that they do not belong. Once again, the dynamics of inclusion and exclusion prove irrevocably intertwined in national identity construction.

In Extract (10), British columnist Sarah Vine employs a conceptual metaphor of the INNER SELF AS THE EMOTIONAL CENTRE OF A PERSON (Lakoff and Johnson, 1980) to construct herself as, emotionally speaking, Italian. Vine moved to Italy aged five and lived there until she was sixteen; she thus possesses a liminal identity as both a migrant and a British national – a so-called friendly Other (Gibbins, 2014). Vine's experience of living in Europe allows her to step outside of the British cultural sphere to comment positively on the behavioural characteristics and values that give Britain an international reputation for 'civility'. Her dual identity enables her to witness the 'miracle' of British 'civility' as a person from a different culture might: with reverence. Her choice of abstract nouns, 'amazement' and 'miracle', foregrounds the supposed singularity of British cultural practices, marking them as different from, and superior to, life on the continent. In other words, they perpetuate the myth of British exceptionalism. The article's publication coincides with the EU referendum vote; its claims reinforce the Leave campaign's argument that the UK is both geographically and culturally distinct from mainland Europe (Cap, 2019).

While the extracts from 2016 constitute a positive reflection on British characteristics, a threat to British identity unites the three examples from 2019. The material process 'tested (to their limits)', which takes 'great national virtues' as its goal, depicts peril and renders the danger to the collective British character tangible in Extract (12) (Halliday, 1985). British political officials pose the threat to the UK in this narrative: 'those who actually run the country' are blamed for testing the 'great national virtues of reason and decency'. These political actors are charged with 'despising' 'the people' in a populist construction that reveals that the national values being 'tested to their limits' belong to British citizens, not British politicians. Through this subtle linguistic differentiation, the journalist suggests that the political elite is less British, or at least less decent and reasonable, than the ordinary Briton. Context is enlightening here: the article disparages an allegedly pro-EU Parliament, whose inability to agree on withdrawal terms delays Brexit. The act of 'despising' means, in concrete terms, disagreeing with the majority public vote to Leave, as the noun 'minority' suggests.

What is striking about this example is its inversion of British civility; by asserting that elected representatives despise 'the people', the journalist establishes a scenario in which it would be reasonable for Britons to lose their sense of decency. As decency is a core characteristic in the British national identity narrative (Bennett, 2018), losing this value throws the existence of collective Britishness into crisis. In short, the betrayal of political leaders threatens the principles that unite Britain. That the political threat has the potential to dismantle the entire realm is evident in Extract (13), which argues that 'the country' is at risk of being 'seized' by a minority that does not value decency. Extract (13) stands out because it is a rare moment in which the pro-Brexit press quotes a *Remain*-backing politician. After this quotation the journalist goes on to question Ms Soubry's trustworthiness by stating that she 'apologised to the British public after admitting David Cameron and his

Cabinet "arrogantly" agreed to hold the Brexit referendum because they were certain Remain would win'. Nevertheless, the quote importantly illustrates that claims that the nation is under threat were perpetuated by *both sides of the debate*. This supports Hearn's (2017) claim that both Remainers and Leavers mobilized national identities.

In the example, the metonymic nominal group 'the country' reveals that it is not just the culture and norms of Britain that are under threat, but the very existence of the nation. The negative construction of British MPs reveals an emerging 'state-of-the-nation' discourse in the later years of the withdrawal process in which dissatisfaction and disharmony within the UK pose a bigger threat to British identity than any international enemy. The discussion of the No Respect domain below explores this discourse further, but it is worth noting here that it forms part of a discursive shift from supporting the official government line on national identity to framing Britain as a nation divided by an incompetent political elite.

The evaluative language in the Polite semantic domain envisions Britons positively as liberal-minded and tolerant. Perpetuating a belief in united British ideals, values and goals strengthens the collective conception of British national identity (Henderson and McEwan, 2005). Given the ongoing desire for Scottish independence, creating a collective sense of character and belonging that overcomes political disagreements can bolster support for the domestic Union. The semantic domain does more than simply construct a country united in positive, democratic values, however. A discursive shift in 2019 marks the emergence of a scenario in which the British nation is under threat, not from an external enemy, but from people within Britain who allegedly lack the fundamental values of British decency and tolerance. This demonized group consists of pro-EU politicians and people who voted Remain; labelling these social actors intolerant enables the newspapers to shield Leave-voting Britons from post-referendum accusations of xenophobia. However, given that almost half of voting Britons opted to Remain, this discourse demonizes a large part of the population. The radical Othering of pro-EU politicians and voters (Gibbins, 2014), then, engenders a deep-rooted division at the very core of British society. Despite the linguistic construction of a united character, the pro-Brexit newspapers envision and threaten to reify widespread national disunity.

The No Respect semantic domain

The No Respect semantic domain is statistically significant in all four data sets and rises from the seventh most key domain in 2016 to the most key semantic domain

Table 4.3 Statistical information about the No Respect semantic domain

Year	Relative Frequency in C1 per 100,000 Words (Media)	Percentage of C1 (Media)	Relative Frequency in C2 per 100,000 Words (ref)	Percentage of C2 (ref)	Log-Likelihood	Log Ratio
2016	13.3	0.02	2.6	0.00	67.49	2.54
2017	14.8	0.02	2.6	0.00	53.65	2.63
2018	23.2	0.03	2.6	0.00	123.13	3.49
2019	44.9	0.05	2.6	0.00	262.18	4.25

Table 4.4 The four key themes in the No Respect semantic domain

Themes	Overall Instances (2016–19)
The denigration of Britain	86
Contempt within Britain	45
Contempt for democracy	21
Contempt for Europe	5

in 2019. Table 4.3 presents the relative frequencies, log-likelihood values and log ratio values for the semantic domain of No Respect across the four data sets.

The representations realized by the No Respect semantic domain are heterogeneous; there are four key themes which increase in 2019 at markedly different rates. Table 4.4 presents the themes and their overall instances across the four annual subcorpora.

The underlying sentiment of the themes is division, which afflicts all levels of society: international partnerships, alliances between politicians and the public and relationships between citizens. As Figure 4.3 illuminates, the distribution of themes is weighted largely towards the later post-referendum years, where the greatest discursive concerns are the denigration of Britain and contempt within Britain. The only theme dedicated to Europe, Contempt for Europe, remains entirely on the periphery, suggesting that the EU's significance as a social actor is generally much lower than Britain's within concordance lines from this semantic domain. This is unsurprising, given that the articles are from the UK press and the news value of proximity dictates that events which take place in the newspaper's country are more likely to be covered than those that occur at a distance (Shoemaker et al., 2007). That the two most frequent themes depict dissatisfaction and disharmony within the UK indicates a general discursive shift inward in comparison to the earlier subcorpora, towards a focus on

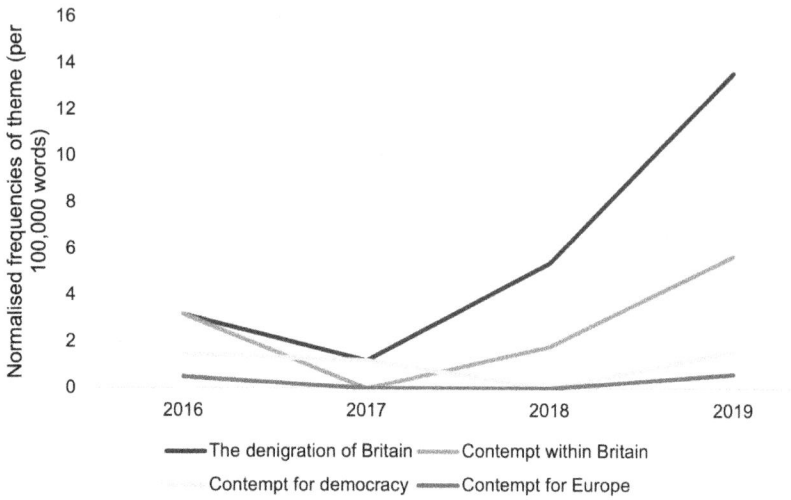

Figure 4.3 Distribution of themes per 100,000 words.

national division and self-perception. This discursive pattern, as it is borne out in the two most salient themes, will be explored in the remainder of this chapter.

The Denigration of Britain

The Denigration of Britain theme consists of two discursive representations: Disdain for Britain and the Humiliation of Britain. There are twenty-one raw instances of the first theme, the majority of which appears in the two earlier annual subcorpora. The latter theme occurs sixty-five times and features most frequently in the two later annual subcorpora.

Disdain for Britain

According to the pro-Brexit newspapers, the most common perpetrator of contempt for Britain is the EU, which appears in eleven pejorative instances of the theme. The depiction of the EU's contempt towards Britain is present in all the annual subcorpora and is based on five main lemmas: 'scorn', 'contempt', 'deride', 'disdain' and 'disrespect'. Four representative extracts appear below.

(14) Meanwhile, our partners (who offered us nothing but **scorn** in their arrogant presumption that we'd vote to Remain) know how heavily they depend on British markets. (*Daily Mail*, June 2016)

(15) Mr Tusk appeared to **deride** the UK for leaving the EU and called on remaining countries to get behind the bloc's failing policies. (*Express Online*, March 2017)

(16) Meanwhile the Brussels machine pours **scorn** on poor lost Britain and for our part we look ready to give in. (*Daily Telegraph*, July 2018)

(17) Brexiteer Tory MP Daniel Kawczynski tweeted: 'Luxembourg PM representing a nation smaller than Birmingham admonishing and being **disrespectful** to a British PM for trying to fulfil will of British people. We need to pull out of EU on October 31 without doubt!' (*Express Online*, September 2019)

A two-pronged discourse of European hypocrisy and British exceptionalism envelops the EU's alleged disdain for Britain in these three extracts. Journalists consistently use a strategy of demontage to derogatorily position Europe as divided, failing and dependent on the UK, a characterization that in turn presupposes British superiority (Wodak et al., 2009). In Extract (15), for example, Donald Tusk asks European countries to support the EU's policies even though they are 'failing'. The supposedly dwindling success of European policy renders Tusk's derision of the UK absurd: Britain can only benefit from avoiding the collapse of the European political framework. In this discourse of British exceptionalism, Britain's vote to leave the EU constitutes political foresight, which contrasts with the myopia of the remaining EU member states, whose blinkered hubris leads them to commit to the EU's failures.

Example (16) similarly depicts alleged European delusions of grandeur: EU countries are said to 'depend' on British economic success while 'arrogant[ly]' pouring 'scorn' on the nation. The cognitive, mental process 'know' (Halliday, 1985) implies that Britain's financial security and the EU's economic dependency are epistemological certainties, a spurious position considering that just weeks before the extract was published, the International Monetary Fund predicted a UK recession if Britain left the EU (Allen, 2016). Nevertheless, the construction of the EU's knowledge forms the crux of its characterization as hypocritical: it highlights a gap between its dependency and disdain, its knowledge and actions. The gulf between the EU's self-perception and its behaviour is alluded to in the nominal group 'our partners'. The relational identification between the UK and the EU ostensibly envisions camaraderie, but the premodifying adjective 'arrogant' and the verbal group 'offered us nothing but scorn' belie the authenticity of the 'partnership'. The adjective and verbal group shroud the noun 'partners' in irony, revealing the extract to be a caustic comment on the purported nature of EU collaboration as bubbling with unpleasantries beneath superficial support.

Extract (17) constitutes a quote from Brexit-supporting MP Daniel Kawczynski. Thinking about perspectivization (i.e. whose views are represented) (KhosraviNik, 2010), this quote clearly aligns *Daily Express* with a Leave-backing agenda. The representation of Luxembourg as 'a nation smaller than Birmingham' in the tweet perpetuates the same attitude of British superiority as the other extracts: the comparison between a European nation and a British city implicitly delegitimizes the Luxembourg prime minister's comments because his country is small. In other words, in this discursive frame 'small' means insignificant. This stance is reinforced by the adjective 'disrespectful', which implies that 'a British PM' is worthy of eliciting respect from a prime minister of a 'smaller' country by nature of his nationality, the size of his territory and his act of 'trying to fulfil [the] will of British people'.

Three of the four extracts above envision the EU as duplicitous. They posit that it is not the political collaboration it purports to be but a demanding entity that presumes support from its member states while failing to offer them robust policies and protection. The prevailing, pejorative depiction of the EU infuses the nominal group 'poor lost Britain' with irony in Example (16). In the extract, the EU is dehumanized and linguistically positioned as an inanimate Other through the metaphor of the 'Brussels machine'. The depiction of EU officials as machinery evokes the Eurosceptic portrayal of the EU as faceless and opaque. More importantly for this reading, though, it supports a depiction of the EU as devoid of emotion. The vision of Britain as 'poor' and 'lost' is attributed to the EU; while those adjectives ostensibly imply empathy, the EU's construction as a machine precludes it from emotional intelligence. As a result, the EU is characterized by pretence; its supposedly supportive nature is revealed to be a performance. In the same vein, the EU's vision of Britain as 'poor' and 'lost' is undermined. The adjectives are used to mock and subvert the pro-EU argument that Britain would suffer because of its withdrawal from the EU. According to this journalist, Britain's departure from the EU does not render it 'lost'. On the contrary, it allows the UK to escape from a Union that thrives on contempt, not collaboration. Despite the EU's perception of Britain, then, the three extracts assert that the UK should thrive outside of the EU.

The extracts were published after the EU referendum vote, at a time when politicians were preparing for and then engaging in Brexit negotiations. In this context, the inferior EU-superior UK dichotomy bolsters public support for UK negotiators taking a tough stance towards the EU in Brexit negotiations.

That the *Daily Telegraph* exhorts readers to support a more resolute position in negotiations is evident in the verbal group 'give in' in Extract (16). The phrase depicts the UK's central problem not as EU derision, but as UK negotiators' apathy and lack of assertiveness in the face of that derision. Through the ironic tone, the journalist questions ostensible political incompetence and implies that Britain should achieve more during UK–EU talks because it is not negotiating from a position of weakness. (The second theme from this representation, Humiliation of Britain, will explore the media portrayal of British political ineptitude further.)

Nevertheless, it is worth considering the diplomatic implications of constructing the EU, and its constituent countries, as radical Others (Gibbins, 2014). Although disparaging the EU as an enemy of the UK might garner support for a post-Brexit British identity, it could hinder relations between the EU and the UK moving forward. That is, increasing globalization demands that the UK develop a trading relationship with a bloc that part of its press has explicitly condemned. EU officials will not be ignorant of the anti-EU sentiment expressed in the pro-Leave press; explicitly belittling the EU could persuade its officials to adopt a more hostile approach to negotiations. The relational nature of national identity construction thus proves double-edged: on the one hand, constructing an EU out-group allows pro-Leave journalists to strengthen support for a non-EU British identity, but on the other hand, it problematizes the development of future international relationships, which are vital for national prosperity in a globalized world (see Chapter 5 for further exploration of governmental constructions of international relationships).

A homogenous group of pro-EU British political officials constitutes the second source of disdain towards Britain; it features in ten of the twenty-one concordance lines. Intranational contempt for Britain is situated within a National Traitor frame, or fifth-column discourse (Chernobrov, 2019), in which support for non-British entities becomes an expression of national self-loathing. The National Traitor discourse is particularly prevalent in the *Daily Express*, as Extracts (18)–(20) exemplify.

(18) His [Tony Blair's] eagerness to invade Iraq was matched by his **disdain** for our British identity, reflected in his devotion to the EU, foreign aid and ever greater immigration. (*Express Online*, July 2016)
(19) Such anguished language is revealing. It proves the argument that there was a large streak of unpatriotic **disdain** running through the Remain campaign. The pro-EU brigade tried to deny this, pretending that a

patriotic case could be made for rule by Brussels. But such a claim was always bogus. (*The Express*, July 2016)
(20) On a deeper level key Remainers sought the embrace of Brussels because, in their **contempt** for traditional Britain, they wanted to make our country more European, more continental. (*The Express*, July 2016)

Three nominalizations, 'devotion to the EU', 'foreign aid' and 'ever greater immigration', form the basis of Tony Blair's 'disdain' for a collective British identity in Example (18). Through the linguistic strategy of association (van Leeuwen, 1995), the journalist implies a relationship between pro-EU sentiment, approval of foreign aid and support for high levels of immigration. Using Blair as evidence, the journalist warns about the perils of supporting pro-EU politicians or political parties. That is, they imply that support for the EU also entails a propensity for national disloyalty that culminates in uncontrollable immigration levels. Immigration is securitized in the pro-Leave press, in a discursive construction of immigration as a threat to British infrastructure (see Extract 1); recontextualizing pro-EU sentiment as support for migrants constructs Remainers as traitors who threaten to unravel their nation, a so-called fifth column (Chernobrov, 2019). Given the salience of immigration during the EU referendum campaign (Geddes, 2017), the threat of greater immigration is a promising rhetorical strategy for persuading pro-Leave readers to support a Leave-backing candidate to replace David Cameron as then prime minister. After all, this would protect the nation from dissolution according to the pro-Brexit press, and is, therefore, the ultimate act of patriotism.

Extract (19) directly accuses the 'pro-EU brigade' (with the noun 'brigade' framing Remainers as belligerent and an army – for more of this, see Parnell (2022a)) of 'unpatriotic disdain' by arguing that patriotism and support for EU membership are incompatible. EU membership is framed as 'rule from Brussels' in a discursive framing of the EU as a 'quasi-imperial power' (Hawkins, 2012: 565). The conclusion that 'such a claim was always bogus' intimates that Remain campaigners have lied to the public by 'pretending that a patriotic case could be made for rule by Brussels' and in doing so, trying to obscure their lack of patriotism.

Example (20) continues the tirade against 'key Remainers', who are charged with 'want[ing] to make our country more European, more continental' because they view 'traditional Britain' with contempt. The attributive adjective 'traditional' intimates that there is a uniquely British history that exists outside of European culture and geography. This discursively constructed history distinguishes between a pre-European British identity and a homogenous mainland European existence. The adjective 'continental' is paramount to this differentiation; it draws on the connotations of geographical distance to emphasize a distinction between Britain and mainland Europe. Geography represents culture in this discursive frame, with geographical distance implying cultural difference. At the time this extract was published, Nigel Farage had been making claims about the UK's cultural singularity based on its geographical distinctiveness for at least three years (Cap, 2019). The identical media and political arguments illustrate that *The Express* aligned its vision of Britain with the most overt of Eurosceptic ideologues. As *The Express* constructs the identities of Britain and Europe as oppositional, it argues that wanting to be part of the EU represents a desire to become more European and so, inevitably, less British. This desire for the Other is conceptualized as taboo through the noun 'embrace'; the connotations of physical intimacy frame the acceptance of a supposedly homogenous European culture as an illicit romantic affair. Although this example differs from the criticism levelled at Tony Blair, it renders an image of the same social act, betrayal of the nation, based on the idea that pro-European sentiment inevitably equates to anti-British beliefs.

Depicting Remainers as unpatriotic and a threat to the nation encourages intolerance of pro-EU sentiment in the UK, both in political leaders and in members of the public. It primes Brexiteer readers to associate Remainers with national betrayal, an attitude which could lead to the social exclusion of large swathes of the British public. The National Traitor frame encourages pro-Brexit readers to support a tougher stance in Brexit negotiations to prevent pro-EU politicians and political parties from driving the country towards higher levels of immigration. All three extracts were published immediately after the EU referendum; there was no longer a need to prove the importance of voting Leave for the UK. Instead, as the country geared up for unprecedented negotiations, the pro-Brexit press employed discursive strategies to augment support for a post-Brexit British identity by narrating a pre-European, collective national history.

The Humiliation of Britain

The two social actors that feature in the Disdain for Britain theme, the EU and British political officials, also appear in the Humiliation of Britain representation. However, there is a reversal in their salience; the most prolific instigator of British humiliation in the pro-Brexit press is a group of pro-EU British MPs.

This collective agent appears in forty-three of the sixty-five instances of the theme, while the EU fulfils the discursive role of the perpetrator in the remaining twenty-two examples. Unsurprisingly, all extracts from this theme centre on the lemma 'humiliate'. The depiction of the EU humiliating Britain is a strategy of demontage that draws on the tropes of perpetrator and victim to construct the EU as a villain and a threat to the UK (Wodak et al., 2009). Six concordance lines draw on lexis from a semantic field of violence, such as the processes 'punish', 'blast' and 'intimidate' (Halliday, 1985), to depict the EU's desire to humiliate Britain as a targeted act. The noun 'henchman' and the material process 'thwarting' in Extract (21) exemplify this discursive pattern:

(21)   Juncker duly became EU President in 2014, despite a strong campaign against his candidacy by David Cameron. His henchman Selmayr has been thwarting Britain ever since. He wants victory for the EU and **humiliation** for us. (*MailOnline*, July 2018)

In this example, the nominal group 'his henchman Selmayr' refers to Martin Selmayr, who was chief of staff to the then president of the European Commission, Jean-Claude Juncker. The pronoun–noun combination enacts relational functionalization (van Leeuwen, 1995). That is, it constructs Selmayr in terms of the social role he performs as a 'henchman' and associates his actions with Juncker. The journalist does not mention Selmayr's institutional title; rather, the writer recontextualizes his job from political official to member of a violent, underground group through the premodifying noun 'henchman'. The illicit connotations of the noun characterize Selmayr as an individual who perpetrates violent acts on behalf of a larger organization: the European Commission. The acts, *MailOnline* insinuates, are commissioned by Juncker, who occupies the discursive role of European institutional kingpin in his position as president. Through the simple depiction of Selmayr as a 'henchman', then, the journalist undermines Juncker's credentials, disparages Selmayr and envisions the EU as an institution that will stop at nothing to get what it desires. The representation of Selmayr as a 'henchman' feeds into the construction of the EU's *gangsterism* that Zappettini (2021) locates in an article by *The Sun*; the present analysis shows that this discursive depiction of the EU extends beyond a single newspaper.

The *MailOnline* journalist employs the first-person personal pronoun 'us' as an inclusive, national form of 'we' to unite the writer, reader and other imagined members of the nation in a single in-group. The pronoun's inclusivity is collusive and coercive; it positions readers as the victims of national humiliation, personalizing the threat and increasing public indignation towards EU actors. The parallelism of the circumstances of Cause (behalf) (Halliday and Matthiessen, 2004) in the prepositional phrases 'for the EU and . . . for us' creates a binary of grammatical beneficiaries in which the EU is the out-group. By splitting the beneficiaries, the journalist explicitly asserts that for Selmayr, and so for the EU, success in negotiations is not an option for both parties; the EU achieving 'victory' in negotiations inevitably involves humiliation for the UK. Characterizing the EU's position in negotiations as antagonistic and selfish enables *MailOnline* to advocate for a similar response from UK negotiators. Framing British resistance as a reaction places the blame for any unfavourable consequences of a hard Brexit (i.e. a withdrawal that results in 'a radically different economic relationship between the UK and the EU' (UK in a Changing Europe, 2020b)) on the EU's original, uncompromising negotiating position and not on Britain's diplomatic decisions.

As president of the European Commission between 2014 and 2019, Jean-Claude Juncker symbolized the European political elite throughout the Brexit process; the pro-Brexit press regularly disparaged him as the epitome of the European 'uber-bureaucrat' (Hardman, 2017: n.p.). Indeed, in this article from *MailOnline*, Juncker is said to 'make no secret of his own contempt for the UK' (Hardman, 2017: n.p.). It is fair to say that Juncker did not shy away from expressing his disappointment at the Leave vote and his progressive weariness with Brexit negotiations (BBC News, 2018b; Adler, 2019), political views which contradicted *MailOnline*'s pro-Brexit sentiments. Juncker's willingness to talk about Brexit, often in terms which were unflattering for Britain, made him a useful tool for the newspapers' discursive framing of a hard Brexit as an inevitable consequence of the EU's treatment of Britain. For example, by demonizing Juncker and his associates as violent bullies in Example (21), *MailOnline* envisages the ongoing Brexit negotiations as a battle against an enemy, rather than a collaborative enterprise intended to produce a favourable deal for both parties. This argument, in turn, persuades the audience that a hard Brexit deal is the only option that will protect Britain against EU antagonism.

Although the EU is constructed as violent and tyrannical in its attempt to humiliate Britain, six extracts exude a derisive tone that undermines the Union's prospects. Examples (22) and (23) represent this argument:

(22) The EU is desperate to **humiliate** us 'pour décourager les autres', as France's President Macron might put it. (*Daily Mail*, July 2018)
(23) Nigel Farage delivered an excoriating barrage at EU 'pipsqueaks' trying to **humiliate** Britain today during a stormy battle in the European Parliament. (*MailOnline*, September 2019)

The verbal group 'trying to' (22); the intensive relational process 'is desperate to' (22); and the desiderative, mental process 'wants' (21) perform distancing, marking the EU's humiliation of Britain as a hypothetical event rather than a reflection of reality (Halliday, 1985). In other words, the Other is represented in its wishes and attempts rather than material actions. The relational and mental processes minimize the threat of intimidation because they frame the EU's humiliation of Britain as a desire rather than a certainty. Positioning Britain's degradation in the future indicates that there is an opportunity to save the country from disgrace. Example (23) strengthens the insinuation that Britain can avoid defeat. In its metaphorical recontextualization of a European Parliament debate as a 'stormy battle', the extract conceptualizes ARGUMENT AS WAR (Lakoff and Johnson, 1980). Nigel Farage embodies the archetype of the hero in 'delivered' – a metaphorical material process that concretizes a literal verbal process. The linguistic attribution of agency acts as a commentary on the socio-political power dynamic between UK and EU politicians; the UK, *MailOnline* suggests, has the advantage. The negative epithet 'pipsqueaks' casts an ironic shadow over the EU's attempt to humiliate the UK by evoking connotations of insignificance and weakness. Simultaneously, the nominalization 'barrage' connotes overwhelming bombardment, revealing that in the battle of words taking place in the European Parliament, Farage is triumphant.

It is clear from Extracts (22) and (23) that despite the EU's characterization as Britain's enemy, the *Daily Mail* does not consider the bloc a serious threat to the UK's international standing. The discursive diminution of the EU threat represents an optimistic view of Britain's ability to thrive outside of the Union, even in the case of a hard Brexit deal. However, the UK's success in negotiations is as contingent on the competence of British politicians as on the EU's alleged incompetence. It is the awareness of this dependency that underpins the widespread representation of British MPs as causing national humiliation.

The pro-Brexit press depicts Theresa May as the individual responsible for Britain's shame most frequently, although often through the pronoun 'her' or the official title of 'Prime Minister' rather than by name. Fifteen concordance lines feature a condemning depiction of May, her cabinet and the deal she has negotiated, as shown in Extracts (24)–(26).

(24) The entire handling of the Brexit negotiations has been a national **humiliation**. Even calling them 'negotiations' is a stretch. The Prime Minister's Withdrawal Agreement hands over our country's self-respect along with control of our future. (*Telegraph Online*, March 2019)

(25) Oh and 90 per cent of Brits think her [May's] handling of Brexit has been a national **humiliation**. What's been sacrificed here is Britain's reputation on the world stage. (*The Express*, March 2019)

(26) Jo Johnson has written that the deal risks being a national **humiliation** on the scale of Suez. He is right. (*Telegraph Online*, November 2018)

In March 2019, journalists describe May's humiliation of Britain chiefly in the present perfect tense: 'has been a national humiliation'. In addition to the nominalization 'humiliation', the present perfect tense in Extracts (24) and (25) depicts May's disgrace as a pre-existing reality – an act which has already occurred, and which has ongoing consequences for the nation. This representation incites a dual sense of helplessness and indignation among readers: envisioning the public as powerless contests the UK's status as a parliamentary democracy. Example (26) constitutes a warning of the national humiliation as its publication occurred before MPs scrutinized May's deal in Parliament. This timeline reveals how the pro-Brexit press undermined May's authority as prime minister even before she unveiled her vision for Brexit. By forewarning the public about May's inevitable failure, the newspapers prepared readers to accept calls for her resignation. During this period, many Conservative MPs publicly voiced concerns about May's deal; in December 2018, she faced a vote of no confidence. That *The Telegraph* chose to paraphrase this specific quote from Conservative MP Jo Johnson indicates that editors saw ideological value in his comparison between the Suez crisis and Britain's international standing in 2019.

There are several events in British political history that Jo Johnson could have cited to symbolize the dire consequences of political decision-making mistakes. That he chooses the Suez crisis signifies that the collective interpretation of British national history includes this historical event. Many historians consider the Suez crisis to be a political miscalculation that adversely affected the nation's position as a world power and triggered a loss of national self-confidence (Peden, 2012; Maccaferri, 2019). As the crisis occurred in recent history, Britons born before the 1950s will likely remember the effect of the Suez crisis on the national psyche. Jo Johnson's comparison consequently resonates on a political and personal level for older members of the public who, of course, were more likely to have voted Leave (Ashcroft, 2016). Given the shared perception of Suez as a political failure, discursively associating it with May's Brexit deal persuades readers that if the deal is passed in Parliament, Britain's international standing will further disintegrate. In this argument, journalists and politicians draw on British history to generate public concern for the future and entreat Britons to support a change in the present political make-up as a preventative measure. Undermining May steadily convinces readers that a different politician, who would negotiate a more ambitious deal, would better steer the UK through Brexit. As a result, the representation is calculated to agitate the public and incite political dissatisfaction. By citing right-wing detractors rather than the opposition, the *Telegraph Online* reassures readers that they are not betraying their political position by criticizing the current Conservative leader.

Although May takes most of the blame for her failure to pass a Brexit deal, the pro-Brexit press also condemns British parliamentarians for their inability to agree on amendments. This social actor representation appears in seventeen concordance lines and is exemplified by Extracts (27)–(29):

(27) In the process, the politicians are destroying faith in democracy, making a mockery of the ballot box, heaping **humiliation** on our country and turning Britain into an international laughing stock [*sic*]. As a failure of statecraft, comparisons have frequently been drawn with Tony Blair's disastrous invasion of Iraq in 2003 or the Winter of Discontent in 1979, when trade union power paralysed the economy. But this Brexit fiasco is far worse. (*Express Online*, 2019)

(28) You – our clueless elected representatives – have created this purgatory. You – the most pathetic shower of MPs in British history – have contrived to bring about this national **humiliation**. (*The Sun Online*, 2019)

(29) OURS is an immensely rich language with literally thousands of adjectives. Two of them are 'stupid' and 'cowardly'. Can they ever be used together? Oh yes. When someone in high office refuses over and over again to admit a stark reality because it is a disagreeable one, that merits both epithets. And those words precisely describe the behaviour of Parliament as we grovel our way to defeat and national **humiliation** over Brexit. (*Express Online*, 2019)

As with the Suez example above, in Extract (26), the alleged national humiliation caused by parliamentary indecision is compared to (relatively) recent historical examples of political unrest: the Iraq War and the so-called Winter of Discontent. The readers of the *Express Online*, 42 per cent of which are aged between fifty-five and seventy-four (Hurst Media, n.d.), are likely to remember the fallout of these political decisions. By labelling the 'Brexit fiasco' as 'far worse' than war and mass protest, readers are encouraged to see the delays in the Brexit process as an unprecedented level of political crisis. The blame for this crisis, according not only to *Express Online* but also to *The Sun Online*, lies with 'our clueless elected representatives', 'Parliament', 'the most pathetic shower of MPs in British history' and 'the politicians'. These political actors – many of whom were in favour of remaining in the EU in contrast to most of their constituents – are framed, through the superlative 'most [pathetic]' and the adjectives 'stupid' and 'cowardly', as afraid of making difficult decisions. The adjective 'clueless' is remarkable in its populist implicature that political elites lack the knowledge and understanding of what is best for Britain. Indeed, politicians' refusal to respond to public opinion and insight is framed as anti-democratic ('destroying faith in democracy', 'making a mockery of the ballot box'). As parliamentary democracy is repeatedly positioned as the cornerstone of British identity in political discourse (Marcussen et al., 1999), a loss of democracy entails the loss of a collective sense of Britishness. The imagined community of Britain is therefore said to be threatened by the undemocratic behaviours of the largely Remain-backing political class.

It is worth making an aside here to comment on the language directed towards the politicians in these examples. Negative adjectives like 'pathetic', 'stupid', 'clueless' and 'cowardly' form part of an expression of mediated anger, which is a political emotion that is 'performative, discursively constructed [and] collective' (Wahl-Jorgensen, 2018: 2071). As Wahl-Jorgensen (2018: 2074) notes, there are significant ideological consequences to the mediated construction of emotions because they act as an 'emotional compass' that readers can use to 'orient' themselves. In other words, journalists' use of mediated emotions can facilitate the 'sharing of particular legitimate ways of talking about our feelings' which, in turn, shape the conditions for shared action (ibid.). At the time of the EU membership referendum, when British Labour MP Jo Cox was sadly murdered by a far-right activist, news outlets started to question the use of impolite language in politics. News outlets such as *The Guardian* published articles titled 'How did the language of politics get so toxic?' (Bland, 2016). These discussions continued up to 2019, with the BBC reporting on 'MPs' fury at Boris Johnson's "dangerous language"' (BBC News, 2019). There was some awareness in the media, then, that negative political language could have consequences. Despite this, we see from the examples above that newspapers continued to use negative language as a form of mediated anger towards politicians throughout 2019. I would argue that the use of this language in *The Express* and *The Sun*, while admittedly influenced by news values of negativity and tabloid sensationalism, forms part of a disruptive and destructive use of mediated anger; a new, less belligerent language needs to be found and agreed upon.

As I argue elsewhere (Parnell, 2021), these articles ultimately undermine public confidence in MPs' ability to agree a Brexit deal that will support the country's global role. Indeed, in the 2019 Audit of Political Engagement, conducted by Ipsos MORI for the Hansard Society, only 25 per cent of the 1,198 adults surveyed had confidence in British MPs' handling of Brexit (Hansard Society, 2019). As the relationship between discourse and social practice is dialectic (Fairclough, 2015), the media depiction of political ineptitude ('pathetic', 'clueless', 'stupid') likely both reflects and reinforces this distrust among readers. In other words, the newspapers do not just discursively construct a political crisis, 'they threaten to induce one by cultivating public distrust in political representatives' (Parnell, 2021: 63).

In sum, the Humiliation of Brexit theme uncovers a discursive construction of division between an inept political class (i.e. the prime minister and *pro-EU* members of Parliament) and a national public with the political know-how and foresight to see that Brexit is the best option for the country. It reveals the construction of Brexit delays as the foremost political crisis in British history and the source of a hitherto unprecedented level of national humiliation.

Contempt within Britain

The Contempt within Britain theme depicts a nation divided along a single, simplified, populist axis: a pro-EU, metropolitan and political elite, labelled 'Remainers', and a hardworking, disillusioned public referred to as 'Brexiteers' or 'Leavers'. Across the annual subcorpora, there is a diachronic shift towards the greater saliency of 'Remainer*' and 'Brexiteer*': there are only 12.8 instances of 'Remainer*' per 100,000 words in the 2016 annual subcorpus but 86.2 instances per 100,000 words in the 2019 subcorpus. Likewise, there are 19.5 instances of 'Brexiteer*' per 100,000 words in 2016 and 70.8 instances per 100,000 words in 2019. That the two terms appear in 2016 is perhaps unsurprising, given that they represent the two opposing sides of the EU referendum campaign. However, that the divisive nouns persist after the referendum takes place indicates that the identities that they index have become what Zürn and De Wilde (2016: 284) term a 'cleavage'. A cleavage refers to a situation in which a myriad number of conflicts are subsumed under a single dimension between opposing groups, 'reinvigorating a new sense of identity politics which may bring back previously disillusioned citizens to the political sphere' (Zürn and De Wilde, 2016: 284).

In the subcorpora, the 'Remainer' identity indexes a group of upper-middle-class, highly educated people who have benefited from globalization and may be part of the so-called political 'elite'. 'Leavers' or 'Brexiteers', in contrast, index a politically aware but oft-disdained group of 'ordinary' citizens. The relationship between these two identities is what the Contempt within Britain theme captures; the theme largely rests upon the lemma 'contempt', which appears in twenty-six of the forty-five concordance lines and is particularly prevalent in the *Daily Telegraph*. Extracts (30)–(33) demonstrate the consistency of this divisive rhetoric between 2016 and 2019:

(30) Much of the discourse has become tainted by a barely concealed form of class warfare, oozing **contempt** for anybody who doesn't have a postgraduate degree and who is therefore too stupid to see the truth. Special bile is reserved for the class traitors – the eminent economists or lawyers who back Brexit. Trendy London society in particular has imported the worse values of modern US politics: the hate, division and credentialism are out of control, making it impossible for both sides to agree to disagree. (*Telegraph Online*, June 2016)

(31) At Tate Britain, the Brexiteers were booed by visitors to the gallery who stood on the steps and signalled a thumbs down. Here was seemingly London's metropolitan elite **jeering** the largely out-of-town Leavers as they walked past. Perhaps nothing so much summed up the nation's divide. When the Remainers booed, the Leavers shouted back: 'Losers'. (*Telegraph Online*, March 2019)

(32) Yes, something nasty in the woodshed has been revealed about a sizeable section of British society – and that thing is not the alleged racism of my fellow Brexiteers, as Remainers would have you believe. No, it is the long-concealed **contempt** of the Remainers for most of their fellow citizens. They have felt free to indulge in the forbidden taste-thrill of bigotry for once in their self-censoring lives. (*Daily Telegraph*, March 2019)

(33) LEAVE voters have been unfairly stigmatised as racists and bigots, and **deriding** their 'legitimate' desire for the UK to quit the EU risks fanning the flames of genuine right-wing extremism, a Swiss politician has warned. (*Express Online*, September 2019)

These examples reveal that the emerging political identities of 'Remainer' (31, 32), 'Brexiteer' (31, 32) and 'Leaver' (31) do not solely reflect attitudes towards the EU, even during the EU referendum campaign. Rather, they symbolize a range of national and social divisions in the pro-Brexit press, particularly in terms of education and class. For example, Extract (29) uses the conceptual metaphor of ARGUMENT AS WAR (Lakoff and Johnson, 1980) to envision the EU referendum campaign as a social class battle for the monopoly of knowledge and intelligence. Within this oppositional frame, Remainers are intellectuals who cannot appreciate intelligence that exists outside of the academy; their unwillingness to see past the lack of 'a postgraduate degree' leads them to undermine Leave arguments as an inability to grasp the complexities of the EU. Within the EU referendum context, the depiction of Remainers as academics with a superiority complex bolsters Michael Gove's claim that the British public has 'had enough of experts' (*Financial Times*, 2016: n.p.) to convince readers that 'Remainers' are sneering at them. Consequently, it lends credence to the Leave campaign. Read outside of that context, it acts as a criticism of a class system that privileges educational attainment. That the argument appears in the *Daily Telegraph* is pertinent because the newspaper is more popular among readers who have higher-paid jobs than those from lower social classes (Ofcom, 2017). Pro-Leave readers of the *The Telegraph* are especially likely to feel frustrated by Remainers' alleged belief that Leavers are intellectually inferior. Through this argument, *The Telegraph* reinforces the class division it describes.

The writer of the editorial from which Extract (30) derives repeatedly frames the division between Remainers and Brexiteers in terms of intellect, class and morality by emphasizing what Siles-Brügge (2019: 423) terms the 'malleability of expert knowledge'. They explicitly argue that the Remainer tactic of 'reasoned argument' is 'not enough' because 'nobody agrees on the facts any more [*sic*]'. The claim that facts are open to debate undermines the very underpinnings of the knowledge economy; it questions the ethos of 'credentialism' that positions certain 'experts' as intellectually superior by suggesting that there are alternative, equally valid interpretations of the facts among the educated middle classes. Indeed, the writer evaluates the economists and lawyers who support Brexit as 'eminent'. This argument adds nuance to the reductive perception of the 'Remainer' identity as the domain of the intellectuals, legitimizing the Brexiteer perspective by aligning it with 'alternative facts'. Even while dismantling the claim that there is a one-to-one relationship between the 'Remainer' identity and the educated middle classes, the journalist reveals the depth of the division they see in the UK both between and within social classes. There is no disputing that the divisions they describe are *national* problems but subsuming them under the terms 'Remainer' and 'Brexiteer' gives the illusion that the problem relates to the EU. After all, at the most literal level, the terms refer to attitudes towards Britain's membership of the EU.

The Telegraph's recontextualization in Extract (30), then, links Brexiteers' discontent with national and intranational divisions to EU institutions. By scapegoating the EU, the journalists can position Brexit as a panacea for the public's palpable frustrations at divisions in the UK and present post-Brexit Britain as the promised land. In other words, they can position national policies as the solution rather than the problem. This argument is persuasive for readers because, as Hearn (2017: n.p.) argues, 'people look for the concrete agents of their troubles, and states and other large institutions are more visibly available to take the blame for people's woes'. In short, EU institutions provide a concrete entity towards which people can direct their frustrations; framing them as the cause of Britain's problems minimizes the discontent expressed towards national policymakers. It is worth noting, though, that the references to class and knowledge in this example align with Clarke and Newman's (2019) argument that Brexit amplified existing frictions in addition to opening new fissures.

I have analysed Extracts (31) and (32) in depth in Parnell (2021). As I argue there, Extract (31) draws on the spatial imaginary of 'Left Behind Britain' (Sykes, 2018) to distinguish London citizens from those living in rural counties. While this discursive differentiation aligns with patterns regarding which regions voted to Leave (often counties and towns) and Remain (London and other big cities), it also draws on grievances about Westminster's economic policies which 'facilitate the prosperity of London and its "metropolitan elite" at the expense of other cities and towns (Calhoun, 2017)' (Parnell, 2021: 65). As such, the extract enacts socio-spatial and socio-economic divisions between members of the British public. The emotive lexis in both examples ('jeering', 'nasty', 'contempt', 'bigotry') arouse emotional attachments to the political identities of Remainer and Leaver (which command a stronger allegiance than traditional political parties among Britons (Kelley, 2019)), cultivating a sense of outrage that requires a passionate, indignant reaction. That three of the examples above are from articles published towards the end of the data collection period reveals that, contrary to its suggestion that Brexit will resolve the UK's problems, the pro-Brexit press still perceives and encourages division in Britain even as it approaches its withdrawal from the EU.

Finally, Extract (33) comes from *Express Online*, demonstrating that the framing of Leaver-Remainer relations is not solely unique to *Daily Telegraph*. In this example, Leave voters are framed as the victims ('unfairly stigmatised') of the kind of narratives that, according to Tyler et al. (2022), were circulating in pro-Remain public discourses around the referendum: that Leavers are 'racists' and 'bigots'. This extract, then, simultaneously taps into and (re)produces the 'polemical cycle of denial and affirmation of racism that is at the crux of the seemingly irreconcilable opposition between Leavers and Remainers'

(Mintchev, 2021: 124). As indicated by the adjective 'legitimate', this extract is also one example of what Mintchev (2021: 124) refers to as a 'counter-critique' of Brexit 'as a legitimate political project'. The ideological position that Leave voters' desires are 'legitimate' is strengthened by the acknowledgement that it is a 'Swiss politician' – that is, a European – who is voicing its legitimacy. This type of legitimization is a version of *authorization* (van Leeuwen, 2007) that I would term *supranational authorization* – authority is invested in a person because of the tradition of their (supra)national identity. In other words, quoting a Swiss politician and foregrounding their national identity allows *The Express* to explicitly argue that 'even Europeans' recognize that the pro-Brexit stance is legitimate.

Notably, the adjective 'genuine' in the noun phrase 'genuine right-wing extremism' downplays the severity of the right-wing views of some Leave voters, pushing the boundaries of 'extremism' further to the right and thereby, potentially, mainstreaming more far-right views. In fact, the article from which this extract derives goes on to say, 'Mr Koppel [the Swiss politician] also dismissed the suggestion that former Italian interior minister Matteo Salvini and Viktor Orban, Hungary's Prime Minister, both known for their tough stance on immigration, were extremists in their outlook' (*Express Online*, 2019). By including this quote from the same voice as the person who legitimizes the victimization of Leavers, *The Express* further pushes the boundaries of what constitutes extreme views, legitimizing more far-right ideologies (see Brown and Mondon (2021) for a consideration of this practice in an anti-Brexit newspaper – *The Guardian*).

Conclusion

The analysis in this chapter reveals a diachronic shift in the construction of British, European and EU identities in the pro-Brexit British press. In the earlier years, Britain and the EU are dichotomous identities: journalists demonize the EU, Europeans and migrants and depict them as endangering the national infrastructure. By encasing the two identities in an Invaded Nation frame (Charteris-Black, 2019), the pro-Brexit press conceptualizes EU membership as a threat and a Leave vote as a proactive way to protect the British nation. Later, journalists portray the EU's stance in Brexit negotiations as antagonistic, framing calls for a more hostile position from Britain as an inevitable reaction to the EU's continued mistreatment of the nation. While bolstering public support for a hard Brexit deal, this representation also pre-emptively shifts the blame for any negative consequences of a Brexit deal away from Britain and towards the EU.

The discursive exclusion of European identities threatens to legitimize the social exclusion of 'non-native' British citizens and Europeans living in the UK. The increase in xenophobic hate crimes after the EU referendum certainly suggests that the anti-EU and anti-migrant rhetoric spouted during the referendum campaign emboldened some Britons to discriminate against those they saw as ethnic Others (Home Office, 2019). In this context, it is useful to apply Baker et al.'s (2008) theorization of anti-migrant rhetoric as 'public rivalry discourse' to Europeans in the UK. In maintaining the political argument that European equals bad, the pro-Brexit press reduces Europeans who live in the UK to the collateral damage of (often legitimate) anger towards the EU.

While the oppositional representation of the UK and the EU in the early subcorpora incites division between Britons and Europeans, it fosters a sense of cohesion within the UK that contradicts international relations. The EU referendum prompted a resurgence of Scottish nationalism; the pro-Brexit press responds by diminishing the threat to the domestic Union. Journalists construct a collective British national identity rooted in innate civility, institutional collaboration and a childhood love of crisps. Consistently positioning Scotland at the centre of British institutional success, the press rewrites a cohesive British history that challenges the Scottish nationalist claim that Anglocentric policies weaken Scotland. The historical focus also feeds the English desire to recover a golden age of political hegemony (Calhoun, 2017), by conceptualizing the post-Brexit future as a return to a unified, powerful past.

The chapter reveals how the pro-Brexit press employs and manipulates nationalist discourses to react to socio-political circumstances. Journalists downplay the threat to the domestic Union through a civic nationalist discourse that writes into being a homogenous British institutional identity. At the same time, they reinforce the Leave campaign's cultural distinction between the UK and mainland Europe through ethnic nationalism. This blend of nationalist discourses underpins the main argument in the early subcorpora – that the EU is to blame for issues in Britain that the public might otherwise interpret as the consequences of national austerity policies and global forces of neoliberalism. These social problems include bitter class divisions, intranational threats to the domestic Union and depleted public resources. By blaming the EU for these problems, the pro-Brexit press presents national policies as the *solution* rather than the problem: the press argues that if Britain can reduce EU control, it can improve the national problems that its politicians are currently too powerless to fix. In this scenario, Brexit offers a glimmer of hope for the future of the nation and a cure for a wealth of public problems.

The early optimism towards Brexit begins to deteriorate in November 2018. Theresa May's initial Withdrawal Agreement and Parliament's inability to agree on a more favourable deal prompt the shift in discursive technique. The focus turns inward, away from the international UK–EU dichotomy towards an intranational reflection on the state of Britain. The EU's role in the discourse decreases substantially; British politicians assume its position as a threat to the UK. This threat is more severe; irony minimizes the danger that the EU poses to the UK in the early subcorpora, but no such relief exists for the threat of the pro-EU politicians. The rhetoric exploits public anxieties about immigration by implying that pro-EU politicians are national traitors who inevitably betray their country by supporting uncontrollable immigration. It argues that the ineptitude of existing MPs constitutes a national humiliation that threatens to undermine Britain's reputation for decency by causing widespread indignation. A populist dichotomy of a political elite and ordinary citizens underpins the argument; the politician–public relationship seemingly radiates mutual contempt. This divisive discourse captures and reinforces the public mood; 50 per cent of people surveyed in the 2019 Audit of Political Engagement felt that the main political parties do not care about people like them (Hansard Society, 2019).

Depicting a fractured relationship between politicians and the public supports the newspapers' political agenda to shift the balance of power towards a new prime minister. The rhetoric cultivates public dissatisfaction with the existing parliamentary make-up, a sentiment Theresa May cannot afford to ignore after facing a vote of no confidence. However, the pro-Brexit press does not only depict division between politicians and the press. Under the EU-related guise of the nouns 'Remainer' and 'Brexiteer', it envisions a public cleaved apart by social class and educational disparities. The *Daily Telegraph* and *Daily Express* persuade their readers that Remainers consider them intellectually inferior. There are consequences to this divisive rhetoric. The Remainer–Brexiteer dichotomy nurtures a belief in an unjust gulf in British society between those who benefit from globalization and those who do not, which risks creating a deep-rooted bitterness in the UK. Notably, the aftermath of Brexit has not brought 'evidence of conciliation or convergence in public attitudes' or shown that 'underlying issues of distrust, disconnection and division' have been addressed (Wincott, 2019: 16). It is not far-fetched to suggest that the discourses I have identified in this chapter have contributed to the sustained sense of division in the UK post-Brexit.

In sum, the positive, homogenous Britishness present in the earlier subcorpora disappears by 2018; in its place is a nation that is more splintered than ever. New labels, 'Remainers', 'Brexiteers' and 'Leavers', reduce a range of political, socio-economic and educational positions to a bitter binary of 'elites' and 'ordinary people'. The identity labels relate national problems to the EU, reinforcing the perception that international officials, not British politicians, are to blame for the state of the nation. This discursive effect is useful for the pro-Brexit press because it addresses public concerns without compromising political alliances. Nevertheless, discursive exclusion often engenders social exclusion. The divisive rhetoric of the pro-Brexit press (and, as Extract (13) suggests, some Remain-backing politicians) mobilizes EU-related identities for political gain but, in doing so, risks fomenting a resentment in UK society so deep that it may be difficult to harness a collective post-Brexit national identity after the withdrawal process is complete. Whether a 'single vision of Britain' is necessary for stability or 'futile' given the complexities of Britain's 'plural identities, narratives, and traditions' is an entirely different question (Ashcroft and Bevir, 2021: 118) and one to which I will return in Chapter 7.

5

Constructing Britain and Europe in UK Government Documents

Introduction

In this chapter, I examine how Britain and Europe are represented in the UK government's narrative of 'Global Britain' – a plan to make the UK 'a problem-solving and burden-sharing nation' that remains open and global (Cabinet Office, 2021: n.p.). Applying key semantic domain analysis to government documents, I uncover a diachronic shift in the representation of Anglo-European relations, prompted by rising political tensions as Brexit negotiations reach a stalemate. I reveal a turn away from the positive portrayal of a transactional UK–EU relationship, towards antagonism and uncertainty about future ties. I argue that the increasing improbability of negotiating a stronger UK–EU partnership triggers the unravelling of the Global Britain narrative – international and intranational tensions render Britain a less attractive ally, forcing it to become an 'outsider' and 'supplicant' (Daddow, 2015: 75). I demonstrate that despite the dwindling argumentative value of Global Britain, the government remains faithful to its narrative, producing a vision that lacks precision and detail, and is often contradictory. I contend that the tensions underpinning the Global Britain vision fail to provide national audiences or prospective trading partners with a coherent blueprint for post-Brexit Britain. I conclude that this could weaken the UK's international standing – the opposite of the promise to reinvigorate Britain's golden-age reputation as a global trading nation.

Britain and the world in UK government documents: A diachronic analysis

The Alive semantic domain

The keyness of the Alive semantic domain diminishes slightly over the years. In the 2016 subcorpus, Alive is among the ten most key domains in the keyness list but by 2019, it places twenty-fifth. The log ratio values in Table 5.1 reveal that the domain consistently occupies over twice as much space in the target subcorpora as in the reference corpus; it is distinctive, then, of the government's Brexit-related documents. Nevertheless, the relative frequencies across the four subcorpora are low compared to the other key domains. The lower frequency values reveal that although there is an identifiable, cohesive set of discourses that centres on the lemma 'life', the 'incremental effect' (Baker, 2006) of these discourses is less perceptible than for other key domains.

In the government subcorpora, the Alive semantic domain consists of the noun 'life' and its plural counterpart 'lives'. The two nouns contribute to three discursive representations, which were identified through a manual thematic and linguistic analysis of the concordance lines that focused on social actors and actions. The three discursive representations are: 'Shared experiences between Britain and Europe', 'Europeans in Britain' and 'British life after Brexit'. The nouns build towards the three representations in slightly different ways. In the first discursive construction, the plural noun 'lives' refers to a collective way of being among Britons and Europeans, such as the claim that 'we live in prosperous countries, whose inhabitants enjoy great lives' (Davis, 2016: n.p.). In the second representation, both the singular and the plural nouns construct experiences

Table 5.1 Statistical information about the 'Alive' semantic domain in the government subcorpora

Year	Relative Frequency in C1 per 100,000 Words (gov)	Percentage in C1 (gov)	Relative Frequency in C2 per 100,000 Words (ref)	Percentage in C2 (ref)	Log-Likelihood	Log Ratio
2016	28.1	0.03	7.1	0.01	22.51	2.03
2017	26.6	0.03	7.1	0.01	78.53	2.22
2018	9.6	0.03	7.1	0.01	50.15	1.88
2019	21.1	0.02	7.1	0.01	44.36	1.64

for migrant groups 'who've made their lives and homes in our country' (May, 2017: n.p.). In the final construction, the singular noun 'life' refers to the material practices that will underpin 'life outside of the EU' (Davis, 2017: n.p.). This chapter focuses on two of the discursive representations: shared experiences between Britain and Europe and British life after Brexit. An analysis of the discursive representation of Europeans in Britain can be found in Parnell (2022b).

As Figure 5.1 indicates, representations of the shared practices and histories among British and European citizens appear most frequently in the documents from 2016. The cohesive stance that is anchored around the discursive construction of shared experiences disintegrates by 2017 and is barely perceptible by 2019. In 2017, the introduction of the British life after Brexit theme indicates that as negotiations begin, the government responds to pressure to outline plans for Britain's future.

According to the UK government, Britain and Europe's shared experiences include 'losing lives' (four instances), a 'cultural life' (six occurrences) and 'saving lives' in the Mediterranean Sea (eight cases). The discursive construction of these experiences highlights three unifying processes: military sacrifice, cultural integration and preventing 'illegal entry' into Europe. The war-related representations feature exclusively in the 2016 subcorpus in ministerial statements. They narrate European cooperation in the Second World War and the fight against terrorism, invoking historical precedents to support calls for

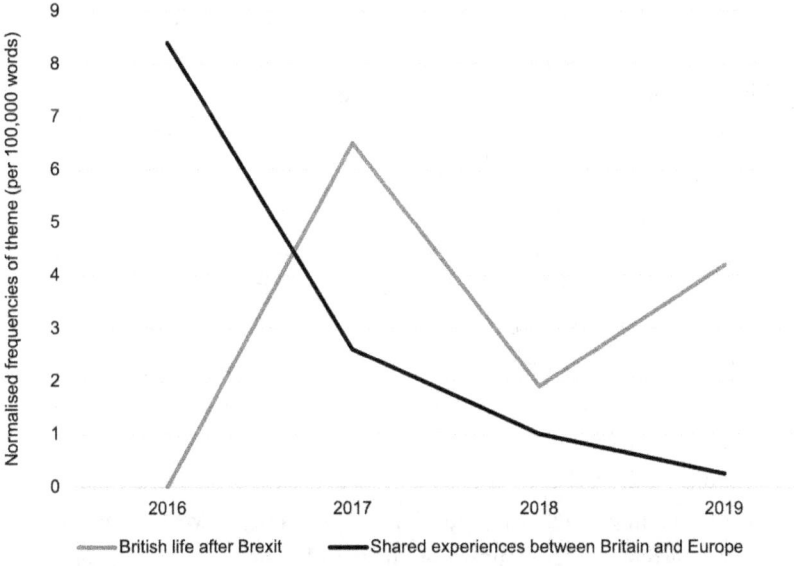

Figure 5.1 British life after Brexit and shared experience themes per 100,000 words.

stronger bilateral defence relationships after Brexit. Depictions of European officials saving migrants' lives recur between 2016 and 2018 in a greater variety of documents, including statements, speeches and White Papers. The representation of a European culture emerges in 2017 and persists through to 2019; it features in speeches, written editorials and statements.

Ethnocentric ideologies underpin various representations in the 'Shared experiences' theme. Ethnocentrism conceptualizes the world through rival social groups (Sumner, 1906; Sobolewska and Ford, 2020). It constitutes the view that 'one's own group is the center of everything' (Sumner, 1906: 13) and is superior (Joseph et al., 1990). As the term '*Euro*centrism' indicates, ethnocentric ideologies inform the construction of transnational in-groups with shared interests, memories and knowledge (Ifversen, 2019). Extracts (34)–(36) exhibit Eurocentrism in their depiction of a European in-group endangered by conflict, terrorism and illegal immigration. Constructing a threatened in-group legitimizes the government's call for renewed bilateral defence relationships between Britain and European countries after Brexit:

(34) We have a shared history, as the Prime Minister said, we were able this morning to recognise those many Polish men and women who sacrificed their **lives** to help keep us safe and secure here in the UK, as well as Europe safe and secure. And we recognise that and there is much that we share in our values that we can take forward together with that greater strategic relationship. (Theresa May, Statement in Poland, November 2016)

(35) This, first of all, we owe it for those who died, Father Jacques, who lost his **life** while he was celebrating the Eucharist, and to the many victims in Europe, and also the many victims of our citizens throughout the world. I'm thinking about those British who died in Tunisia just a year ago, and the Italians who died in Dhaka just a few weeks ago. Terrorism is trying to disintegrate our **lives** and when they are enabled to do that, they try to create fear and terror. We have to reaffirm our values, our identity, and we have to continue fighting, aware that our first challenge is not to give in. We have to remain strong and solid, believing in our culture. (Matteo Renzi, Statements in Rome, July 2016)

(36) In addition, the UK uses its military assets to support Operation SOPHIA, the EU's countering illegal migration operation in the Mediterranean. The UK is one of a few countries to have had a ship continuously assigned to the operation, and its naval assets have destroyed 172 smuggling

boats, saving over 12,000 **lives**, since the Operation began. (The Future Relationship between the United Kingdom and the European Union, July 2018)

Although all three extracts above appear on the UK government's website, not all authors are British officials. Extract (35) is from the then Italian prime minister Matteo Renzi, while Example (34) alludes to a comment by the Polish prime minister, Beata Szydło. The UK government's style guide stresses that statements should only be published online when it is in the public interest to know the entire content; when only a single message needs disseminating, alternative formats are available (Government Digital Service, 2020). Publishing the statements from non-British ministers in full suggests that policymakers deem Renzi and Szydło's arguments worth communicating to the British public. This is unsurprising: as the analysis below reveals, there is a strong convergence between the UK, Polish and Italian arguments, which reflects positively on the government's ability to re-establish ties with European countries after Brexit. It makes sense, then, that these statements are part of the government's officially curated, public-facing content.

In Extract (34), Theresa May makes an intratextual reference to an earlier comment from the then Polish prime minister, Beata Szydło. At the press conference during which May delivered her statement, Szydło said:

(37) So first of all, thank you very much for accompanying me to lay flowers in front of the monument commemorating Polish pilots who lost their **lives** in the Battle of Britain fighting for the freedom of the United Kingdom but also for the freedom of Europe, for all of us. (Statement in Poland, November 2016)

In contrast to the British media framing of European history as a series of cross-continental conflicts (Marchi and Partington, 2012), May and Szydło frame military 'sacrifice' positively as evidence of European collaboration; they argue that it 'help[ed] keep us safe and secure' and brought 'freedom' to the continent. Through recourse to the highly emotive discourse of suffering (through the verb 'sacrificed' and the verbal group 'lost their lives'), the two leaders create a moral responsibility to collaborate on European defence. By foregrounding 'sacrifice', the politicians undermine the claim that Britain's transactional approach to the EU lacks 'underpinning emotive content' (Siles-Brügge, 2019: 426). The commemorative event to which the ministers allude renders the image of sacrifice meaningful for present-day UK–EU relations: that the Second World

War strengthened the Anglo-Polish partnership signals that European relations improve when nations face conflict. The collective memory, then, offers hope that Britain can reconfigure its European relationships despite the potential for intra-European tension caused by Brexit.

May and Szydło construct Britain and Europe as independent yet friendly 'Others' (Gibbins, 2014) – that is, as two *distinct* social actors who share cultural and historical affinities. They foreground the absence of a collective political identity for Britain and Europe through the linguistic differentiation of 'here in the United Kingdom, as well as Europe' (May), and the syntactic parallelism of 'for the freedom of the United Kingdom but also for the freedom of Europe' (Szydło). In distinguishing the UK from mainland Europe, the politicians evoke the myth of the geographically unique British Island Nation, a spatial imaginary that accounts for the nation's defence against Hitler in popular retellings of European history (Bogdanor, 2020). British policymakers employ the British Island Nation imaginary to situate the country at a distance from any single foreign power, arguing that its geography should allow the UK to engage with different 'circles of influence on a "transactional" basis' without being tied to one partner (Gaskarth, 2013: 67). In the context of Brexit, situating Britain outside of Europe mirrors May's desire for a flexible, pragmatic approach to forging relationships after Brexit – one that balances the public desire for sovereignty and independence (Miglbauer and Koller, 2019) with the realities of a globalized world.

May and Szydło's statements demonstrate how policymakers reformulate the boundaries between the national self and foreign other(s) to fit their needs, albeit within the constraints of existing identity positions (Gaskarth, 2013; Atkins, 2022). By situating Britain within Europe ideologically and outside of it geographically, May creates and legitimizes a liminal status for her nation as both an insider and outsider in Europe (Shackleton, 2016). May's speech acts as an 'identity-reinforcing activity' (Gaskarth, 2013: 61) by reproducing and celebrating the stability of a long-enduring Anglo-Polish partnership. Through her delivery, May performs the role of an extra-EU ally that she covets for post-Brexit Britain, constructing the future in the present (Watkins, 2015). She legitimizes her role conception by drawing on a long-established tradition, dating back to Thatcher, of conceptualizing Britain as both a part of European heritage and an exceptional case (Daddow, 2015). By rooting Britain's distinctiveness in history, May frames Brexit as the ratification of a long-existing norm of British exceptionalism, rather than a radical departure from the status quo. Overall, then, May elucidates her vision for post-Brexit Britain as a constructive, extra-European defence partner (Gaskarth, 2014).

While retaining the emphasis on collective threats, Extract (35) shifts the focus to interactions between European and extra-European social actors. In the excerpt, Matteo Renzi responds to a European journalist's question about the viability of a unified, post-Brexit response to terrorism after an attack which occurred in France the day before. Although the journalist asks about 'what happened in France', Renzi shifts the locus of terror away from Europe as he speaks: after acknowledging the 'many victims in Europe', he expands to 'our citizens in the world' and then narrows the lens to two specific place imaginaries (Watkins, 2015): 'Tunisia', and 'Dhaka' in Bangladesh. By relocating the terror attacks to 'Eastern' places, Renzi constructs terrorism as an extra-European phenomenon to which Europe must respond, rather than a threat which also comes from within the continent. The calls to action, 'reaffirming our values' and 'believing in our culture', frame terrorism through a cultural discourse of difference, in which European leaders react peacefully to foreign agents who incite 'terror' and 'fear'. The postcolonial relationships between Europe, Tunisia and the Bengal imbue this Eurocentric, cultural interpretation of terrorism with an imperialist spirit of European superiority, in which Europeans are the innocent, 'civilized' victims of an 'Eastern' threat to a shared 'culture', 'identity' and 'values'.

Despite situating the terror attacks in North Africa and South Asia, Renzi linguistically suppresses (van Leeuwen, 1995) the extra-European victims, including the two Tunisians who died in the former attack and the seven Bangladeshis who died in the latter. This act of discursive exclusion implies that extra-Europeans only occupied the roles of perpetrators, reinforcing the Eurocentric conceptualization of terrorism as an act that is done to Europe by extra-European others. British public opinion exhibits a similar Western-centric view of terrorism: 48 per cent of British YouGov respondents (3,574 adults) cited international terrorism as the great 'threat to the West' in 2018 (YouGov, 2018: n.p.). Given the mutually reinforcing relationship between discourse and social practice (Fairclough, 1989), Renzi's statement strengthens the perception that 'non-Western' actors pose a terrorist threat to European nations. Although constructing a European in-group based on collective threats might foster intergovernmental solidarity between Britain and Italy, then, it could also perpetuate interpersonal divisions between Europeans and non-Western migrant groups. That this statement appears in full on the UK government website suggests an ideological alignment between British and European policymakers on the status of non-Western migrant groups.

As Excerpt (36) appears in a policy paper, it represents the UK's official negotiating position rather than the views of individual politicians. Its audience is not the public but interested groups who will likely be invited to consult on the proposals. Despite its greater formality, the document continues to structure UK–EU relations around shared threats. In the extract, Britain occupies the role conception of a maritime power within the broader role orientation of an influential, international actor (Gaskarth, 2014). This discursive construction centres on the repeated noun 'assets' in the nominal groups' 'military assets' and 'naval assets'. The evaluative connotation of 'asset' as a useful tool, in conjunction with the noun 'support', depicts Britain as a constructive partner and reliable ally to Europe (Gaskarth, 2014). Britain's generosity is allegedly rare: the nation is 'one of a few countries' to 'continually assign a ship to the operation'. Describing the UK's willingness to pool 'assets' as unusual subverts the oft-cited conceptualization of Britain as an 'awkward partner' to Europe (George, 1990). In this novel discursive frame, the UK is so active a collaborator that without its 'assets' and willingness to cooperate, the EU's defence against illegal immigration would be weaker. In other words, the government intimates that Britain can withstand the absence of a 'future [defence] relationship' much better than the Union. Despite this national posturing, the policy paper emphasizes Britain's attractiveness as a partner, indicating a return to the nation's pre-accession orientation of 'outsider as supplicant' (Daddow, 2015: 74). This role is far removed from the Vote Leave vision of a country 'taking back control' (Vote Leave, 2016: n.p.). In sum, the excerpt elucidates a tension between the rhetoric of Britain as a powerful maritime force and the use of this image to persuade European countries to collaborate with Britain after Brexit.

Though implicit in each case, Extracts (34)–(36) outline the need for future bilateral collaboration in the ideological and physical defence of Europe by arguing that the fight for freedom is ongoing. The excerpts establish the role conception of a reliable ally (Gaskarth, 2014) for Britain, Poland and Italy, citing deaths which occurred during symbolic battles against extra-European values as evidence of allyship. Britain occupies a liminal place within Europe in this discursive construction, allowing the UK government to balance its promise to protect Britain's sovereignty with its post-Brexit, internationalist narrative of Global Britain.

Where Extracts (34)–(36) construct a European in-group based on hard power and collective threats, Excerpts (37) and (38) reveal a culturally constructed European in-group. In this discursive frame, soft power – the diffusion of ideas and knowledge between communities (Unesco, n.d.: n.p.) – unites Britain and Europe.

(37) And Danish culture can be seen in all parts of British **life**. Television dramas like Borgen and The Bridge are screened on the BBC, our children

play endlessly with Lego and hygge is the new buzzword for coffee shops and eateries across the UK. So, as Britain leaves the EU, the relationship between our two nations will continue to thrive, not least because of the shared interests we have in this globalised world. (David Davis, Statement in Denmark, March 2017)

(38) We can continue the whirl of academic exchanges that have been a feature of European cultural **life** since the middle ages, and whose speed of cross-pollination has been accelerated by the internet as well as by schemes like Horizon or Erasmus, all of which we can continue to support, and whose participating scholars are certainly not confined to the EU. (Boris Johnson, Uniting for a Great Brexit, February 2018)

In Extract (36), from a speech delivered in Denmark just thirty days before official negotiations began, David Davis reflects positively on the effects of cultural globalization across Europe. He offers 'lifestyle evidence of the Europeanisation of Britain' (Garton-Ash, 2001: 9). By identifying Danish influences on the English language through linguistic borrowings ('hygge'), entertainment consumption through television programmes ('Borgen', 'The Bridge') and childhood play ('Lego'), Davis creates a role for Denmark as an international cultural leader (Gaskarth, 2014). The emphasis on the benefits of Anglo-Danish contact constructs Britain as a country that welcomes diversity and views multiculturalism as the natural result of globalization. That is, Davis's glorification of Denmark reworks Gibbins's (2014) concept of the friendly Other, assigning Britain the role of a friendly Self that acknowledges and amplifies the strengths of its international partners. In other words, it conciliates Danish leaders while emphasizing Britain's willingness to champion its European counterparts after Brexit. Through this two-pronged approach, Davis performs a soft, cultural power version of the extra-EU ally role that his government desires for Britain, evincing a coherent, albeit tenuous, foreign policy strategy throughout May's tenure as prime minister.

Boris Johnson's 'Great Brexit' speech reinforces the positive evaluation of European soft power. Where Davis focuses on the products of cultural globalization, Johnson highlights the processes through which a European cultural sphere has emerged. Although the nominalizations 'exchange' and 'cross-pollination' linguistically background the process of sharing academic knowledge, they frame the UK–EU relationship in terms of active cooperation. That is, they support the view of Europeanness as constituted through action – a performance, rather than an innate supranational identity. The plant-based metaphor of 'cross-pollination' naturalizes European collaborative endeavours, a linguistic choice which Johnson strengthens by representing the exchange of ideas through the grammatical structure of objectivated naturalization (representing an action, through nominalization, as a natural process of development, evolution or fusion) (van Leeuwen, 2008). Johnson depoliticizes the European academic community by arguing that it pre-existed the political Union, with research exchange forming the basis of 'cultural life since the middle ages'. By situating Britain within a long-enduring European intellectual tradition, Johnson identifies institutional collaborations that could continue if the ongoing negotiations between the UK and the EU do not end in a trade deal. In other words, he makes the case for cultural unity to distract from the potential for political division.

While Johnson's construction of a European research community is integral to his call to 'continue' cross-continental 'academic exchanges', focusing solely on European social actors would imply a Eurocentric conceptualization of knowledge. A Eurocentric focus would undermine the government's construction of Britain as an outward-looking, global nation (see below). To avoid the criticism of Eurocentrism, Johnson alludes to 'participating scholars' from outside of the 'EU'. By widening the research community to extra-EU countries, Johnson assigns the UK a role conception of an international bridge (Gaskarth, 2014). In this position, Britain encourages EU member states to expand their scope to extra-European nations, facilitating a strongly interconnected international community. In short, the excerpt elucidates the belief that the UK can use its soft power to expand its sphere of influence throughout the globe while continuing to shape Europe.

Extracts (37) and (38) reveal that in its quest to create a global trading nation, the UK government naturalizes and embraces cultural globalization, positioning it as evidence of the need to sustain bilateral relationships with EU member states. This stance is most overt in David Davis's idealized spatial imaginary of 'this globalised world' (Watkins, 2015), a discursive construction which presupposes an already interconnected planet. The government's pro-globalization attitude recognizes that the UK must intensify its relationships to survive economically after Brexit (Bogdanor, 2020). Framing globalization in cultural rather than economic terms renders this fact more palatable to a public that, in part, may have voted to leave the EU out of frustration at feeling economically 'left behind' (Goodwin and Heath, 2016). Nevertheless, if the UK government pursues deeper ties with individual nations after Brexit, Britain's exposure to the economic forces of globalization will increase. Ironically, this could compound feelings of dissatisfaction and marginalization among the 'left behind' in the UK (Bogdanor, 2020). In short, greater international cooperation could lead to further *intranational* division of the kind that the Eurosceptic media envisions in Chapter 4.

In contrast to the Eurosceptic media's construction of a uniquely British way of life based on democratic values and institutional innovation (see Chapter 4), the UK government envisions Britain as a nation whose experiences and culture are naturally influenced by the continent. The six examples above outline the need to strengthen Britain's bilateral relationships with Poland, Italy and Denmark while maintaining cultural exchange and expanding the European research community to extra-EU scholars. The excerpts intertwine British exceptionalism, evident in the discursive differentiation between Britain and the continent, with the awareness that the UK must intensify its global relationships to survive economically after Brexit (Bogdanor, 2020). Politicians argue that post-Brexit Britain will use its hard and soft power to act as a link between EU and extra-EU countries. That soft power becomes more salient after negotiations begin suggests that officials search for cultural common ground to offset political tensions.

British life after Brexit

'British life after Brexit' elucidates the government's vision for Britain's role after it leaves the EU. Unsurprisingly, given the importance of this theme for bolstering Britain's post-Brexit reputation, examples appear in a variety of documents. Of the fifty concordance lines, eighteen are from policy papers, fourteen from speeches and twelve from statements. The remaining six appear in press releases (five), and a government-produced news story about the EU (Withdrawal) Bill receiving Royal Assent. Although the theme is most quantitatively salient in 2019, these examples are merely variations of the claim that British and European migrants can 'continue to live their lives broadly as they do now' after Brexit. This assertion appears in sixteen extracts (from nine documents) in the context of guaranteeing citizens' rights despite the breakdown in UK–EU negotiations. While this consistency reveals a desire to reassure migrant communities, the examples which expose argumentative contradictions are more ideologically illuminating – they reveal the challenges that the government faces in legitimizing its Global Britain vision. Excerpts (39)–(42) reveal two principal disagreements in the plan for post-Brexit Britain:

(39) Of course, we recognise that we can't leave the EU and have everything stay the same. **Life** for us will be different. But what we do want, and what

we hope that you, our European friends, want too, is to stay as partners who carry on working together for our mutual benefit. (Theresa May, Speech in Florence, September 2017)

(40) And the certainty that Britain's plan, its blueprint for **life** outside of the European Union, is a race to the top in global standards. And not a regression from the high standards we have now. (David Davis, Foundations of the Future Economic Partnership Speech, February 2018)

(41) The implementation period is not only about providing certainty in the short term. It's also about beginning **life** outside the European Union, serving as a platform on which we build our future relationship. Which is why, as Michel said, the United Kingdom will be able to step out, sign and ratify new trade deals with old friends – and new allies around the globe – for the first time in more than 40 years. (David Davis, Statement in Brussels, March 2018)

(42) Now the reason I took the job of Brexit Secretary is because at this crucial moment in our history, I want to see the UK leave the European Union in the best possible way. Preferably with a deal, but prepared, on any eventuality, to manage the risks and grasp the opportunities of **life** outside the EU. (Dominic Raab, Speech on No-deal Planning, August 2018)

The construction of Brexit as both a departure from and continuation of the status quo in international relations is the most salient contradiction across the examples. In Extract (39), Theresa May expresses a desire to maintain Britain's relationship with the EU through the verbal phrases 'carry on' and 'stay as partners'. Despite conceding that 'everything [cannot] stay the same', the connotations of stability and continuity underpinning these verbs suggest that May's vision for a new UK–EU relationship largely echoes the one already in place. These contradictions can be partially explained by May's audience ('our European friends') – EU leaders have repeatedly stated that post-Brexit Britain cannot continue to enjoy the same benefits as member states. Nevertheless, May's emphasis on equality and continuity jars with David Davis's metaphorical conceptualization of Brexit as Britain 'step[ping] out' (41) into the world in a speech that is also delivered to European leaders. Through this metaphor of onward movement, Davis personifies the nation and underscores political action and agency.

Adapting the Eurosceptic metaphor of EU MEMBERSHIP AS ENTRAPMENT (Charteris-Black, 2019), Davis pejoratively frames the existing UK–EU power dynamic to establish a basis for changing its terms. For Davis, emerging from the shadows of the EU means ratifying new trade deals 'for the first time in more than 40 years' (41). In other words, Britain's post-Brexit status is not a new role but a return to its pre-accession standing. Davis's plan for post-Brexit Britain thus marries the ideas of progress and rising standards, expressed through the conceptual metaphor of INTERNATIONAL POLITICS AS A COMPETITION ('race to the top') (Charteris-Black, 2019), with the restoration of a lost imperial reputation as a global trading nation. In uniting the two conflicting images, Davis acknowledges part of the public's desire to return to a golden age of British power (Calhoun, 2017) while eschewing criticism that this constitutes 'regression'.

The inconsistent conceptualization of Brexit as both continuity and rupture renders unclear the government's vision for post-Brexit Britain: it is not obvious whether the UK will continue down its pre-referendum path, transform or return to its former glory. The argumentative tension is unlikely to be a rhetorical choice. Rather, it reflects competing pressures on the UK government to maintain a trading relationship with the EU while delivering on the Vote Leave promise to sign new trade deals with 'key allies like Australia or New Zealand, [and] growing economies like India, China, or Brazil' (Vote Leave, 2016: n.p.). It also mirrors a broader inconsistency in Theresa May's rhetoric about Brexit during her premiership (Brusenbauch Meislová, 2019a). The incongruities could be diplomatically useful: by informing EU leaders that Britain still values its trading partnership while also illustrating its desire for more equal relationships, the government placates both EU and extra-EU allies. However, the lack of clarity could also indicate that Brexit Britain is unsure of its place in the world; perceived instability could weaken Britain's international standing and lessen its attractiveness as an ally.[1]

A further tension emerges in Excerpts (40)–(42) between viewing Brexit as a risk and an opportunity. The abstract noun 'certainty' recurs in Davis's speeches, promising that the government has a 'blueprint' for Brexit Britain that entails rising global standards and financial security. In both examples, Davis foregrounds the government's preparedness to leave the EU on favourable terms. However, just four months after delivering his speech in Brussels, Davis resigned, citing concerns about giving away too much to the EU (Walker, 2021). Replacing him as Brexit secretary was Dominic Raab, who, in Example (42), offers a more balanced statement on the 'risks' and 'opportunities' of Brexit. Although Raab reassures Britons that the UK is 'prepared' for its withdrawal, his use of the phrase 'on any eventuality' expresses greater uncertainty about a future trade relationship than any of the previous speeches. This temporal shift in the discursive construction of Brexit corresponds to an impasse regarding the Irish border in Brexit negotiations, which led to a greater probability of the UK leaving the EU without a trade deal. Together, Raab's more temperate view of Brexit and the conflict that he alludes to challenge the feasibility of the government's Global Britain vision: they problematize the nation's role conception as a mediator between EU and extra-EU countries by highlighting the increasing precarity of the UK–EU relationship.

As the analysis above indicates, very few tangible policies appear in the government's vision for life in Britain after Brexit. In the early years, ministers conceptualize post-Brexit Britain as a global trading nation whose reach will expand after it 'step[s] out' from the shadows of EU membership. This image rests on two conceptual metaphors, INTERNATIONAL POLITICS AS A COMPETITION and PROGRESS AS ONWARD MOVEMENT, which disguise the lack of detail behind a general image of development. In the later years, the Global Britain spatial imaginary unravels as negotiations between the UK and the EU reach a stalemate. Given that the only concrete plan the government articulates is to act as a point of connection between EU and extra-EU countries, the vision for life in Britain after Brexit becomes hazier as the withdrawal day approaches.

The examples from the Alive semantic domain reveal that, in the early years, the government pursues bilateral relationships with European nations. Politicians construct a European in-group which collaborates to defend itself against three shared threats: conflict, terrorism and illegal immigration. The UK is represented as occupying a unique, liminal position as both an insider and outsider to this group (Shackleton, 2016). This discursive placement balances the public demand for independence (Miglbauer and Koller, 2019) with the realities of collaborating on foreign policies with other nations. Although the primary unifying factors are hard power and collective danger, politicians also depoliticize European sociocultural ties and naturalize cultural globalization. They envision the UK as a facilitator of an interconnected global community. While a pro-globalization stance is necessary for Britain's economic survival after Brexit (Bogdanor, 2020), it is unlikely to ameliorate the feeling of being 'left behind' which may have led some Britons to vote to leave the EU in 2016 (Goodwin and Heath, 2016). Paradoxically, then, the government's internationalist 'Global Britain' vision threatens to intensify the intranational discontent that contributed to the decision to leave the EU.

As Extracts (39)–(42) reveal, once official negotiations begin, the government's optimistic tone towards the UK–EU relationship disintegrates. Complexities and contradictions increase in the later subcorpora, as ministers offer conflicting visions of post-Brexit Britain. There is little clarity or detail about where Britain fits into international politics; the only tangible plan, to reignite the UK's reputation as a global trading nation, becomes increasingly unlikely as Brexit negotiations reach a stalemate. A diachronic analysis of the examples thus uncovers a turn away from a hopeful, unifying view of Anglo-European relations, towards confusion and uncertainty about Britain's ability to fulfil the role it covets as a bridge (Gaskarth, 2014) between EU and extra-EU countries.

The Personal Relationship: General domain

Much like the Alive semantic domain, the keyness of the Personal Relationship: General domain diminishes over the years. In 2016, it places twelfth in the keyness list but by 2019 it drops to thirty-eighth. As Table 5.2 shows, the domain does not reach the 1.0 log ratio threshold in 2019. Although the 0.87 value indicates that the domain contributes almost twice as much to the target subcorpus as it does to the reference corpus, it demonstrates a marked reduction in the salience of relationships in the data relative to the earlier years. This discursive pattern mirrors the breakdown in UK–EU negotiations – as tensions rise, the government's emphasis on international relations decreases.

The Personal Relationship: General semantic domain consists of lexical items used to describe international alliances. Depictions of the UK–EU relationship feature in 1,052 of the concordance lines; representations occur in speeches, parliamentary statements, policy papers, editorials and withdrawal bills. Four nouns describe UK–EU ties: 'relationship' (65 per cent), 'partner*' (23.8 per cent), 'friend*' (10.7 per cent) and 'ally' (0.5 per cent). All four terms connote less emotional attachment than the 'European family' metaphor that the European Commission adopts (Charteris-Black, 2019). For the UK government, then, Brexit involves a release from some of the affective ties and moral obligations

Table 5.2 Statistical information for Personal Relationship: General domain

Year	Percentage of C1 (gov)	Relative Frequency in C2 per 100,000 Words (ref)	Percentage of C2 (ref)	Log-Likelihood	Log Ratio
2016	0.37	93.2	0.10	255.57	1.93
2017	0.42	93.2	0.10	891.79	2.11
2018	0.24	93.2	0.10	263.69	1.33
2019	0.18	93.2	0.10	123.73	0.87

that bind together EU member states; the lexical choices used to frame UK–EU interaction reflect a more transactional, pragmatic approach than EU membership entailed.

Representations of UK–EU relations decrease over the years: there is a decline from 163 to 55.2 instances per 100,000 words between 2016 and 2019. 'Relationship' is the only term which experiences a renaissance in use over the years, as Figure 5.2 illustrates. This uptick corresponds to the publication of the Withdrawal Agreement, which includes a section dedicated to 'the future UK–EU relationship' in which the phrase is repeated. Use of the other three nouns peaks in 2017 when the formal negotiation process begins.

Three extra-European alliances also appear in the government data: partnerships with unspecified countries (136 instances); relationships with specific countries outside of the EU (93 occurrences); and relations between Ireland, Northern Ireland and the UK (88 cases). The former category consists of vague references to 'the rest of the world' or 'international partners' – these phrases appear most frequently in 2016 and decrease consistently thereafter.

The second group includes twenty named countries or continents, reflecting the government's attempt to position Britain at the centre of a sprawling network of bilateral relationships. The most frequently cited nation in this category is Japan (eighteen instances), with evaluative claims that compare the friendship of the politicians to the nations: 'I have seen your rich traditional culture and

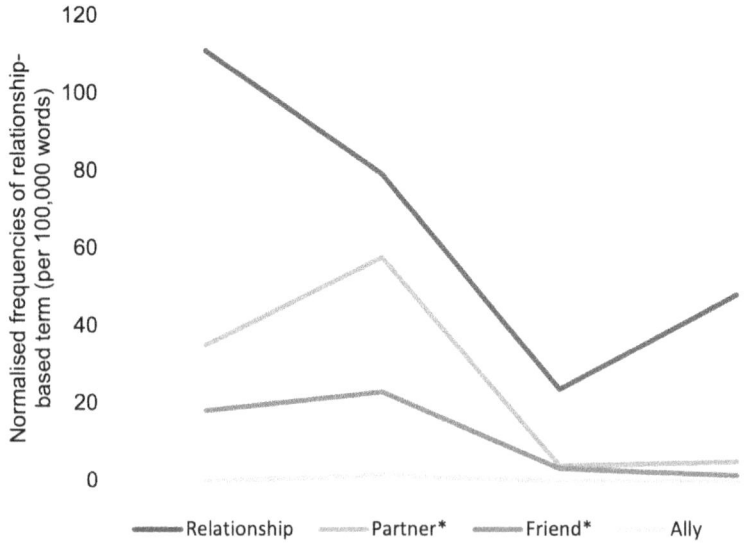

Figure 5.2 Normalized frequencies of relationship-based terms per 100,000 words.

the modern dynamism of Japan, and our personal **friendship** reflects the deep **friendship** and bonds between our two countries.' Perhaps unsurprisingly, given the discourse of the 'special relationship', the United States appears in fifteen instances, in statements asserting that 'President Trump told me how much America values its close **friendship** with Britain'. A relationship with Canada is construed in nine instances ('I hope that shows how much we prize our precious **friendship** with Canada and the Canadian people'), while Gibraltar ('the close **relationship** between Gibraltar and the United Kingdom'), China ('it is a golden era of the **relationships** between China and the UK') and Switzerland ('Switzerland is a close international **partner** to the UK') appear in eight instances each. The mix of non-English speaking and Anglophone countries somewhat problematizes Siles-Brügge's (2019: 422) claim that the Global Britain vision involves 'bringing the UK ... closer to its "kith and kin" in the Anglosphere'.

In its choice of extra-EU countries, the government aligns its plan for Global Britain with public opinion about the UK's closest allies and the most trustworthy nations: some 60 per cent of Britons surveyed view Japan as the most trustworthy and responsible nation, while 29 per cent of British respondents believe that the United States is the UK's best friend (Gaston, 2020). Instances of specific extra-EU relationships decrease overall, although there is a slight increase between 2018 and 2019. This growth reflects the greater likelihood of a no-deal Brexit, the consequences of which the government seeks to counteract by brokering more extra-EU partnerships (see below). Representations of the Ireland–Northern Ireland–UK nexus follow the same pattern of declining overall but rising slightly between 2018 and 2019. In this instance, the uptick reflects a growing discussion about the effects of a potential hard border on Anglo-Irish relations after Brexit.

The government alters its construction of the UK–EU relationship in line with the changing socio-political context. In 2016, politicians positively evaluate bilateral relationships with European countries while acknowledging that higher-level UK–EU interactions will change after Brexit. Government documents from this subcorpus repeatedly construct prospective security relationships (in 134 concordance lines) and trade relationships (in 148 concordance lines) between the two parties after Brexit. In their emphasis on security threats that both the UK and the EU face – and which necessitate a close, strategic relationship between the two actors – these concordance lines echo those which appear in the 'Shared experiences' subtheme of the Alive semantic domain. Together, the two domains present a long-established history of security cooperation. In the context of the Personal Relationship: General domain, the concordance lines often express a desire to maintain 'the closest possible economic **relationship** between our countries' (May, 2016) and to engage in 'close **cooperation** on global challenges' (UK Government, 2016). As these two brief examples indicate, the government typically frames future UK–EU interactions as mutually beneficial and goal oriented, while remaining optimistic that negotiations will produce a 'better relationship' (Davis, 2016). Excerpts (43) and (44) encapsulate this duality:

(43) Now is the time to build a new and productive **relationship**, based on **friendship** and free trade, and a new European **partnership** where we continue to develop our work on things that matter to all of us in Europe. (Johnson, Speech, 2016)

(44) Simply, we will do what independent, sovereign countries do. It will be a negotiation, and it will require some give and take, but we want a deal that reflects the kind of mature, cooperative **relationship** that close **friends** and **allies** enjoy. I have been clear to my European counterparts that we approach the negotiation in a spirit of goodwill and a desire to see the EU succeed politically and economically. In exit we are not seeking a bitter divorce, but a better **relationship**. (David Davis, Speech, December 2016)

Extracts (42) and (43) – which I discuss at length in Parnell (2022c) – demonstrate the rhetorical tendency of politicians to combine several relationship-related terms in a single utterance to emphasize the importance of future ties. Extract (42) unites the ideas of pragmatism (expressed through the adjective 'productive', noun phrase 'free trade' and verb phrase 'develop our work') with an emphasis on emotive bonds ('relationship', 'friendship' and 'partnership'). The alliterative union of 'friendship and free trade', connected through the simple conjunction 'and', places both on an equal footing. As free trade is an important aspect of national identity in Britain (Trentmann, 2008), relating it to friendship with Europe highlights the importance of a 'new and productive relationship' to the British national identity narrative. The recognition of the future relationship is further reflected in the adjective 'European' and first-person plural pronoun 'us', which create an in-group centred on *Europe* (but not EU-rope). This exclusive use of the noun 'European' to mean the continent rather than the political alliance reflects the broader argument made by the Conservatives at this time that the UK was leaving the EU but not Europe. At the same time as the proper noun creates a sense of inclusivity, then, it subtly points to political distancing. Underpinning the extracts is a sense of confidence in the ability to achieve what politicians desire – a *strategic* international relationship based on congruent interests (Oelsner and Koschut, 2014: 13–15) – from future UK–EU ties. This is achieved, as I note in Parnell (2022c: 400), through the framing of the UK–EU relationship as a *normative* relationship 'based on ideational and emotional ties'.

In 2017, official Brexit negotiations begin. The positive and optimistic view of future UK–EU relations found in the 2016 documents continues with the repeated claims that bilateral relationships will become 'stronger' after Britain's withdrawal and the new UK–EU relationship will be rooted in trust. Extracts (45)–(47) exemplify these discourses:

(45) This is why, in addition to stronger relations with EU member states, we also envisage a strong UK-EU **partnership** on foreign and defence policy following our departure. This will allow us to continue our work in tackling the shared challenges we face worldwide. (Johnson, 2017)

(46) As the Prime Minister said last week, our shared future can only be founded on **partnership**, **friendship** and most importantly trust. (Davis, 2017)

(47) Indeed, we want to be your strongest **friend** and **partner** as the EU, and the UK thrive side by side. (May, 2017)

These examples frame Brexit simultaneously as a process of political distancing (taking the UK from *part of* the EU to *partner to* the EU) and of enhancing relations. That is, we see the repeated use of the adjective 'strong' (45), comparative 'stronger' (45) and superlative 'strongest' (47) to refer to the future UK–EU relationship, envisioning Brexit as a process of *intensifying* ties rather than weakening them. However, this is somewhat problematized by the nouns 'partner(ship)' and 'friend(ship)', which represent the UK and the EU as distinct but equal entities,[2] and 'side by side', which provides an image of balance and equality, but also distinctiveness. The tensions paradoxically suggest that it is possible to have a closer relationship with the EU when outside of it than within it. The imagined relationship remains rooted in pragmatism, with the focus on 'foreign and defence policy' and 'work in tackling the shared challenges'. Foreign and defence policies reflect the emphasis on shared threats from the Alive semantic domain, suggesting a relationship based primarily on hard power.

Whereas representations of the UK–EU relationship exude confidence and optimism in the 2016 and 2017 subcorpora, recognition of discord and the potential failure to reach a deal begins to emerge in the 2018 subcorpus and continues into 2019. Extracts (48)–(50) illustrate these themes:

(48) But there's one aim I want to particularly concentrate on today – and it's the need for this new **partnership** to stand the test of time. Because while

we can get bogged down in the day-to-day grumblings, we must not lose sight of that goal during these negotiations. (Davis, 2018)

(49) Now, I think in reality, many of the no deal challenges will affect the EU in similar or the same ways. For our part, if the negotiations fail, we would continue to behave as a responsible European neighbour, **partner** and **ally**. (Raab, 2019)

(50) Some in the UK have the mirror worry that the backstop is evidence that the EU will not handle the negotiation of our future **relationship** energetically or ambitiously, or even that the EU will down tools altogether and leave the UK permanently in the backstop arrangements. (Johnson, 2019)

David Davis's use of the noun phrase 'day-to-day grumblings' in Extract (48) draws attention to disagreements in the negotiations for the first time (see Chapter 1 for context). However, the temporal juxtaposition between 'test of time' (with its connotations of longevity) and 'day-to-day' reveals an attempt to trivialize and minimize the level of conflict being experienced between the UK and the EU. While the nouns 'goal' and 'aim' express hope for the future, the noun 'need' and deontic modality of the modal verb 'must' underscore the importance of the deal at a time when the possibility of leaving without one is increasing.

As explored in depth in Parnell (2022c), the possibility of a no-deal scenario leads Dominic Raab to emphasize the UK's commitment to remaining 'a responsible European neighbour, partner and ally'. While this could be read positively as a reaffirmation of dedication, 'for our part' and the hypothetical 'if the negotiations fail' place the onus – and therefore the blame – on the EU. This is supported by the following extract:

(51) We approach these negotiations with a spirit of pragmatism, compromise and indeed **friendship**. I hope, I trust that the EU will engage with our proposals in the same spirit. (Raab, 2019)

As I lay out in Parnell (2022c), this extract represents an attempt to coerce EU negotiators into conceding to Britain's desires. On the locutionary level, the speech acts 'I hope, I trust' (Searle, 1979) perform friendship through expressing trust in the EU's desire to compromise with the UK and reach a deal. However, on the illocutionary level, the speech acts introduce doubt that the EU will respond in the same 'spirit of pragmatism, compromise and . . . friendship'. I argue here that the same subtle framing of the EU as the potential problem in negotiations is achieved in Extract (48). The logic underpinning the extract(s) is that if the UK remains a 'responsible European neighbour, partner and ally', there is no reason why it should not reach a deal with the EU, unless the EU refuses to compromise. This encourages British listeners to associate failure in Brexit negotiations with EU leaders.

Extract (50) is somewhat different, in that it comes from a letter from then prime minister Boris Johnson to then presidents Tusk and Juncker – both part of the EU – about the Northern Ireland backstop, a topic which was causing concern on both sides of the negotiation table. Naturally, with such a different audience from Davis and Raab, who are speaking to the nation, the framing of the UK–EU relationship is somewhat distinct. In the example, Johnson recognizes the fears that some British critics have that 'the backstop is evidence that the EU will not handle the negotiation of our future **relationship** energetically or ambitiously, or even that the EU will down tools altogether and leave the UK permanently in the backstop arrangements'. In other words, he verbalizes the doubt that simmers beneath Extracts (48) and (49) – he overtly envisions an EU that is *un*ambitious, lazy and disinterested in the UK's future. While this supports my reading of the rising tensions leading to a recognition of discord between the UK and the EU and thereby highlighting the UK's position of weakness in negotiations, it is important to acknowledge that Johnson goes on to say that he 'firmly believe[s] that the [fear] about the EU's intentions is unfounded'. The national posturing and more negative framing of the EU that is evident in Extracts (48) and (49) is not conducive to positive UK–EU relations and, as such, Johnson presents a more ambivalent framing of current ties. When taken together, Extracts (48)–(50) highlight some of the contradictions in the UK's rhetoric surrounding the UK–EU relationship during the negotiation process.

By 2019, British politicians have shifted from questioning the possibilities of a future UK–EU relationship to sidelining the EU as a partner and focusing efforts on extra-European alliances. Extracts (52)–(54) reveal this transition:

(52) As we strive for a better deal with the EU, we need to view that relationship in the context of our wider vision for the UK after Brexit. Fifteen years ago, when I was posted as a Foreign Office lawyer to The Hague, I remember my counterparts from Japan, Australia, South Korea and Brazil lamenting the introverted perspective of the EU and the UK – at the expense of the rest of the world. It was a salutary warning. Today, the UK wants a strong **relationship** with our European **partners**. But

Brussels isn't the only game in town. It's time we broadened our horizons, and my first visits as Foreign Secretary – to the US, Canada, Thailand and Mexico – have shone a light on the opportunities for a truly global Britain. (Raab, 2019)

(53) But if we are going to restore faith in our institutions, we must make sure that Britain leaves the EU on 31 October. Politicians of all parties promised the public that they would honour their vote, and if we are to have any hope of restoring faith in our governing institutions it is imperative that we uphold the democratic mandate of that referendum. I hope, and believe, that we will leave with a deal. We have set out a bold, fair offer to our European **friends** and I look forward to engaging with them on the detail of what we have set out. But, whatever happens, we must be prepared to leave on 31st October, even if that means leaving without a deal. (Johnson, 2019)

(54) When I picture how others see Britain right now, I suspect old friends are shaking puzzled heads. The clash and thunder over Brexit is not an appealing spectacle. (Hunt, 2019)

The examples from 2019 introduce the idea that the UK–EU relationship is just one facet of a broader internationalist Britain, as expressed through the idiom 'isn't the only game in town' and the metaphor 'broaden our horizons' (52). In Extract (52), Dominic Raab alludes to the long-standing Eurosceptic argument that the EU is 'regional' in outlook rather than international (Teubert, 2001) by claiming that the EU (and by extension the UK as a member) has been 'introverted'. This personifying adjective is interesting, since it does not necessarily imply *wilful* ignorance of other trading partners but rather a shyness and meekness which does not typically lend itself to successful foreign policy. This is an important framing of the UK as a member of the EU since it tells extra-EU actors that the UK was never intentionally exclusive and that it appreciates their 'salutary warning'. At the same time, it avoids directly blaming the EU for a 'regional' outlook. Ultimately, in the argumentative frame of the extract, leaving the EU means transforming from a nation held back by an introverted EU to an extroverted foreign partner – a 'truly global Britain' – and Brexit is subtly depicted as the (re)birth of an internationalist Britain (see Zappettini, 2019).

It is worth noting that despite the grandstanding rhetoric underpinning these examples from 2019, there is an underlying sense of national division permeating them. For instance, in Extract (53), Johnson alludes to a lack of public faith in UK institutions, linking this to British MPs' delays in passing Brexit legislation (which is described in lexis from the semantic field of chivalry – 'honour'). This extract, together with Extract (52) which was published in *Washington Post* (and which I analyse in Parnell (2022c)), foregrounds domestic divisions not only between British politicians but also between members of the public and their political representatives. Foregrounding divisions and a lack of public faith in political institutions arguably forces the UK into a place of political weakness, airing its dirty laundry in national speeches and international newspapers. As a result, although Extract (53) illustrates that UK policymakers depict Britain as a nation capable of 'offer[ing]' (and therefore determining the contents of) a 'bold' and 'fair' deal to the EU, Extract (54) demonstrates the reversion of the UK to its role as an outsider and supplicant to other countries.

Extracts (53) and (54) are also interesting because they demonstrate a shared discursive construction of the UK in the later years of the government and media corpora. Johnson's claim that the public now 'lack[s] faith' in British institutions reflects and is reflected in the newspapers' depictions of politicians as 'clueless', 'stupid', 'cowardly' and 'pathetic'. This parallelism suggests that representations of British division – at least between politicians and the public – were circulating beyond the pro-Brexit press and were more widely accessible than just to readers of these newspapers.

Of course, there is some evidence to suggest that Britons *might* have been losing faith – or rather trust – in political institutions. For instance, Gaskell, Stoker, Jennings and Devine (2019: 4, italics in original) argue that citizens' 'expectations politicians or government could be trusted to deliver a better life for them are *generally low*'. In fact, their focus group research found that anxiety and cynicism were the dominant themes in response to the prospects of a post-Brexit deal (Gaskell et al., 2019). Meanwhile, in 2019, the Hansard Society found that 'opinions of the system of governing [were] at their lowest point in the 15-year Audit series – worse . . . than in the aftermath of the MPs' expenses scandal' (2019: 3). On the one hand, acknowledging these views to a national audience allows Johnson to imply that he is trying to win that trust back and is therefore an important attempt at authenticity. On the other hand, discursively constructing divisions in *Washington Post* is only likely to *extend* the view of Britons as divided beyond the UK. This likely weakens the UK's international standing by presenting it as a nation that cannot agree on who it is and who it wants to be.

At this point, it is necessary to question to what degree the 'Global Britain' vision can be considered as tenable and, importantly, coherent: How can the UK claim to be a global trading nation when it is experiencing division with its former closest trading partner and within its public? How can the vision lead to rising trust in the UK's future when it is fraught with contradictions? It is perhaps not surprising, considering the argumentative shift between 2016 and 2019 and the contradictions between documents published at the same time, that in 2019, some 28 per cent of Britons surveyed by the British Foreign Policy Group said they did not understand what it means to be a global nation (Gaston, 2020). Those who claimed to comprehend did not agree on the criterion for being labelled a global nation (Gaston, 2020).

Despite the argumentative shift between 2016 and 2019, which reveals a rising self-consciousness that the ongoing trust breakdown in UK–EU negotiations and parliamentary disagreements over Brexit are rendering the UK a less attractive trade partner, the government remains committed to the Global Britain vision as it barrels closer to its withdrawal. In 2019 documents, the 'global' modifier is used to evaluate Britain forty-nine times. Although contextually, the Global Britain identity narrative appears ever more precarious as the years progress, the UK government remains committed to its internationalist discourse. However, at the time of writing, in October 2023, there appear to be fewer constructions of Global Britain in government discourses about international cooperation – perhaps reflecting a belated recognition of the weakening of the narrative. For instance, although the Integrated Review of Security, Defence, Development and Foreign Policy published in 2021 was titled 'Global Britain in a competitive age' (HM Government, 2019), Hadfield and Whitman (2023) note that there are fewer references to Global Britain in the second version published in spring 2023, which is simply titled 'Integrated Review Refresh 2023: Responding to a more contested and volatile world' (HM Government, 2023).

Conclusion

This chapter reveals a discursive shift in the government's Global Britain narrative, brought about by a stalemate in Brexit negotiations and discord in the UK Parliament over the Withdrawal Agreement. In the early years, government documents envision a transactional UK–EU relationship that protects both entities from threats of terrorism and illegal migration. Within the construction of a European in-group, the UK occupies a liminal position as both an insider and an outsider (Shackleton, 2016). The government argues that the UK's liminal position allows it to fulfil a role as an international linchpin, uniting EU and extra-EU countries in a strongly connected global community. This argument requires the government to embrace globalization – the process which may have led some Britons to vote to leave the EU because they felt economically 'left behind' (Goodwin and Health, 2016; Bogdanor, 2020). Although politicians frame globalization in cultural terms to render its inevitability more palatable, an internationalist identity could compound the feelings of dissatisfaction among the British public. Paradoxically, then, the Global Britain plan could foster intranational divisions of the kind that the Eurosceptic media envisions (see Chapter 4).

In the later years, the ability to strengthen the UK–EU relationship becomes increasingly precarious. Documents reveal an increased positioning of the UK as an international 'outsider' and 'supplicant' (Daddow, 2015: 75). Politicians foreground sociocultural ties between Britain and Europe, but the focus on cultural unity cannot mask the palpable uncertainty about reaching a trade deal with the EU before the transition period ends. Politicians begin to foreground disagreements between the UK and the EU and within domestic politics as the process extends. Forced to address Britain's weaknesses, officials illustrate that their plan for Global Britain is becoming untenable: Britain cannot claim to be a global trading nation without strong international relationships, but ongoing disagreements could compromise future deals by negatively affecting Britain's reputation.

Despite the dwindling feasibility of the Global Britain vision, the government remains faithful to its narrative of post-Brexit national identity up to the withdrawal date. While consistency might suggest that there is a coherent blueprint for life outside of the EU, the Global Britain rhetoric lacks detail and is often contradictory. Politicians provide contradictory interpretations of Brexit as both departure and continuity, risk and opportunity; metaphors of onward movement create a vague image of progression in an attempt to mask a lack of detail about life outside of the EU. Given these inconsistencies, it is perhaps unsurprising that, in 2019, 28 per cent of Britons stated that they did not know what being a global nation entails (Gaston, 2020). Think tanks have responded to public confusion by calling on the government to publish a values statement to demystify the Global Britain vision (Gaston, 2020; Hug, 2020). At the time of writing, no such statement has been produced and as noted above, the rhetoric of Global Britain in government discourse appears to be slowly disappearing.

The inconsistencies in the government documents and the dwindling argumentative value of the Global Britain vision fail to provide the British public or future trade partners with a coherent blueprint for Britain outside of the EU. The lack of precise details about the government's plan for its global nation leaves the UK at risk of losing its international standing – a far cry from the early promise that Brexit would reinvigorate Britain's historical identity as a global trading nation.

6

Discursive Constructions of Britain and Britishness in Oral Interviews

Introduction

Moving on from the corpus-assisted critical discourse analyses of media and government texts, in this sixth chapter, I conduct a discourse analysis of narratives to examine the ways in which people with ties to Nottinghamshire tell stories to position themselves within national social groups, legitimize their political stance towards Brexit and perform their identities as Leave and Remain voters. When conducting the interviews, I noticed the prevalence of narratives as responses to open questions that did not explicitly request narrative replies. It was through these stories that participants largely contested, negotiated and performed national and political identities. While all participants told at least one narrative, often Remain-voting interviewees told several per interview. As a result, the stories that I analyse in depth in this chapter are most often told by Remain voters. The higher number of Remainer stories is partly due to the Remainer self-selection bias (ten of the fifteen interviewees voted to Remain). Potential Leave-backing participants expressed a greater level of suspicion towards the research aims than Remain voters, expressing concerns about being framed as racist or xenophobic. In general, my five Leave-voting participants were more likely to give minimal responses to questions during the interviews.

To analyse the narratives, I categorized the stories thematically based on the representations of Britain and Europe that they contained. This process resulted in the identification of four key themes: remembering a great British past, inequality, discrimination, and division and difference. The micro-linguistic analysis of the narratives that follows explores these themes across stories that were selected for the representativeness of the key discursive representations of Britain, Britishness, Europe and Europeanness. While many stories tell of national identities in relation to Brexit, several others tell of national identities in *times* of Brexit; both contribute to positioning the interviewee as a Leave or Remain voter.

Below, I reveal how my participants negotiate, perform and contest national and political identities through the stories that they tell during the interview. In their stories, the lived experience of being British and the dynamics of inclusion and exclusion that accompany it are very much dependent on the spaces and places that characters occupy. Given the highly localized nature of the stories, the plots typically centre on quotidian activities such as conversations with friends or shopping excursions. I argue throughout the chapter that what unites the stories is a sense of dissatisfaction with the present state of the British nation as participants imagine it, whether that is due to a lack of global trade, the underfunding of English regions and towns, or the social exclusion of Black and minority ethnic people.

Most often, the stories include representations of Britain as divided: the participants claim that English regions are as different as countries and that some accents index otherness while Others index Britishness. Notably, although participants construct Britain as divided and its meanings as contested, eleven of the fifteen interviewees still self-identify as 'British' and claim that this identity has emotional significance for them. Of the remaining four, two identify as 'English', and two say they do not subscribe to national identity as a concept.

Remembering a great national past

'They have got their points when we were, you know, we was in Europe. They have been helpful in a lot of ways and that. It's just that we felt that we wanted to be our own country again and to be like we used to be many years ago', explains Participant C, an eighty-six-year-old, self-identifying English woman from Nottingham who voted Leave in the EU membership referendum. This quote illustrates something which became clear to me throughout the interviews I conducted for this project: that representations of (supra)national identity – and often *stories* about (supra)national identity – are used to legitimize how a person voted in the EU membership referendum. Through this legitimization, the stories play a key role in constructing the participants' national and political identities.

In the quotation above, Participant C appears to be constructing a national in-group through the first-person plural personal pronoun 'we' and the noun phrase 'our own country' and placing it in opposition to 'Europe', which is

Othered through the third-person pronoun 'they'. In this way, she is ostensibly drawing on a long discursive history of constructing Britain in opposition to Europe (Spiering, 2014). However, reading the full claim – 'we wanted to be our own country again and to be like we used to be many years ago' – indicates that the first use of 'we' in conjunction with the verb 'wanted' is, in fact, used to refer to Leave voters. In this way, Participant C elides national and political identities, constructing a narrow version of the national public consisting of Leave voters – much like Theresa May's rhetoric when she was prime minister (Atkins, 2022). This representation of national identity disregards the fact that almost half of the voting public voted to Remain; it is a subtle form of discursive exclusion that simultaneously signals a strong sense of belonging to a Leave-voting in-group.

What is notable about this quotation is the story underpinning it: by saying that we 'used to be' 'our own country', Participant C draws on a broader Eurosceptic narrative of EU membership as stripping the UK of its agency and identity (see, e.g., Hawkins, 2012 on a 'quasi-imperial' EU representation). By claiming that 'we felt that we wanted to be our own country', Participant C legitimizes her Leave vote through *mythopoesis*. While van Leeuwen (2007: 105) defines *mythopoesis* as 'legitimation achieved through storytelling', Bennett (2022: 371, italics in original) provides a more specific definition of *mythopoesis* as '*a form of legitimation through history* or, more specifically, through narratives of history that are taken as truth and accepted as canonical stories that are the bedrock of social groupings'. While the quotation from Participant C above is not in itself a story, it does *legitimize through history* by implicitly drawing on a broader master narrative or myth of British national identity: that of the great British trading nation.

Several stories told by the older Leave-voting participants in this project draw on the broader master narrative of the great British trading nation. In the case of Participant C, there is a striking juxtaposition between stories she narrates of a poor childhood with a collegial, neighbourly atmosphere that she 'loved', and Britain as having once traded widely with far-flung countries. For instance, in the narrative below, Participant C speaks fondly of the 'lovely lovely atmosphere' of her childhood, when people who were struggling financially banded together to form tight-knit support networks (transcription conventions can be found at the front of the book):

> when we were younger no one had got very much money (.) everybody was in the same boat (.) so you'd got your neighbours used to help you out if you ran out of anything (.) you used to do the same for them (.) nobody would see you struggle if they could help (.) it was a lovely <u>lovely</u> atmosphere in that respect.

When prompted to compare this 'lovely <u>lovely</u> atmosphere' with the present – 'do you think that that's still true of what it's like to live in England today?' – Participant C emphatically replies, 'no', before adding that 'people are better off today'. Remarking that children go out to restaurants with family now, she recalls that the 'fish and chip shop was the best we ever did'. The claim that people are 'better off today' is important considering another story that Participant C tells – an Observation of when Britain 'used to trade all over the ^world':

> we used to trade all over the ^world and that (.) I <u>quite</u> remember (.) New Zealand butter being on the shelves in the shops and Australian this and that and the other you know and (.) you could you could trade with anyone and that's the one thing we're <u>pleased</u> about coming out of Brexit <u>hopefully</u> that's what we're going to be able to do again we're going to <u>work</u> at it but (.) hopefully that's how it's going to be where we can trade with <u>any</u> country we want to

There is arguably a contradiction at play when these stories are considered together: Participant C constructs a time when Britain was trading widely but 'no one had got very much money', and a time when the UK is part of the EU and people are 'better off'. Despite this contradiction between individual finances and the economy, the participant expresses nostalgia for a country that 'used to be' and that she hopes in the future 'can trade with any country we want to'. Underpinning this nostalgia is a sense that Britain is not what it once was – the past tense verb 'used to' implies that the nation no longer trades globally, which is reinforced by the past-oriented verb 'remember'. In many ways, then, this is a story of national decline. Nevertheless, the temporal adverb 'again' ties the country's trading past to its future, framing Brexit as a return to a more internationalist past for the nation. Through this temporal connection, the participant's narrative becomes *retrotopian* – 'a nostalgic vision for the future based upon a lost but undead past' (Beaumont, 2017: 380).

Participant C is not the only older Leave-voting interviewee who tells stories of feeling more strongly connected to Others in the past. For instance, Participant E, a seventy-six-year-old woman from Nottinghamshire, tells an Exemplum of when she lived at home with her parents and her 'mum and dad used to go up the road to vote'. Participant E voices her childhood 'excit[ement]' at seeing her neighbour going to vote: 'Oh look! There's Mrs so and so, she's just going up to vote.' She then contrasts this image with present-day relationships between compatriots to make a point outside of the story: 'I don't think there's that camaraderie so much now with people. Or [there] just doesn't seem to be. Everybody seems to be living their own lives and getting on with it and it's particularly so with the younger generation.'

The similarity between Participants C and E's conceptualizations of the past as more interconnected suggests that remembering a great British past is not only linked to an economic argument about the desire for more international trade, but also a sociocultural argument about the effects of greater individualism on the participant's sense of national togetherness. In other words, as Beaumont (2017: 382) puts it, 'Brexit cannot be reduced to economics.' Part of constructing the present-day nation is narrating a sense of isolation – as personal relationships become increasingly mediated through technology and face-to-face interactions are (at times) replaced by online connectivity, older participants are voicing a feeling of *losing* connections. While the participants do not position themselves as 'left behind', then, the critical analyst might argue that greater individualism and being 'better off' are framed by these participants as a threat to a previously experienced, neighbourly – or even class-based – solidarity.

Later in the interview, Participant C states that she is, at the time of interviewing, 'just proud to be an English person'. Conversely, stories by Participants E and D – a husband and wife who identify as 'British' and were interviewed together – locate pride in the nation at specific moments in the past. For instance, Participant E tells the following Observation of her 'school days':

I can remember feeling very proud to be British particularly (.) in school days we had (.) Empire Day I can't even remember now but I think it was sometime in April (.) you know when all the children did (.) displays and proud to be British and everything that was British was good (.) and St George's Day we used to celebrate that and you know y I I was British and just proud to be British (.) I suppose I didn't know anything else really but I think I was brought up to believe that way

While Participant E's representation of herself as 'British' is straightforward in indexing her national identity, her alternating pronoun use is striking. In the storytelling world, Participant E repeatedly refers to herself through the singular first-person personal pronoun 'I' whereas in the story world of her 'school days', she frequently employs the plural personal pronoun 'we' to metonymically construct a national in-group of British children who were socialized to believe that 'everything that was British was good'. The shift in pronouns, tense and stance marks a move away from a collective national identity in childhood towards a less nationally connected adulthood. That Participant E is constructing a more ambivalent stance towards Britain in the storytelling world is clear from her assertion that she no longer celebrates St George's day ('used to'). It also emerges through the juxtaposition between the child character who 'didn't know anything else' and the storytelling adult who (it is implied in the adverb 'else') is aware of an alternative interpretation of British history. Through this coming-of-age story of a transition from collective patriotism to a more ambivalent adulthood, Participant E narrates an analogous shift away from support for British influence in the national psyche.

Participant D continues the theme of British decline by narrating a Recount of travelling to New Zealand by ship and feeling proud to 'see the [British] ensign flying':

> When I went to New Zealand to visit by ship the journey took about six six weeks (.) it hit many ports on the way out there (.) and and in every port you know there was a British cargo ship with the ensign flag (.) and that that made me feel proud because that was influence to me of (.) of England because we were at that time we were still a kind of a really global trading country I mean this is go this would be around 1960 62 (.) obviously I don't think there'd be an English or British merchant ship now (.) but in those days yes and yes it was good to see the the ensign flying

Participant D's Recount narrates a loss of British – or English – influence since the 1960s. The adverbs 'obviously' and 'now' position the argument that Britain is no longer 'a really global trading country' as common sense. The past tense verb 'made' in the clause 'that made me feel proud' indicates a potential loss of pride in the storytelling world. The elision between 'English' and 'British' serves as a reminder that this story – and indeed all the stories narrated in this chapter – is an *English* narration of Britishness and often those identities are discursively conflated in the narratives.

The stories I analyse above (re)produce similar constructions of Britain. The participants interweave economic and sociocultural arguments with a narration of a powerful British history rooted in the spatial imaginaries of the British Empire and Global Britain (Sykes, 2018). Two of the stories convey the affective stance (Du Bois, 2007) of lost pride in the nation. Two participants articulate a sense of lost camaraderie between neighbours. While all the stories provide *some* support for Calhoun's (2017: n.p.) interpretation of the Leave vote as 'a vote for the good old days, in complaint against a frustrating present', not all participants voice a belief that Brexit will help Britain return to its past glory. For instance, Participant D states 'that we don't make anything anymore' while Participant E notes that 'there's not so many British or English factories around nowadays and we don't make so many goods as we used to'. Not all Leave-backing stories are *retrotopian*, then. The stories above were narrated *after* Britain left the EU. In that sense, even for Participant C, who constructs Brexit as the means through which Britain could trade widely again, leaving the EU had not led to a tangible sense of national reinvigoration at the time of interviewing. The same can be said for the slightly younger Leave-voting interviewees, one of whom (Participant O, a white, middle-aged male) argues that Britain still needs to 'roll up its sleeves and get into the fight' for a place in the world after Brexit. For these participants, then, one might suggest that Britain has 'lost an empire and not yet found a role' (Acheson, 1962: n.p.). In other words, what are being constructed in these stories are what are referred to by Mann and Fenton (2017) as *discontented national identities*. The authors (2017: 4) argue that discontented national identities are best identified through 'popular sentiments which can include references to everyday lives and neighbourhoods'. I would go further and state they are best identified through the *narrative accounts* that people tell about their everyday lives.

Inequality

Whereas Participants C, D and E tell stories in which they remember a successful pre-accession British past, Participants A and H tell narratives which capture a sense of inequality between different regions in the UK. Within these stories, areas in the UK are represented as neglected by the government and supported by the EU. For instance, a Remain-voting interviewee in her mid-thirties who has lived in Powys, Manchester, Birmingham and Nottinghamshire – referred to here as Participant A – tells an Exemplum in which rural Wales has been neglected by London-centric government officials. This Exemplum is representative of the kind of stories told by Remain voters that encapsulate inequality:

> a small part of it is a route back into ch^ildhood growing up in mid-Wales (.) which is not a very prosperous area in some ways and it didn't attract a lot of government funding you know so you had this quite polarised community sometimes very poor and and quite wealthy (.) and (.) I remember learning to drive (.) up and down Powys (.) and my dad was quite keen that I get some experience driving on (.) busier fast roads and not just poddling around the the hills which is quite sensible (.) and we did this big drive one day and I remember seeing signs built with Europe EU money built with EU money and so (.) it and that was the time of a Tory government as well and it just made me realise that

actually we we are reliant on the Europe European Union to do the right thing because we (laughs) can't rely on our government (laughs) always to do it you know (.) and so (.) so there was a gut instinct (.) but it was rooted in in a kind of factual fact-based memory

Participant H, a white, Remain-voting British man in his mid-twenties, relates an almost identical Exemplum of growing up in a 'poor' area and seeing signs for developments funded by the EU:

definitely growing up we saw a <u>lot</u> of (.) <u>signs</u> around of (.) areas <u>being</u> developed because a lot of where I grew up was is poor and there were all these <u>developments</u> that was like funded by the EU and it was like you could <u>see</u> that and most of these w we had more investment from the EU than we did from Westminster so it's like (.) I could <u>see</u> that and I was <u>aware</u> of that and I'd <u>read</u> that (.) and it's just ridiculous to then (.) ignore it

Participants A and H relate a 'childhood' experience of domestic inequality brought about by the economic policies of a ('Tory') government. In Participant A's story, the association of mid-Wales's poverty with a lack of governmental support establishes a discourse of blame in which supposedly representative politicians are implicated in the act of poverty-making. The informal premodifier 'Tory' evokes a sceptical attitude towards the main right-wing British political party, the Conservatives, indirectly indexing the interviewee's left-wing political views. The phrase 'as well' makes relevant the political leaning of the government in the storytelling world, discursively associating the participant's youthful political attitudes with her contemporary stance towards British politics. In other words, there is a temporal continuity to the government's behaviour in the participant's narrated childhood and her adulthood; in the story world and the storytelling world, the 'Tory government' occupies the role of an immoral villain ('do the right thing') on whom the British public 'can't rely'.

Unlike the sense of decline in the Leave-voting participants' stories above, Participant A's story constructs poverty and inequality as a *longer-term* state for Britons. The same continuity is achieved in Participant H's story through the repair 'was is poor' which suggests economic stagnation is still a feature of contemporary British society after the participant's youth is over. The negative evaluative stances (Du Bois, 2007) underpinning the adjectives 'poor' and 'unequal' evoke dissatisfaction with the nation based on the effect of funding policies on regions outside of the political centre of London. In these stories, then, individuals index a pro-EU stance by discursively constructing the EU as the saviour of an economically neglected British public whose lives have been negatively affected by the (right-wing) policies of 'Westminster'. By taking this stance towards the EU, the participants perform their identities as left-leaning 'Remainers'.

While some quantitative research about Brexit has associated feelings of economic neglect with a pro-*Leave* stance (Goodwin and Heath, 2016), Participants A and H invoke the spatial imaginary of left-behind Britain (Sykes, 2018) in their Orientations to support a discursive construction of the EU as a saviour and Britain as socio-economically unequal. In contrasting politicians in 'Westminster' with their 'poor', 'rural' areas, the participants draw on the same cosmopolitan versus provincial distinction (Jennings and Stoker, 2016) that some academics invoke to distinguish between Remain and Leave voters. However, they undermine the homogenous equation of entire 'out of town' areas with a Leave stance by tying their pro-EU opinions explicitly to their youthful experiences of regional poverty.

It is worth noting that there are some similarities between the stories told by Participants C, D and E and those told by Participants A and H: the stories are underpinned by an economic argument and are rooted in narrations of childhood and youth. Looking back on the past, then, is not in itself characteristic of a Leave-backing story. Rather, across these stories the difference lies between *positive* reflections on the past as a time of collegiality and great national trade (despite personal situations of poverty), and *negative* reflections on the past as a time of wealth inequality and government neglect that required additional EU funding to redress. Just as Richards et al. (2020: 74) argue that it 'is the substance of the nostalgia that matters, not the looking towards the past per se' in the distinction between Leave and Remain voters, the narrative exploration in this book problematizes a common framing of only Leave voters as oriented towards the past (Tyler et al., 2022).

Discrimination

In addition to the tendency of the stories told by my interviewees to be rooted in the past, there is a common theme which unites several of the narratives in the interviews: discrimination. Participants tell stories of other voters' discrimination, discriminate against others and deny being discriminatory. In this way, they support Andreouli et al.'s (2019: 318) claim that 'constructions of prejudice occupy a central role in structuring, justifying, or delegitimizing positions toward Brexit'. For example, Participant A, who labels her national identity as 'fluid', tells an Observation of Leave voters' supposedly discriminatory rhetoric. She argues that when she hears the 'dog whistle' of Leave voters she thinks, 'oh they're all white van man Sun-reading (.) red-faced gammon types'. Repeatedly referring to her views as 'types' and 'stereotypes', she continues to describe 'the amount of people that can't spell like really simple stuff and are going gah (.) we want our cuntwy back or I don't know where the country went'. Her characterization of Leave voters is extended over several utterances:

> perhaps I'm stereotyping them as you know poorly educated semi-literate (.) pretty xenophobic and I I don't think even whilst there are racists who are shouting about Brexit (.) and that's that's very prevalent and obvious (.) I think there's also people who (sighs) I don't know if it really comes as xenophobia but it's there's a sort've (.) something about a desperation to believe that that you know Britain is this great empire and or could be again and that we built the world and and you know all the rest of it and (sighs) yeah okay anyone who's studied anything like that knows (.) the racist and xenophobic elements of our past and and the terrible abuses but I don't think people are always thinking of it from that view I think I think there's something about hope and desperation being projected onto you know (lowers pitch) oh yeah we could be great again and (reverts to normal pitch) we could be going back to those amazing days that never really existed you know so (.) so it's easy for me to sort've stereotype people as being gammons but I think there's there's just a lot of desperation and sadness and anger as well

What is most notable about Participant A's habitual Observation is the stereotypical characterization of a Leave voter that she provides. Participant A introduces her Leave-voting protagonists into the story world, describing them through collectivization (van Leeuwen, 1995) in the extended noun phrase 'white van man Sun reading (.) red-faced gammon types' and the repeated third-person pronoun 'them'. Her use of the nouns 'types' and 'stereotypes' indicate a general silhouette of Leave voters that is homogenous, gendered ('man') and racialized (depending on your reading of 'white', it could be evaluating 'van' or 'man'). In addition to the racial and gender markers, Participant A indexes a Conservative, anti-immigration ideology for Leave voters through the allusion to the pro-Brexit tabloid *The Sun*. Her repeated use of the informal political noun 'gammon' is particularly important, as it indirectly indexes her identity as a 'leftie' Remainer (as she refers to herself) who is critical of right-wing and pro-Brexit ideologies. That is, 'gammon' is commonly used by Remain voters to refer to those who support Brexit by conceptualizing them as having a 'flushed face, similar to a type of pork meat' (Demata and Zummo, 2020: 178). Through this single noun, then, Participant A produces a disparaging caricature of Leave voters and distances herself from the political and social views she assigns to them.

In her Observation, Participant A offers two explanations for the Leave vote. First, she argues that Leavers are nostalgic for the British Empire, drawing on a common representation of Leavers among Remain voters (Meredith and Richardson, 2019; Andreouli et al., 2019), and a dominant socio-political narrative of Leave voters as desiring a return to a British golden age (Calhoun, 2017). Second, she attributes the Leave vote to an expression of 'hope' and 'desperation', evoking another dominant narrative of Leave voters as economically left behind (Hobolt, 2016). Both reasons are rooted in discontent with the present state of the nation and a desire for change. In this sense, Participant A also captures some of the feelings expressed by my Leave-voting participants in their stories. However, her construction of the Leave voter aligns with the classicism that pro-Brexit outlets such as *The Telegraph* accuse Remain voters of exhibiting (see Chapter 4). There is a degree of educational superiority and belittlement in the ventriloquation of 'cuntwy' (Bakhtin, 1981), the shift to a lower pitch when voicing 'hope' and 'desperation' and the adjectival phrases 'poorly educated' and 'semi-literate' which contribute to a derogatory construction of Leave voters as incapable of rational debate and thought (see Meredith and Richardson (2019) for this construction in Remain voters' comments on news websites). There is also a juxtaposition between knowledge ('anyone who's studied anything') and Leave voters who glorify Britain's 'racist and xenophobic' past which feeds into the broader idea of Remain voters as rational and Leave voters as emotional (Manners, 2018). Despite accusing Leave voters of discriminatory beliefs (xenophobia, racism), Participant A reproduces social exclusion through her story. In short, by representing Leave voters as nationalist, xenophobic and yearning for empire, and performing her own identity as an intellectually superior, less patriotic Remain voter, Participant A both constructs and reifies polarization within the imagined national community (Anderson, 2006).

In parallel to the similarities between Participant A and Participant H's stories about inequality, Participant H echoes Participant A's stories of Leave voters' discrimination in an Observation and an Exemplum. Participant H tells the stories below in response to a question about a speech delivered by Theresa May which is being used in the interview as a stimulus. The interviewer asks whether the participant has encountered any Leave voters saying, like Theresa May, that they want Britain to become a more tolerant nation after Brexit. Participant H claims that, on the contrary, people who voted to Leave embrace intolerance, a common charge levelled at Leave voters by Remain voters (Andreouli, 2020):

> no tolerance was (.) the opposite they they of often embraced the intolerance erm I witnessed people that I ^knew shout at er:m people in the ^street (.) telling them to go back home and like I I witnessed a lot of the xenophobia erm it was really awful erm one of my friends erm who is again (.) he's of Pakistani descent so it's totally irrelevant anyway but he was actually (.) erm (.) punched and told to go back to where he came from erm (.) because (.) it's our country again now erm (.) so it's like yeah (.) tolerance is not (laughs) the experience that I heard or saw or witnessed

Participant H introduces his character into the story world by positioning the first-person personal pronoun 'I' as the Senser of two mental processes, 'witnessed' and 'knew' (Thompson, 2013). Although 'I' is the grammatical subject of these clauses, the social actions that the participant performs are passive; they forge a role for the character as an observer of Others' actions rather than an agent of change within the story world. In contrast to the participant's passivity, the protagonists ('people that I knew') are collectivized, activated (van Leeuwen, 1995) and positioned as Sayers of the verbal processes 'shout at' and 'telling' (Halliday, 1985). The aggressive connotations of 'shout' provide a pejorative moral evaluation of the characters. However, their political leanings are not explicitly introduced into the story world; it is only through the interviewer's question, which asks for information about 'Leave voters', that the political affiliations of this social group become clear. Much like the protagonists, the third group of actors, the Receivers, are collectivized through plural pronouns ('them') and nouns ('people') (van Leeuwen, 1995). Once again, the participant provides no identifying information for these characters. By constructing both perpetrators and victims as generic silhouettes, the participant positions the verbal assault as a general event rather than an isolated incident. In other words, his story narrates what 'people that [he] knew' habitually did to Others. Through the representation of verbal abuse as a recurrent event, Participant H cements intolerance as a core personality trait of the social group of Leave voters, rather than a behaviour specific to a single Leave-voting person in a particular context.

Although the participant refrains from providing explicit identifying factors for the characters in his first Observation, his recontextualization of the speech acts of 'shouting' and 'telling to go back home' as 'xenophobia' permits the audience to infer some demographic information about the characters. As 'xenophobia' connotes prejudice against people from other countries, the participant indicates that the perpetrators assume their victims are immigrants. Their motivation for 'shouting', then, is ethnonationalism: the belief that only 'native' citizens (who share a common ancestry) belong and have a right to be in a country (Le Bossé, 2021). While this ideology might be racially motivated, it can also underpin the social exclusion of white immigrants, providing an additional group of people whose belonging in the UK is contested. Through his story, then, Participant H indicates that the identity of 'Briton' is not just problematized in racial terms, but that there are some white people whose right to call the UK 'home' is also challenged.

Immediately after the first Observation, the participant narrates an Exemplum which, through the temporal proximity of its telling, is positioned as thematically and ideologically related to the first story. In this Exemplum, Participant H is not a character or an observer, but a heterodiegetic narrator who is distanced from the action (Carranza, 2015). He is involved in the story on an emotional level, though, because the main character is introduced as 'one of my friends'. By indexing a close personal relationship with the main character, Participant H subtly prepares the interviewer for an alignment with the friend and a share in the effects of the events that happen to him. In contrast to Participant H's previous story, in which the ethnicities of the characters are ambiguous, the narrator explicitly describes his friend as 'of Pakistani descent'. The adjective 'Pakistani' serves as a racial marker, signalling that the character is part of an ethnic minority group. It is not, however, a national marker because, as the noun 'descent' indicates, the character's non-whiteness does not equate to non-Britishness. The racial marker indexes ancestry rather than the birthplace of the character.

It is worth noting at this point that while there is an albeit vague perpetrator in the Observation, the participant discursively suppresses the actor in the Exemplum through passive agent deletion in the clauses 'he was actually punched' and 'told to go back to where he came from'. Deleting the agent from both clauses precludes the interviewer and analyst from accessing any identifying information about the perpetrator (aside from the inference that they voted Leave in the EU referendum). Nevertheless, the context and the racialization of the victim allow for an interpretation of the perpetrator as a white British person.

The most significant aspect of the story for understanding the relationship between the EU referendum and constructions of Britishness is the direct speech: 'because it's our country again now'. Through this explanatory clause, the participant indicates that what is in question in the Exemplum is not just who can call themselves British, but also who can decide what 'Britain' and 'British' mean. In other words, the implicature in the reported speech, particularly the imperative 'go back' and the noun phrase 'our country', is that the EU referendum was not only about remaining in or leaving the EU – it was also about choosing which interpretation of 'Britain' should be hegemonic. In this story, the unnamed perpetrator argues that the referendum result imbued those who voted to leave with the right to decide who belongs in the country and what values are associated with it. For the perpetrator, the prevailing interpretation is a country from which minority ethnic people are excluded. The adverbials 'again' and 'now' tie the contestation of Britishness to the historical context of the EU referendum, recontextualizing 'Brexit Britain' as a return to a monoethnic nation that never existed (Bhambra, 2017). In this way, the stance indexed in the reported speech intertextually echoes the broader Vote Leave campaign slogan of 'Take Back Control', which also links the Leave vote to 'decid[ing] who can come here – and who can't' (Vote Leave, 2016: n.p.).

The participant concludes the story by reasserting the stance the story justified: that he never 'heard', 'saw' or 'witnessed' tolerance from Leave voters. In associating Leave voters with prejudice and Remain voters (like himself) with tolerance, Participant H reproduces a dominant interpretation among Remain-voting Britons of the Brexit vote as caused by prejudice (Andreouli, 2020; Andreouli et al., 2019). His positions towards the political identity categories of Leaver and Remainer, and towards the broader socio-political context, are thus both locally rooted in personal experience and related to dominant political narratives being disseminated across the UK. In other words, there is an intermingling of bottom-up and top-down constructions of Brexit that enable the participant to make sense of political, national and ethnic identities during the critical juncture (Capoccia, 2016) through which he is living.

In Participant H's stories, the discursive construction of post-Brexit Britishness involves the social exclusion of minority ethnic Britons and white immigrants. As minority ethnic and immigrant are the marked identities, the unmarked (and linguistically suppressed (van Leeuwen, 1995)) identity is a white, British-born person. Even though unmarked identities possess cultural privilege and symbolic capital (Bourdieu, 1991) – that is, accumulated prestige – Participant H argues that being a white, British-born male does not preclude him from the effects of the exclusion in his stories. After narrating the ethnic and racial abuse, Participant H laments that 'it's like the England I respect is being erased', a position shared by Higgins' (2018) pro-Remain British ex-pats. Even though Participant H occupies the same social position as the unmarked British identity in his stories, the appropriation of Englishness to signify the discursive and social exclusion of minority ethnic Britons and white non-Britons leads him to feel alienated and disorientated. What Participant H's two stories indicate is that constructing national identity is an inherently political and ideological project, the effects of which extend beyond social groups that are explicitly Othered to exclude even those whose right to claim Britishness is not discursively challenged. Feeling alienated from the ideological project of post-Brexit Britishness, Participant H states that that 'the best thing [he] could do for [England] would be to not be in it'. He plans to move abroad after completing his university education.

While Participants A and H tell stories of Others' discrimination (and in the case of Participant A, (re)produce social exclusion), Participant F, a middle-aged Remain voter, tells a story which includes racist language to describe people from Pakistan. Notably, the story comes just after the participant remarks on the 'really, really worrying' nature of contemporary 'racial tension':

> you know I can remember where we had very <u>very un</u> (.) PC words you know the local shop was called the Paki shop (.) erm and stuff like that (.) but it was <u>never</u> (. .) it it as <u>stupid</u> as it sounds it wasn't d meant derogatory (0.1) whereas <u>now</u> you'll hear somebody call somebody a smelly (.) Paki (.) and you just think wh where's that come from

Referring to racist language euphemistically as 'very <u>very un</u> PC words' downplays the force of the utterance and avoids acknowledging 'Paki' as racist – it is what van Dijk (1992) would label a specific form of denial of racism called *mitigation*. In this way, it acts as a reputational shield, attempting to prevent an interpretation of the participant as racist. Wikström (2016) finds a similar construal of 'PC' as desirable and used to pre-empt negative responses in Tweets. While 'Paki' is the racist term, the participant implies that it could historically be used neutrally as long as the speaker did not intend to be 'derogatory'. Indeed, the repetition of the term in a different context – 'smelly Paki' – suggests that the only negative associations of the word are from the attributive adjective 'smelly'. The participant distances himself from what he frames as the more pejorative or 'derogatory' meaning through voicing what 'somebody' will 'call somebody'. Despite the vagueness of the pronouns providing a distancing effect, the participant appears to recognize the possibility that his defence could be contested through the phrase 'as <u>stupid</u> as it sounds'. The use of the adverb 'now' is striking; in the same way that Participants C and E refer to the past as a time of collectivism, Participant F constructs the past as less racially 'tense' than the present despite the racist language use. Remarkably, then, the implicature is that 'Paki' in the past was non-racist because it was not meant derogatorily, whereas 'now' the term has negative connotations. This problematically erases the racism from the past use of the term and supports the participant's reading of the present as a moment of more heightened 'racial tension'.

The pauses and prosody in the extract are also worth comment – the emphasis on '<u>very un</u> PC' recognizes the severity of the language (in juxtaposition with the euphemistic quality), while the pauses before and after the second use of 'Paki' help to frame this use of the epithet as more problematic. Overall, then, there is a clear tension between the participant's identity work – in which he tries to portray himself as non-racist – and his language use. This story is important because it counters simplistic narratives of Leave voters as racist or xenophobic and Remain voters as morally superior; it, like Participant A's story, demonstrates that Remain voters also (re)produce discriminatory language and denials of discrimination.

The final story I have selected for this section comes again from Participant C, who narrates a story of a 'chappy living in England called the Hook'. Following the narrative, which I (re)produce below, Participant C says that she does not 'feel any racism' because she 'can get on with people no matter where they come from' but is 'glad that we might have some say' on immigration 'otherwise our country's gonna be flooded eventually'. As Taylor (2018) notes, water metaphors are common in immigration-related discourses, construing migration as a form of natural disaster in which the host country is overwhelmed by the influx of migrants and is unable to respond to the demand. The narrative is as follows:

> for an example we had a a chappy living in England (.) living in England called the hook and he was a br a person that was always encouraging people to be evil you know (0.2) and that and we really wanted to get him out of our country (.) because you know he wasn't born here I think he just came kind've thing when he was able to (0.4) he was a sikh (.) yeah and erm so he he was creating problems and he was encouraging yo youth to go into these terrible things like blowing places up and things like that [inaudible] in the ^open street not just the the erm mot the muslim the er muse er what are they called where they pray (0.1) that's not just there they used to stand in the streets in London (0.2) and all this evil (0.1) and we really wanted to get him out of England (0.2) it was on ISIS that's it that's the one and erm so of course we didn't want him here (.) cos he was creating a lot of problems with the youth (.) the Sikh youth and that he was encouraging them to do these evil things that they some of them did (0.3) er though erm but the EU said no you can't do that you've you've got to let him stay where he is (0.2) and fortunately eventually we did he did he went

to America (0.2) but the thing was they stopped us sending this man who was causing problems in our country out (0.2) and that to me cannot be right (0.2) but you know the government could do nothing about it

The discursive discrimination in this story is worthy of note for its religious and nationalist connotations. The participant begins by arguing that 'we really wanted to get him out of our country' – the pronouns 'we', 'him' and 'our' demonstrate a clear discursive Othering of the character, as does the villainizing adjective 'evil' which is repeated several times throughout the story. The participant goes on to explain that 'we' wanted the character to leave partly 'because . . . he wasn't born here'. This frames who is welcome in the country through ethnonationalism – the belief that only 'native' citizens are allowed to reside in a nation (Le Bossé, 2021). This ethnonationalism is then intertwined with religion in the clause 'he was a Sikh'. 'Sikh' is the first religious category introduced in the story. The participant discursively links being 'Sikh' to the encouragement of 'blowing places up' by saying that the character 'encouraged youth' to 'go into these terrible things'. Notably, the participant then claims that it isn't just 'the Muslim' place of the mosque where this encouragement is taking place. In this utterance, the participant conflates the religious categories of Sikh and Muslim as though they are interchangeable (and implies – although not explicitly – in the adverb 'just' that the mosque is a place where people are encouraged to 'blow places up'). Finally, the participant then introduces 'ISIS'. Through the elision between the categories of Sikh, Muslim and ISIS, the participant conflates these identities and positions them as a single out-group of people who 'blow places up', are 'evil' and are not welcome in the country. In other words, she perpetuates a discourse of Islamophobia – 'the growing mistrust and often belligerent animosity towards communities with a Muslim background' (Kallis, 2013: 61), even if she often refers to this community as 'Sikh'. In simple terms, then, the religious identities of 'Sikh' and 'Muslim' are discursively associated with the category of 'terrorist', albeit implicitly.

Although it is not possible, using the methods I have chosen, to measure the degree to which this story is influenced by media discourses, the man to which Participant C is referring – Abu Hamza al-Masri – was referred to by British newspapers as 'Captain Hook' (e.g. Hume, 2004; Bucktin, 2013). It *is* possible, then, to note the intertextuality between the media representation of Hamza and Participant C's discursive construction of 'a chappy living in England called the Hook'. Reporting on ideologies of deportability in the pro-Leave press around the time of the 2016 membership referendum, Radziwinowiczówna and Galasińska

(2021: 77) state that the newspapers' narrative was that 'EU deportations are impossible because the United Kingdom was not a sovereign country when it remained in the EU'. A similar ideology of deportability is present in Participant C's story – the EU is framed as a 'quasi-imperial' (Hawkins, 2012) power which can tell the UK that it cannot deport foreign criminals. The UK government, in contrast, is framed as powerless ('could do nothing about it') to fulfil the will of the people ('we really wanted to get him out of our country'). This representation of the EU as interfering also aligns with Eurosceptic discourses in the British press, as shown by Dugalès and Tucker (2012) and Zappettini (2019).

It is worth mentioning at this point that discrimination did not just occur in stories, and participants tended to acknowledge when the words or discourses they were employing were contested or controversial (as was the case in Andreouli et al.'s (2019) study of lay discourses about Brexit and prejudice). For instance, Participant E remarks that 'people who lived on the council estates didn't seem interested in the state of the country' before adding, 'I hope I haven't spoken out of turn'. Similarly, Participant B – who lives on a council estate and is working class – states: 'I think that the working class sometimes are a lot more vocal, and I think the working class and I don't mean to be judgemental are a lot more easily led by newspaper articles, by the media, by what they're watching and seeing . . . I think they're a lot less analytical than the middle classes (.) maybe it's an educational thing.' The aside 'I don't mean to be judgemental', like Participant E's concern at speaking 'out of turn', shows a self-consciousness at labelling people deemed to be Other based on class differences. Nevertheless, the language of difference is rife, not least in the use of the third-person pronoun 'they' by both participants. Ultimately, this discursive exploration of narratives of discrimination achieves the same goal as Andreouli et al.'s (2019: 318) analysis of lay constructions of Brexit-related prejudice: it shows that the stories 'resist neat dichotomies such as tolerant Remain/prejudiced Leave'.

Division and difference

Closely related to the stories of discrimination are stories of division and difference, which are most frequently told by Remain-voting participants. While Leave-voting participants do not necessarily tell *stories* of division, the younger Leave voters do argue in the interviews that division exists in the UK. For instance, Participant O posits that there's a 'real division' between Scotland and England and that 'it's hard to call both sets of people British when they clearly have such different opinions'. He goes on to state that the divisions between Remainers and Leavers are 'still there' at the time of interviewing and are 'very, very raw'. Conversely, while Participant N claims that Britain is 'divided', he argues that 'we've always been' that way as 'that's the nature of democracies'. The dominant way that division is articulated within and across stories is through the discursive contestation of Britishness along racial, linguistic and national lines; there are fifteen stories related to this topic. In these stories, participants address macro-level questions about identity and belonging by relating stories of personal experience in highly localized contexts, such as conversations with friends or incidents they have witnessed in the street. In this way, they support Mann and Fenton's (2017) claim that discursive constructions of national identity often include references to daily lives and local places.

Five of the race-related stories are narrated by Participant G, a 'non-white', Remain-backing participant in his twenties. In these tales, the racialized dynamics of Britishness are presented without foregrounding the temporal and political context. While the events in the stories typically take place against the backdrop of Brexit, identity contestation transcends the sociopolitical context to become an ongoing question of belonging in Britain. In other words, for the participant recounting these stories, as for Benson and Lewis's (2019) minority ethnic interviewees, expressions of xenophobia in the time of Brexit cannot be separated from a longer history of racialized exclusion in the nation.

Participant G was born in London but moved to Nottingham as an undergraduate student in 2014, just months before the General Election that secured the EU referendum vote (see Chapter 1). At the time of interviewing, Participant G lived in Beeston in Nottinghamshire, a town that is part of the majority Leave-voting parliamentary constituency of Broxtowe. His grandparents are first-generation immigrants from India. Throughout the interview, Participant G repeatedly interprets the UK's majority Leave vote as 'strongly' related to attitudes towards immigration. In particular, he argues that there is 'quite a lot of segregation' between 'the non-white' – specifically Pakistani immigrant – 'and white communities in Nottingham' due to 'both sides segregating themselves from each other'. He posits that this 'segregation' leads to erroneous assumptions about what being a minority ethnic immigrant means. To support his argument, he compares what he sees as the socio-economic 'status' of Pakistani immigrants in Nottingham – workers in the 'service industry' such as 'taxi drivers' – with the 'wealthy' Indian immigrants that live in northwest London, his birthplace. In doing so, the participant introduces a geographical dimension to his interpretation of race relations in the UK, a dimension which proves to be ideologically meaningful in his stories.

Against a backdrop in which place and race intersect, Participant G tells a Recount and an Anecdote of occasions when his identification as 'British' has been contested by members of the 'non-white' and 'white' communities in Nottingham. In the first Recount, Participant G narrates a trajectory from growing up in multicultural London to moving to and living in a smaller city with a very high majority of white residents – 95.5 per cent in the 2011 Census (ONS, 2011):

> (0.5) erm (0.5) it's (.) it's kind of (0.5) I didn't (.) so I didn't think about it nearly as much until I came to (.) Nottingham (.) I don't know if that's like it's partly probably because of my age like erm you know being a teenager I didn't really think about (.) very many things (laughs) erm so erm but like also when I was at schoo:l my school was like (.) er (.) like fifty per cent (.) brown er like forty per cent (.) er like white Jewish and then like the rest was just like like Christian white so like it was like a minority like a small minority erm (.) so (.) I didn't ^think about it as much because it and also my school was very much (.) erm it was (.) accepted by everyone in the school and the teachers included that like everyone was a bit casually ^racist but in not in a in not in a derogatory way in like a an accepting way because (.) everyone (.) there was so much diversity to the point where it was like (.) people could people would make jokes that would (.) you know that (.) that weren't offensive and it was a bit there was a bit of a different like standard for it and but then it was generally also accepted like (.) don't continue that outside of this school (laughs) erm co you know erm cos like mates would be able to make these jokes and then was like you know outside of that just like don't do that erm (.) but yeah no erm (0.5) but coming to Nottingham it's (.) I've felt (sighs) (1.0) I've definitely felt like a (.) divide because (.) there's less (.) minority ethnic people (.) erm I've often been like the only minority ethnic person in the room erm and like I've (.) and that it's more to do with that so if anything like (. .) I've I've I it's not about my personal identity because I've still felt British but I've felt more like (.) scrutinised by others who might think I'm not

The story above is a coming-of-age Recount during which Participant G narrates a transition from ignorance of the exclusionary dynamics of Britishness to being conscious that white people contest his national identity because he is a 'minority ethnic person'. The story begins with a long Orientation during which Participant G introduces himself as a naïve, young character in the story world – a 'teenager' who 'didn't really think about (.) very many things'. This character is situated within the chronotope (Bakhtin, 1981; Blommaert, 2015) of 'my school', a space which, over the next forty lines, becomes symbolic of the ethnic diversity experienced during the participant's youth.

Participant G begins the Record of Events by discursively constructing the 'casually racist' behaviour that routinely takes place within the school. Throughout this part of the story, collectivization (van Leeuwen, 1995) is used, discursively constructing the students and teachers in the school through the generic pronoun 'everyone', the mass noun 'people' and the plural noun 'mates'. Alongside impersonal, passive declaratives such as 'it was accepted', and adverbs which connote generalization ('generally'), this collectivization constructs a sense of communality and solidarity, signalling a community of practice within which all members are aware of the rules that govern appropriate behaviour inside and outside of the shared space. The generic, impersonal language also allows the participant to avoid sole responsibility as an individual for what could be a face-threatening act – revealing that as a teenager, he partook in 'racist' communication practices. By distributing responsibility for the racism across many dimly sketched characters, the participant mitigates the likelihood that the interviewer will position him as a racist in the storytelling world.

The moment of social awakening occurs with the repetition of the conjunction 'but', which marks a contrast between the previous action at the school and the upcoming action in Nottingham. The ideology conveyed in the free direct speech – that 'outside of this school' racial discrimination is unacceptable – forms the basis of the moral underpinning the story. After his character 'com[es] to Nottingham', the participant shifts from solidarity to isolation through the repeated first- person singular personal pronoun 'I'. The change in the discursive construction of social actors mirrors the character's emotional trajectory in the story towards feeling 'a divide'. The emotional effect of being 'the only minority ethnic person in the room' is performed by the participant at the interactional level through a sigh and eleven pauses, including one 0.5-second pause and one 1.0-second pause. The spatial vagueness of 'the room' in this segment contrasts with the specificity of the London private school to index the generality and habituality of the experience of being racially Othered in Nottingham. In other words, as the definite article 'the' implies, being the only minority ethnic Briton in a room could happen anywhere in a city with over 90 per cent of white residents (ONS, 2011).

Alongside an isolated self, the participant employs collectivization (van Leeuwen, 1995), discursively constructing white Nottingham residents as a homogenous group of 'Others'. This group is constructed as performing the cognitive mental processes (Thompson, 2013) of 'scrutinis[ing]' the participant and 'think[ing]' that he is not British. The first verb connotes a microscopic interest in the participant's racial identity and, relatedly, his national identity, which contrasts with the tacit acceptance of racial diversity in the London-based segment of the story. The verb also indexes an unequal power relationship in which white residents perceive themselves to be the typical, unmarked Briton and so assign themselves the right to judge Participant G's claim to belong to the in-group. It is the focalization of events through the eyes of white residents, alongside the prosodic emphasis on the possessive determiner 'my' in the negative clause 'it's not about my personal identity', that frames the story as a tale of contested belonging (Anthias, 2008), or of ascribed identities (Blommaert, 2005), rather than an individual sense of identity. The participant reinforces this interpretation when he argues that he 'still felt British' despite facing scrutiny about his nationality. The use of the emotive mental process (Thompson, 2013) 'felt' constructs national identity as a subjective, lived experience that exists outside of others' discursive contestations of it.

What the participant presents through this story is a highly regionalized and localized understanding of national identity where the lived experience of feeling British differs depending on the place and space that the participant occupies and the people with whom he interacts. Among friends from ethnic minority groups, questions of identity can be formulated through discriminatory language without posing a threat to the protagonist's national identity. However, what signals solidarity and communality in the multicultural context of a London private school can be experienced as discrimination when the participant is the only minority ethnic Briton in the room in Nottingham. Although the experience of having white people think he is not British does not alter the participant's feeling of being British, it does lead to the perception of a 'divide' between a white British in-group and a minority ethnic British out-group. In other words, the participant's sense of identity, which he essentializes as an internal state, remains consistent in the story, but the sense of national belonging that he constructs is negatively affected. In Participant G's story, the lived experience of being a Briton is constantly in flux; the dynamics of inclusion in and exclusion from a British in-group depend on social context.

Importantly, Participant G makes clear that it is not only the white community in Nottingham that questions his claim to be British. Immediately following the story above, the participant narrates a second story (Arminen, 2004) during which a 'minority ethnic' taxi driver assumes that he is Punjabi. Throughout the Anecdote, Participant G performs complex identity work which constructs and reproduces a position for himself between the 'non-white and white communities' in Nottingham that he identified earlier in the interview.

> erm (.) and the ^other thing (.) is that (.) n minority ethnic (.) people who I've talked to for example people in like a taxi who I'll talk to will gravitate ^towards me as like erm another (.) like Indian or punja Punjabi guy (.) and then try and speak to me in Punjabi and then like get really happy if I can like understand them and whatever and like and like but they will (.) you know (.) that's a unique experience that I've had so like that community gravitated towards me erm which I thought was quite interesting

Participant G narrates the story above in response to the same question about instances in which his Britishness has been foregrounded. The participant opens his story with an Orientation that situates the events of the story world 'in like a taxi'. The significance of this space is not clear if the story is decontextualized from the rest of the interview. However, the space is imbued with meaning when considered in relation to the participant's previous construction of Pakistani immigrants in Nottingham as taxi drivers who are segregated from white communities. In the specific context of this interview, then, the Orientation establishes that the dynamics of inclusion and exclusion are going to be racialized.

Following the Orientation, the main construction of social action unfolds in a Remarkable Event. It is during this Event that the participant introduces a second character into the story world: himself. Throughout the interview, the participant repeatedly and explicitly self-identifies as British, maintaining that he has a 'strong British identity'. It is noteworthy, then, that the participant constructs himself in the story world as 'another (.) like Indian or punja Punjabi guy'. The determiner 'another' is meaningful on two levels. First, it presupposes that the other person in the taxi is from the Punjab areas of India and Pakistan and identifies as Indian or Pakistani. Second, the determiner positions the participant as sharing this identity through its connotations of similarity. The juxtaposition between the discursive construction of the participant in the story world as 'Indian or Punjabi' and his construction in the storytelling world as 'British' indicates that the ethnic categorization of the participant as Indian is imposed on him by the 'ethnic minority' taxi driver – it is an ascribed identity (Blommaert, 2005). In other words, the story is narrated through the eyes of the ethnic minority person in the taxi, a character who has mistaken the participant for an Indian because he is also 'non-white'. Although the Indian character's assumption is rooted in solidarity and a desire to include Participant G in an in-group, its result is to exclude the participant from the national group with which he identifies: Britons.

Within the story world, Participant G does not contest the presumption that he is a member of the Indian in-group. However, in the interactional event of the interview, the participant problematizes this categorization in several ways. First, he passivates his character through the repetition of the metaphorical verb 'gravitate towards [me]'. Positioning himself as an object constructs the identification of similarity as a one-way process rather than a mutual expression of sameness. Second, the participant positions the 'people in a taxi' as Others through the third-person plural personal pronouns 'they' and 'them', and the determiner 'that' in the noun phrase 'that community'. Together, these lexical choices construct the Indian people as belonging to a single, homogenous group, of which the participant and the interviewer are not part. Third, Participant G signals that he is not Indian by constructing for himself a limited proficiency in Punjabi: the verb 'try' in the metapragmatic descriptor 'try and speak [to me in Punjabi]' and the conditional clause 'if I can like understand them' index this lack of knowledge. Through this simultaneous positioning in the story world and the storytelling event, then, Participant G indexes his identity as a minority ethnic Briton.

Although positioning the taxi drivers as Others could unite the interviewee and the white interviewer in a non-Indian (or British) in-group, the participant chooses to emphasize his difference from the interviewer throughout the storytelling event. This difference is accentuated lexically through the noun phrase 'unique experience' and prosodically through the emphasis on the personal pronoun 'I' in 'I've'. Together, the adjective 'unique' and the prosodic emphasis on 'I've' recognize that as a white Briton and resident of Nottingham, the interviewer occupies a privileged social position that means that her identification as British is not challenged by Others. As a result, the experience that Participant G describes cannot be fully understood by the interviewer, despite the participant's vivid storytelling.

Through the two interrelated stories above, Participant G narrates a shift in his ethnic identity from being unmarked (Bucholtz and Hall, 2004) in the chronotype of the multicultural London private school, to being marked and Othered in the generic spaces of the 'room' and 'a taxi' in the predominantly white city of Nottingham. Through his positioning in the storytelling event and the story world, Participant G reproduces a liminal identity for himself between minority ethnic immigrants and white British Nottingham residents (a group to which the interviewer belongs). This liminal position is reinforced later in the interview when Participant G states that he 'wouldn't identify with either of those groups'. In reproducing this liminality, Participant G discursively constructs Britishness as inescapably intertwined with ethnicities and indicates that the lived experience of being a Briton depends on the spaces and places an individual occupies at any given point in time. In other words, even though Participant G essentializes national identity as an internal feeling, his performative storytelling constructs identities as multiple (a person can be minority ethnic and British), discursively negotiated and context-dependent.

How do these stories relate to the context of the UK's withdrawal from the EU? Participant G's arrival in Nottingham as an undergraduate university student in 2014 coincided with the lead-up to the 2015 general election. As noted in the political context in Chapter 1, David Cameron's promise to hold the referendum depended on a Conservative win in this general election. As such, Participant G's lived experiences as a minority ethnic Briton in Nottingham have always taken place in the historical context of political contestations of what it means to be British and European. He explicitly notes this socio-political context when he states later in the interview that although he has experienced more racial hostility and Othering in Nottingham than in London, he cannot empirically link this to the referendum context because he has no lived experience in Nottingham prior to this point.

In addition to the discursive contestation of Britishness along racial and ethnic lines, interviewees tell stories in which regional or local identities interact with national identities to engender exclusion. For instance, Participant I narrates an experience in which her regional accent is used to question her claim to be English by an American who thinks she does not 'sound posh'. Participant M tells a similar story of having his Northern identity 'Othered', 'alienated and denigrated' at a university where southern people with 'massive wealth and privilege' redefine his sense of being posh. Participant M also tells a hypothetical narrative in which Scotland, the North-East and the Midlands break away from the South of England and create a new British identity that stands apart from a Southern-inflected Englishness. For him, 'in this hypothetical world where the North of England is breaking off from something, it's always breaking off from the South and London'. This narrative is interesting, in that it confirms Richards and Heath's (2023: 5) finding that 'Northerners appear to demonstrate rather high levels of in-group comradeship alongside unusually negative views of the Southerner out-group' in Brexit Britain. The Exemplum below, narrated by Participant K, a white, self-identifying 'British' man who voted Remain, encapsulates the dynamics of regional and national tensions that participants explore through their stories from a different perspective – that of the Southerner.

Participant K no longer lives in Nottinghamshire but was a student in the city at the time of the EU membership referendum in 2016. In the first half of the interview, he narrates an Exemplum to support his claim that coming from the South of England provides him with certain privileges to identify as British. In contrast to Participant I, whose Englishness is challenged on account of her Midlands accent, Participant K speaks in Estuary English, which, according to the participant, is a culturally recognizable index of Britishness. In the story, Participant K narrates becoming aware of how the symbolic capital of his regional identity and the linguistic capital (Bourdieu, 1991) of his accent allow him and other people from Southeast England to define a culturally hegemonic idea of Britishness.

> I think particularly being from the south of England which is probably the most (.) culturally and economically powerful part of the United Kingdom it's very easy to say that I only see myself as British because (0.5) I guess (.) erm (.) to some extent these people have (.) been (.) instrumental in defining what Britishness is and it's much easier to expect everyone else to step in line with that and say this is the hegemonic identity than to (.) I mean just as an (.) example I (.) one of my friends from Northern Ireland (.) teases me a lot (.) because I went out to (.) stay with her family for a few days (.) and (0.5) we were (laughs) (.) erm (.) o one of her aunties is an Ulster Scot erm who have this quite thick accent and (.) w sometimes has difficulty being understood in Northern Ireland has difficulty being understood in England once asked in England if she speaks ^English and she said (puts on Irish accent) a:h [participant's name] can you understand my accent (reverts to own accent) and I was like (.) yeah I mean like I think the whole time I was there I missed maybe two words she says I sort of said (.) yes of course erm (.) can you understand mine and she laughed at me (puts on Irish accent) ach [participant's name] you sound like that man off the BBC (.) and one of her sisters (.) who (.) was erm (.) not even there (.) teased her about it a few weeks ago (.) erm (0.5) I mean it's not a particularly interesting story but the point is it's how obviously absurd they all found it that I thought they might not understand my accent because of the way I speak right and I tell that to my Northern Irish friends and they a:ll find it funny (.) erm (.) so I mean I'm not denying that it is perhaps easier for me to say well I'm (.) British and I don't really care about anything else

As an embedded story, Participant K's Exemplum does not begin immediately. First, the participant explores the ease with which he positions himself as

British. He invokes the region of his birthplace ('from') through the predicate 'being from the South of England' and evaluates the region as 'probably the most culturally and economically powerful part of the United Kingdom'. Through this evaluation, Participant K imbues the English region with economic and symbolic capital (Bourdieu, 1991) and compares ('most') this sociocultural power with not just other regions in England, but other nations in the UK. In situating himself at once within a region, nation and kingdom, Participant K depicts the regional identity marker as the lens through which he experiences being British. In doing so, he puts forward the same argument as Participants G and H, namely that place affects both the lived experience of being British and the relationship a person has with the meanings of Britishness.

Explaining why he finds it easy to self-identify as 'British', Participant K states that 'these people' were 'instrumental in defining what Britishness is'. Through the shift from the first-person personal pronoun 'I' to the vague determiner 'these' (which has no antecedent), Participant K distances himself from the power to define the meaning of Britishness. In other words, he positions himself as a beneficiary of his region's symbolic power but not personally culpable for the exclusionary, hegemonic meaning of Britishness. Through this implicit positive self-representation, the participant positions himself in the storytelling world as self-aware, moral and tolerant. Participant K's regional marker 'South of England' indicates that he is drawing on the broader cultural representation of the region as 'almost quintessentially English' (Bond and McCrone, 2004: 6).

The participant pits 'these people' and their region against a homogenous, personified image of 'everyone else'. Through this binary construction of Southeast England and every other nation and region in the UK, the participant (re)produces a stereotype of the South(east) of England as a 'very restricted territoriality that designates much of the country as being untypical' (Bond and McCrone, 2004: 6). He posits that all other regions have been expected to accept and adjust to the imposition of a 'hegemonic' interpretation of Britishness which they have had no part in defining. In erasing the roles that institutions, groups and individuals outside of the South have played in contributing to culturally dominant narratives of Britishness, the participant reproduces a narrative of the powerlessness of non-southern Britons even as he tries to perform his awareness of their exclusion from Britishness as hegemonically defined. The participant's conception of the economic and symbolic power (Bourdieu, 1991) to define Britishness as being contained within the South of England draws on broader cultural discourses in which the South is viewed as disproportionately well funded, often at the expense of declining industrial towns (Jennings and Stoker, 2016).

Having established a contextual background in which the South of England has the symbolic power to force other UK nations and regions to perform its interpretation of Britishness, Participant K begins an Exemplum. He establishes through the Orientation that the events of the Incident take place on a 'visit' to a house of a 'friend from Northern Ireland'. Although 'my friend from Northern Ireland' is introduced first, she is not the protagonist of the story – that role is reserved for 'one of her aunties' who is described in precise ethnic terms as an 'Ulster Scot'. The defining characteristic of the aunt is her 'thick accent'. The importance of this characteristic is foreshadowed through the elliptical, syntactically parallel clauses 'has difficulty being understood in Northern Ireland has difficulty being understood in England'. The syntactic parallelism, in conjunction with the prepositional phrases 'in Northern Ireland' and 'in England', emphasizes the marginalization of the Ulster Scot identity – it does not sit comfortably in the geographical and imagined periphery, or in the centre of the UK. The elliptical clause 'once asked in England if she speaks English' places the identity contestation within the realm of accent discrimination. Within the story, then, linguistic difference is constructed as problematic grounds for Britons to position the Ulster Scot as an Other.

Recognizing that place and accent are central to the discursive contestation of Britishness and the politics of belonging surrounding it, Participant K performs the dialogic encounter between his character and the Ulster Scot auntie. Switching between a linguistically symbolic, hegemonic Estuary English accent and the Northern Irish accent he has already framed as incomprehensibly other for some, Participant K prosodically reinforces the character's otherness. In describing the auntie's laughter and ventriloquating (Bakhtin, 1981) her evaluation that the participant 'sounds like the man from the BBC', Participant K indicates that the protagonist internalizes and reproduces otherness for herself. At the same time, he illuminates the linguistic capital (Bourdieu, 1991) of his southern English accent and identity by discursively associating them with the national institution of the BBC. Even though the story is intended to foreground Participant K's self-reflexivity and ambivalence towards his privilege, then, neither his characters nor his performance of their dialogue challenge the Othering of the Ulster Scot. On the contrary, they place her at the fringes of Britishness and reinforce her difference. The conclusion that his Northern Irish friends 'all laugh' upon hearing the joke further cements the idea that Northern Irishness is peripheral and Southern England is central to British identity.

Participant J, a white, Remain-voting 'Londoner' who lives in Nottingham and is in his mid-twenties, also discursively constructs the South of England as a culturally dominant region in the UK. Whereas Participant K focuses on national differences, Participant J narrates a story centred on the dominant cultural narrative of the division of England into cosmopolitan and rural areas (Jennings and Stoker, 2016). The interviewer asks whether the participant felt like an outsider when living abroad, a question to which the participant responds with a discussion of being a *domestic* Other – a topic he had previously introduced in the interview.

The participant's first mention of being Othered when living in the North of England forms part of an argument about the importance of people being mobile. Through a Recount, Participant J contrasts his adventurous mindset with people who live in a village in the Lake District where he used to work. He explains that the people there 'didn't move about at all' but were born, raised, 'lived in a village and died in a village'. He recognizes the advantage of this set-up as providing a 'tightness to the community' but pejoratively evaluates the attitude of the village people as 'insular' in contrast to 'the guy from London who's moved here':

> well when I was abroad I was the outsider as well but it was a differen completely different feeling of (.) being an outsider like when I was er (.) up north (.) erm (.) there was (.) definitely like a low level of suspicion that I was there like going into Greggs or whatever to get lunch and then like I open my mouth and I'm like it's clearly a southern coded accent in these kind of (.) small (.) Cumbrian towns and (.) and then you you know there's a (.) there's a mo there's a there's a slight tension whereas (.) in Germany or or and Austria as well (.) it helped (.) because I could speak (.) German I would just open my mouth and people would be like ^OH there's an English person or British person or you know wherever (.) from the north Atlantic (.) archipelago archipelago who (.) er speaks German who's learnt our language and is like a:h o:h (.) ^yes please so (.) it was er (.) yes also like you can (.) play the outsider card erm which is fun

Participant J prefaces his Exemplum with a comparison of two types of 'outsider' roles he has occupied during his mobile mid-twenties. Through the conjunctive phrase 'as well', the participant discursively renders a likeness between being a Briton 'abroad' and being a Southerner 'up north' in England. However, he constructs the effect of being Othered as a 'completely different feeling'. It is the subjective experience of being the outsider that forms the plot of the Exemplum. The participant's Orientation begins with an emotional frame of reference for the plot through the claim that 'there was definitely a low level of suspicion' that the participant was living in, but not coming from, the north. The noun 'suspicion' frames the participant's presence in Cumbria as unwelcome and out-of-place; its connotations elucidate a fear of the protagonist as an internal Other transgressing the border between the north and the south. What emerges out of the Orientation, then, is the sense that the relationship between the protagonist and the people in the northern village (and at the symbolic level, the relationship between the North and the South of England) is shrouded in an implicit, unspoken hostility or 'tension'. Through his representation of a north–south divide, Participant J's story of personal experience draws on a broader cultural narrative of Englishness in which those outside of the South of England express 'hostility to the power and wealth of London and the Southeast' (Kenny, 2012: n.p.).

The negative experience of the Londoner in Cumbria is compared to being a Briton in Germany or Austria. In this context, accent is replaced by language – the participant states that it 'helped because I could speak (.) German'. Repeating the same verbal construction as he uses to situate the character in Greggs ('I would just open my mouth') the participant explicitly contrasts the 'tension' with the pleasant surprise that an 'English person' or 'British person' has gone to the effort to learn the language. Through the narrative comparison, the participant indicates that in England, knowing the language and being from the same country are not sufficient to be included in the in-group – a person also needs the right accent to fit in. In other words, in Participant J's narrative rendering, European countries such as Germany and Austria are more welcoming of non-nationals than English people are of their fellow citizens. In England, inhabitants are not only suspicious of each other but are also hostile towards one another. A person is ascribed an identity as an Other, whereas in Germany and Austria, a Briton who knows the language is welcomed and can choose to 'play the outsider card' if they wish.

In the stories above – which are as much about national identities in *times of Brexit* as national identities *in relation to Brexit* – Britishness is contested along racial, ethnic, linguistic and spatial lines. The lived experience of 'being British' and the meanings that participants associate with Britishness shift depending on the places and spaces that their characters occupy. For instance, in Participant G's stories, a minority ethnic British character experiences solidarity in a multicultural London school but discrimination in rooms and taxis in the predominantly white city of Nottingham. In these stories, Britishness is tacitly associated with whiteness, which leads to the discursive and social exclusion of the minority ethnic Briton even in cases of attempted inclusion. In Participant H's story, the effects of the discursive and social exclusion of minority ethnic people extend beyond the social group that is Othered to alienate a participant whose whiteness affords him the privilege of not having to defend his right to claim to be British. Similarly, in Participant J's story, a man with linguistic and symbolic capital (Bourdieu, 1991) is Othered when he enters an eatery in Northern England because of his accent. In these stories, then, what is in question is not just who can call themselves British but what Britishness means, and who gets to decide its meanings. While the five stories are diverse, they share the discursive construction of a divided nation in which even characters with social and cultural capital (Bourdieu, 1991) are marginalized at times.

Conclusion

In this chapter, I demonstrate that interviewees tell stories in response to interview questions to navigate the contested meanings and lived experiences of 'Britishness'. Through their stories, participants make sense of the effects of Brexit on their national identities and explore what it means to be British more generally in times of Brexit. In their explorations, the participants unite personal experiences with interrogations of broader cultural narratives, revealing that identity construction takes place at the intersection between 'individual experiences [and] collective visions' (Krzyżanowski, 2010; Zappettini, 2018: 18). Overall, the chapter provides support for Mann and Fenton's (2017: 4) claim that 'it is through people's views of being English, British or otherwise, that we locate deeper sources of resentment – of a world in which they have been left behind or a country that has changed for the worst'.

In the first part of the chapter, I explore stories during which older Leave-voting participants narrate encounters with symbols of British trade in the past (New Zealand butter in the shops; ensigns in ports; displays in schools). In remembering a global trading nation identity that Britain, in their eyes, no longer possesses, the participants lend credence to Calhoun's (2017) suggestion that Leave voters felt nostalgic for a golden age of British influence. There is, however, diversity in the participants' attitudes towards post-Brexit Britain. While Participant C imagines Britain's post-Brexit future optimistically, hoping that Britain will once again trade widely, Participants D and E are doubtful that the UK will reinvigorate its internationalist reputation. Not all Leave-voting stories are *retrotopian*, then.

The stories told by the older Leave-voting participants are, in some ways, similar to two stories told by Remain voters in which the Britain of their youth is framed as unequal. All six of the stories constitute reflections on the past and five are underpinned by an economic argument that legitimizes their Leave or Remain vote. However, the Leave-voting participants' stories reflect *positively* on the past as a time of greater collectivism and trade, whereas the Remain-voting stories tell of government neglect. In the Leave-voting stories, although the EU is *suppressed* (van Leeuwen, 2008) as a social actor, the implicature is that EU membership prevented the UK from trading widely. In contrast, in the stories by Participants A and H, the EU is represented as a saviour – it provides funding to areas that have been 'left behind' – areas like rural Wales and deindustrialized northern towns. Either way, there is a sense of dissatisfaction – of *discontented national identities* – across the stories: Britain is framed as in decline (Participants C and E) with pride located in the past (Participants D and E), or as unequal (Participants A and H). For some participants, Brexit, at the time of interviewing in 2020 and 2021, affords optimism and hope for the future (e.g. Participant C). For others, it signals a descent towards (or an enhancement of existing) prejudices and exclusion in an already largely divided imagined community (Anderson, 2006).

There is a remarkable similarity between the lexical choices and plots told by Participants A and H. Through their stories, these interviewees indicate that their attitudes towards the EU are rooted in personal experiences that contributed to the formation of their political opinions from an early age. It is through these personal experiences that the participants make sense of their responses to broader cultural narratives about the EU. Growing up in underdeveloped towns and counties where government funding is scarce, the two participants interpret the EU's funding for regional developments as saving Britons from the neglect of their national governments. The participants claim that having 'seen' the EU's heroism in action, they could not ignore it and vote Leave. In drawing on the spatial imaginary of left-behind Britain (Sykes, 2018), Participants A and H problematize the broader cultural interpretation of *Leave* voters as those who have been disadvantaged by globalization (Goodwin and Heath, 2016).

In the middle of the chapter, I explore stories of discrimination in which participants narrate other people's discriminatory practices, are discriminatory and deny their discrimination. Like Andreouli et al. (2019), this section importantly problematizes some of the allegedly stable subject positions of Leavers as xenophobic and racist and Remain voters as tolerant. Indeed, Remain-voting participants are just as likely to tell stories of or discursively (re)produce discrimination and prejudice as Leave-voting-interviewees. For instance, while Leave voter Participant C conflates the religions of Sikh and Muslim and associates them with the terrorist group ISIS, Remain-voting Participant F repeatedly uses the derogatory term 'Paki'. Both participants deny racism – the former by arguing that she can 'get along with anyone' and the latter by claiming that his previous use of 'Paki' was 'not meant derogatory'. Meanwhile, although Participant C contends that 'people on council estates' did not care about the state of the country, Participant A refers to Leave voters as 'semi-literate' and people who 'can't even spell really simple things'. Participant B, a working-class person who lives on a council estate, positions working-class people as 'less analytical' than the middle classes and uses the Othering third-person plural pronoun 'they'. These narratives support Andreouli et al.'s (2019: 318) finding that 'constructions of prejudice occupy a central role in structuring, justifying, or delegitimizing positions toward Brexit', irrespective of whether the discourse producer is supporting a Leave or Remain position.

In the final part of the chapter, I explore stories through which participants interrogate questions of identity and belonging in Britain that transcend the socio-political context of Brexit. Some stories reveal an implicit association of Britishness with whiteness, despite the diversity of Britons and the fact that Britain has never been a monoethnic nation (Bhambra, 2017). In other stories, the region is the lens through which the nation is interpreted; what it means to be British is questioned through stories of regional accent discrimination, for instance. What unites the stories is the sense that the meanings of Britishness shift constantly, depending on space, place and time, as well as the context of the interaction. In this way, we might say that there is no single imagined community but multiple communities which coexist, contradict, include and exclude simultaneously. 'Britain' and 'Briton', like 'EU' and 'Europe', then, are floating signifiers. That is, they mean something different to every participant and at different times for the same participant. That does not mean that they are void of meaning. On the contrary, as much as ascribed identities (Blommaert, 2005) of Britishness are open to contestation, almost all participants still identify as 'British' and for them, 'being British' is a source of pride (Participants C, D, E, F and G) or shame (Participants I and L).

What, then, do these stories indicate about national identities in post-Brexit Britain? The stories I examined in this chapter discursively construct national identities as flexible, multiple, discursive and context-dependent. Participants carefully distinguish between ascribed identities (Blommaert, 2005) and internal feelings of belonging to their nation. In distinguishing between what they, as participants, understand as 'British', and what their characters interpret to be British, the participants indicate that there is no single collective understanding of what Britain is or could be among citizens. Nevertheless, to be British means something and for these participants, the Brexit process is about determining what.

7

Concluding Remarks

Introduction

This is the first book of its kind to analyse the discursive construction of Britain and Europe in pro-Brexit newspapers, UK government documents and semi-structured interviews with individual Leave and Remain voters. It uses a novel combination of corpus linguistics, CDA and discourse analysis of narratives told in oral interviews to uncover a narrative of national division in Brexit Britain at a tumultuous time in British politics. Beyond a methodological contribution, the book expands upon a sizeable body of literature that explores identity mobilization in relation to Brexit, such as Zappettini and Krzyżanowski (2019), through a focus on (supra)national identities. In this final chapter, I consider points of commonality and difference in the representation of Britain and Europe across the three data sets. I go on to reflect on methodological challenges, as well as the advances this book has made. I address my position as a researcher undertaking an emotive, political project. Finally, I outline where there is scope for future research.

Shared representations of Britain and Europe

A discourse of difference

A representation that pervades all three data sets is Britain as a nation that is distinct from continental Europe. This depiction was common in pre-referendum Eurosceptic discourses and was also prevalent in political discourses during the EU referendum campaign (Cap, 2019; Spiering, 2014; Wenzl, 2019). In the pro-Brexit media (Chapter 4), it appears when *The Express* accuses Remain voters of wanting to 'make our country more European, more continental'. This geographical argument presupposes that Britain is not fully (culturally)

European because it is not part of the mainland (a view commonly referred to as 'British exceptionalism'). I propose that the discursive differentiation between Britain and Europe in the pro-Brexit media forms part of a Churchillian argument that Britain is 'with Europe but not of it' (Roberts, 2018: n.p.) and therefore should be free from the legal and political directives issued from Brussels. In the government data, the British Island Nation imaginary (Sykes, 2018) is adopted to claim that Britain should engage with different 'circles of influence on a "transactional" basis' (Gaskarth, 2013: 67) and so should not be trading only with the EU. Theresa May and the then Polish prime minister both discursively differentiate between Britain and Europe; their grammatical strategies, such as syntactic parallelism, underpin a discursive construction of the UK and Europe as allies in defence. Despite the shared representation, the governmental construction of the British Island Nation is adopted to support a future UK–EU relationship, whereas the pro-Brexit media use it to argue against continued EU membership.

While the stories told by participants do not necessarily draw on geographical arguments, they too distinguish Britain from EU-rope. For instance, Participant H, a Remain voter, compares a European 'them' who look 'quite nice' to 'the actual government'. The discursive distinction between Britain and EU-rope thus underpins both Eurosceptic and Europhile representations of the UK–EU relationship. This finding supports Wodak's (2018) uncovering of a discourse of difference in Remainer David Cameron's so-called Bloomberg speech, by demonstrating that the British Island Nation imaginary is versatile and can be mobilized to different ends: to disparage the EU and encourage readers to vote Leave, to persuade European political officials to be defence allies with Britain and to justify a Remain vote in the EU referendum.

British decline

A further point of comparison between the data sets is the discursive construction of British decline. A narrative of British decline is not new to the British media – retellings of the Second World War have long been mobilized by tabloids to compare contemporary Britain unfavourably with the past (Conboy, 2006). It is also not a new theme in British political discourse, where the Suez crisis is often evoked as the catalyst for British post-imperial decline (Maccaferri, 2019; Peden, 2012). The representation of decline is subtle in my early media data. It emerges in Priti Patel's argument that there are increasingly limited resources in the UK's health service, the housing market and schools and the *Telegraph Online*'s claim that political officials have done damage to the nation's reputation by refusing to accept a Brexit deal. The sense of decline is more obvious in the later years when *Telegraph Online* and *The Express* argue that May's Withdrawal Agreement has been a national humiliation on the scale of the Suez crisis. These examples from the No Respect semantic domain take further the earlier suggestion that the UK's international reputation is at risk by implying that national humiliation has already occurred.

In the government corpus, decline seeps through in the Alive semantic domain in Theresa May's argument that the future Union needs to be as strong as it was in the past (which subtly implies weakness in the present), and through the assertion that Britain needs to regain its global trading nation reputation. It is particularly evident in the claim that British people have 'lost faith' in national institutions. Both institutional data sets therefore subscribe to the view that Britain needs positive change, and that Brexit *should* be the means through which transformation is achieved.

The narrative of national decline is strongest in my interview data. Leave and Remain voters express dissatisfaction with the present state of the UK due to a lack of global trade (Participants C, D, E and O) and multiple incidents of discrimination (Participants G, H and J). Participant C's desire to trade widely 'again' after Brexit implies a return to a previous period of global trade – it is *retrotopian*. Meanwhile, Participant D's assertion that there would not be British trading ships in ports now, unlike in the 1960s, implies that Global Britain is not, at the time of interviewing, a tangible concept for some citizens despite governmental discourses. Despite Brexit being sold by the Vote Leave campaign as a panacea for British political ills that would return the UK to its former status as a global trading nation, the presence of a narrative of decline in interviews I conducted after the UK left the EU suggests that leaving did not resolve the malaise with the present state of the nation. In other words, Brexit did not achieve the sense of national reinvigoration it was promised it would. The consequences of this broken promise in the long term are likely to be political alienation (or at least disenchantment) and a weaker sense of belonging to the nation among Leave voters. A similar outcome is likely for those Remain voters who are disillusioned by discrimination; several participants expressed an intention to move to mainland Europe after Brexit.

British division

By far the most widely shared representation of Britain across the later years of the media, government and interview data sets is of a divided nation. In the media outlets, this representation is constructed through the No Respect semantic domain, which includes images of divisions between British politicians and the public, and between Remain and Leave voters. Divisions are represented lexically through verbs such as 'humiliate' and 'jeer', and nouns such as 'scorn', 'contempt' and 'disdain'. The Eurosceptic media alleges that politicians increasingly view the electorate with contempt. The UK's intranational divisions are framed as a source of national humiliation the likes of which have never been experienced (a manipulation of British history to serve a Leave-backing agenda). Through this representation of British humiliation, journalists weave an anti-elite, populist discourse of national crisis (Moffit, 2016). They also cultivate a fear of the loss of the UK's international standing. By blaming politicians and members of the public for divides, the newspapers obfuscate the role that their discursive constructions of tensions play in reinforcing and inciting divisions. At the same time as these divisive representations pervade pro-Brexit newspaper articles, the UK government openly acknowledges in a North American newspaper that MPs cannot agree on a Brexit deal through the weather metaphor of 'clash and thunder', and claims that the UK public has lost faith in its political institutions. These arguments expose political weakness and depict the UK as an unstable ally because they point to a lack of direction and consensus within Parliament, and a division between the public and those elected to represent them.

With such a pervasive media narrative of a nation divided between politicians and the public, it is hardly surprising that many of my interviewees communicate distrust of the political class and dissatisfaction with the contemporary state of the nation. For example, Participant A laments that 'we cannot rely on our government' and Participant H implies that 'what the actual government is doing' is not 'nice' in comparison to the EU. While Leave-voting participants do not necessarily tell stories about division, they do argue that Britain is divided elsewhere in the interviews. Only one participant frames these divisions as pre-existing Brexit and a natural consequence of democracies – a more favourable, or at least naturalized, view of national tensions.

Several stories feature divisions between individuals, many of which include pejorative descriptions of voters on the other side of the EU referendum debate. Participant A, for example, caricatures Leave voters as 'white van man, Sun-reading, red-faced gammon types' who are 'poorly educated, semi-literate' and 'pretty xenophobic'. Similarly, Participant H argues that Leave voters 'often embraced intolerance' by shouting at people in the street. These expressions of distrust and judgement, together with the media narratives of intolerance and division, paint a picture of Brexit Britain as a deeply politically fractured nation.

While studies have documented representations of political division in the UK media the day after the EU referendum vote (Koller and Ryan, 2019), this book demonstrates that the narrative of political division goes beyond just the media data to pervade the construction of British society in both political and personal contexts even after the UK has left the EU. The fact that stories of division are more prominent among Remain-voting participants suggests that narratives of division permeate both sides of the debate. In other words, they extend beyond just the pro-Brexit press.

The discursive construction of national divisions in the interview data also extends beyond the political realm. In the participants' stories, there are socio-economic, geographic and racial divides between Britons. For example, Participant A relates a story of economic stagnation in which mid-Wales is simultaneously 'very poor' and 'quite wealthy'. This representation points to a construction of the UK as a financially unequal society. There are echoes of this description in *The Telegraph*'s representation of Remainers as 'metropolitan elites' and 'trendy London society' and Leave voters as disadvantaged out-of-towners. However, *The Telegraph* envisions economic inequality along Remain/Leave lines, whereas Participant A discusses geographical differences that existed before Brexit. Either way, representations of British inequality could lead to greater resentment between social groups, precipitating further polarization between those who have and those who have not.

Participant G narrates two stories that highlight the different experiences of being a minority ethnic Briton in London and Nottinghamshire. His stories indicate that racial and geographical differences can intertwine – multicultural solidarity exists in some spaces but not in others. Further geographical divisions appear in a story narrated by Participant J, who faces 'suspicion' because he is a Southerner living in a small northern town. This narrative points to a North–South regional divide. The images of socio-economic fracture in the stories are not necessarily precipitated by Brexit: two interviewees argue that Brexit is a 'symptom' of existing divides in the UK, rather than the cause. Whichever way the disunity is interpreted, there is a widespread consensus that divisions are rife in Brexit Britain.

As the above sections indicate, the institutional and lay constructions of Brexit Britain largely align in their negative constructions of the nation. There is a sense at all levels of discourse that there are problems within the nation state (and with its relationship with the EU) that need to be rectified. For the pro-Brexit media, the pro-Brexit government and Leave-voting participants, Brexit presents an opportunity for transformation – but, crucially, that transformation is yet to occur. Presumably, Brexit has not reached its full potential for Leave voters by the time of data collection, which is why dissatisfaction with the nation still exists among Leave-backing participants. That sense of discontent among Leave voters is only likely to be exacerbated if a Global Britain foreign policy is not taken forward (and, indeed, it seems not to be – as noted in Chapter 5, the Global Britain rhetoric appears to be dwindling at the time of writing). For Remain-voting interviewees, Brexit represents a worsening of the most negative aspects of British national identity, leaving the UK 'on the precipice', as Participant J puts it. This narrative of division is significant because it suggests that despite what pro-Brexit campaigners, newspapers and politicians promised in the pre- and early post-referendum years, Brexit led not to national reinvigoration but to a greater awareness of socio-political divisions in the later post-referendum years.

There is little chance of an amelioration of feelings in the short term: since the interviews were conducted, there have been further examples of economic decline and division between the UK's constituent countries. For example, the Office for Budget Responsibility has concluded that Brexit will have a worse long-term effect on the UK economy than the Covid-19 pandemic (BBC, 2021c). There have been international shortages of workers in industries like haulage and butchery, due partly to Brexit and partly to '1.3 million foreign born workers [having] left the UK as the result of a pandemic' (Financial Times, 2021: n.p.). There has also been widespread political instability in Westminster, as the UK lurched from prime minister to prime minister throughout 2022, with Conservative MP Liz Truss remaining in office for only forty-nine days. Meanwhile, the UK and the EU have clashed over the Northern Ireland protocol, which has disrupted trade between Great Britain and Northern Ireland (Edgington and Morris, 2021). Perhaps unsurprisingly given these political events, an Opinium research poll from December 2021 found that 44 per cent of the 1,904 adults surveyed thought Brexit had a negative impact on the UK economy (Opinium, 2021).

Differences in representations between Britain and EU-rope

The UK–EU relationship

Representations of Britain and Europe are inextricably linked in all three data sets: EU-rope is the dominant British Other. One key relational representation in the media corpora, which relies on personification and metaphor, is the UK as a victim of EU interference. The UK-as-victim representation is dominant across all years of the pro-Brexit media articles, which employ an Invaded Nation frame (Charteris-Black, 2019) to position the EU as a radical Other (Gibbins, 2014). In the early post-referendum years, the UK's victimization is realized through the Alive semantic domain in the discursive representation of the EU's interference in British life. Material processes (Halliday, 1985) such as 'interferes', 'invade', 'restrict', 'tighten' and 'seized' are used by journalists and politicians who are quoted in newspaper articles to render tangible the EU's legislative dominance over the UK (see Dugalès and Tucker, 2012). These representations, in addition to the metaphor of the EU as the 'Brussels machine', draw on an existing Eurosceptic discourse of the EU as an untransparent, interfering, bureaucratic super-state (Oberhuber et al., 2005; Wenzl, 2019). In the later years, the EU's effect on the UK is represented through the No Respect domain as akin to bullying. The EU's behaviour is depicted lexically through the verb 'deride', the phrasal verb 'pour scorn' and the nominalization 'humiliation'. This disparaging construction of the EU as a bully only appears in the pro-Brexit media, which is not surprising: I contend that the main purpose of the early articles is to persuade readers to vote Leave in the EU referendum by selling Brexit as an opportunity for British emancipation from a quasi-imperial EU (see also Hawkins, 2012).

While the pro-Brexit press constructs the UK–EU relationship as one that victimizes the UK, the government documents in the early post-referendum years envision a secure relationship between equal allies. The discursive construction of equality comes through in the syntactic parallelism and linguistic differentiation used by Theresa May and Beata Szydło, when they portray Britain and Europe as friendly Others (Gibbins, 2014) who face the shared threats of death in war, terrorism and illegal (extra-European) migration. The grammatical strategies that the leaders employ position the UK and Europe as two independent but equal allies. Across the early examples, history is evoked not to discursively differentiate between the UK and the EU, as Wenzl (2019) finds in parliamentary debates, but to unite them. This representation is undoubtedly strategic, as it reflects the government's desire for bilateral trade and defence relationships between the UK and European countries.

Government documents in the early post-referendum years also employ a range of personifying kinship terms, such as 'relationship', 'friendship' and 'partner' to envision positive relations between the UK and the EU. The kinship terms problematize Siles-Brügge's (2019) claim that there is no emotive underpinning to the government's discourses about the UK–EU relationship. Kinship terms are used to obscure increasing tensions during UK–EU negotiations as the years progress. Ministers begin to highlight tensions between the UK and the EU and within the UK between politicians and the public. Eventually, the EU is sidelined and reduced to only one potential (but not necessary) post-Brexit partner. Although the UK government does not use the hard Eurosceptic terminology of victims and villains, or explicitly formulate the construction of the EU as faceless and bureaucratic, the shift towards subtle negative Other representation in the later years brings the institutional narratives of the UK–EU relationship closer together. There are consequences to this negative Other representation for the UK's post-Brexit vision: it is questionable to what degree the UK government can claim that Britain is a global trading nation when it subtly undermines its closest trading partners. Similarly, the implicit antagonistic approach towards the EU is unlikely to result in a positive, fruitful environment when it comes to international trade, something which the UK relies on not just to project a global image but for its economic survival (Bogdanor, 2020).

As the stories told by my interviewees tend to focus on personal experiences, participants seldom discursively construct Britain and Europe as higher-level entities. Where they do, representations differ depending on the attitude of the participant towards the EU. For example, Participants A and H (both Remain voters) represent the EU as a funding alternative to a neglectful national government. For them, leaving the EU inevitably means more stagnation for underfunded or overlooked areas of the UK. In contrast, Participant C implies that Britain's membership of the EU prevented the nation from trading globally in her assertion that 'coming out of Brexit', the UK will be able to 'trade with any country we want to'. In sum, there is no single way of discursively constructing the UK–EU relationship between press, politics and public opinion and in the latter case, representations differ between individuals, depending on their attitudes towards their nation's foreign and national policies.

The nation and national identity

Media and government discourses homogenize Britain through the discursive construction of a British way of life. Their similar representations of the nation align with Smith's (1992) definition of a human population that shares a historical territory, memories, culture and laws; they draw on instances of British history (the Suez crisis, the Second World War) and point to a singular British culture that is distinct from continental Europe. The British society that the journalists and politicians construct is largely civic (in contrast to Rowinski (2017) who argues for increasing ethnonationalism in the British press); there is a focus on democratic institutions such as the National Health Service and Parliament in Theresa May's unionism speech, which is reproduced in full without editing in both *Express Online* and *MailOnline*. The focus on institutions is retrospective, through the present perfect tense of 'we have built'; this lexicogrammar foregrounds a shared, historical, civic identity between England and Scotland that undermines Scottish nationalist claims that Scotland is fiscally and politically peripheral to England (Whigham, 2019). There is a sense of timelessness to the representations, as journalists and politicians elaborate a shared past and provide a vision of a collective future (Anderson, 2006). The nation is frequently flagged through deixis and metonymy (see Billig (1995) for banal flagging of nationalism and Wodak et al. (2009) for micro-linguistic strategies for constructing the nation). Despite the similarities between the media and government data, the media's construction of the nation often excludes Remain voters, depicting an entirely Leave-voting coalition of media professionals and citizens as the national public.

The constructions of the nation and national identity produced by citizens are radically different from those produced by journalists and politicians. The language used by participants constructs the imagined communities (Anderson, 2006) of the nation as multiple, context-dependent and discursive. Britishness and Europeanness, in the stories which centre on difference, are constantly problematized, contested, negotiated and recontextualized. For example, for Participants G and K, what it means to be British differs depending on place and space. In one of Participant G's stories, he explains that he 'still [feels] British' even though others living in Nottingham contest his Britishness by ascribing to him an Indian identity. This story relates an experience of ethnonationalism that contradicts the civic Britishness constructed in the media and government data. Rather than discursively constructing higher-level relationships between UK and EU officials, participants tend to privilege localized, mundane personal experiences that they use to explain and justify their political attitudes. In other words, as Davies (2021) also finds, higher-level relationships in the Brexit context are worked out at the local, personal level.

Importantly, in participants' stories, Britain and EU-rope are floating signifiers that have different meanings for people at different times. There is no one vision of what Britain is or should be within or across the stories. A key contribution of this book is that identity construction in relation to Brexit Britain is found to emerge at the intersection between top-down discourses and cultural narratives, and bottom-up constructions of national identity based on individual experiences (Krzyżanowski, 2010; Zappettini, 2018).

The myth of the tolerant Briton

Journalists and politicians draw on the myth of the decent Briton (Bennett, 2018) in the early post-referendum years, while interview participants construct (other) Britons as intolerant and xenophobic. In the media data, the tolerant Briton construction manifests itself through the Polite semantic domain, which consists of a range of value-laden nouns including 'fair-mindedness' and 'civility'. British civility, marked through the symbol of the queue, is marvelled at by journalists who have lived in Europe. The decent Briton representation is used not only to claim British exceptionalism, but also to shield Leave-voting participants from accusations of xenophobia. In the media during the later post-referendum years, the image of British civility is problematized: *Telegraph Online* claims that politicians' inability to agree on a Brexit deal has damaged 'the famous civility and fair mindedness of British life and 'tested to their limits' the 'great national virtues of reason and decency'. Given that decency is a core characteristic of Britishness in the dominant national identity narrative (Bennett, 2018; Holmes, 1991), this representation implies that a collective Britishness is in crisis due to the Brexit-related decisions of political officials.

In line with the diachronic shift towards images of intolerance in the media data, the stories told by Participants A, H and G reveal a lay Remainer construction of Britain as beset by racial, linguistic and xenophobic discrimination (see also Andreouli, 2020). In other words, my participants contest the institutional myth of the tolerant Briton (Bennett, 2018). While interviewees generally position *themselves* as tolerant (by evaluating the stories they tell and the characters within them, and by denying the racism in their stories), they focus on incidents of racism and xenophobia they have witnessed or experienced to argue that Britain is a fractured and intolerant nation. In one case, a participant refers to Leave voters as 'poorly educated' and 'semi-literate'. This expression of educational superiority lends some credence to the critique of an alleged intellectual division between Remain and Leave voters in *The Telegraph*. In another example, Participant H explicitly labels tolerance 'the opposite' of what Leave voters display. Participant F, while (re)producing the derogatory term 'Paki', speaks of his concern at increasing 'racial tension'. Arguably, in participants' rejection of the tolerant Briton myth and in their perception that Brexit has strengthened or triggered a new crisis of intolerance, there is also a rejection of the media's early discourses of unity and a reinforcement of a narrative of decline.

A great global trading nation

The discursive construction of Brexit Britain as a global trading nation is the core national identity narrative in UK government documents (see Chapter 5). This representation is not new; Teubert (2001) identified a similar discursive construction over twenty years ago. The representation of the global trading nation intertextually relates to (sanitized) historical understandings of Britain's place in the world, as Zappettini (2019) finds in a document published by the Department for International Trade. In other words, the post-Brexit Global Britain vision draws on historical discourses of Britishness to project an influential future identity for the nation (Zappettini, 2019; Eaton and Smith, 2020). Although the government remains committed to a Global Britain narrative up to the end of the data collection period, the rising sense of uncertainty and antagonism in the discourses surrounding the UK–EU relationship suggests a contradiction, or unravelling, of the early promise to reinvigorate Britain's global trading nation status as the years progress. That is, the subtly antagonistic approach towards the UK–EU relationship reflects tensions between negotiators, but it also reinforces them; the UK government, through its language use, renders less probable its own future-oriented national identity narrative.

Given the similar ways in which the government and the media use language and history to construct a civic British national identity, it is notable that the representation of Britain as a trading nation does not appear prominently in the media data. Indeed, while the government discursively constructs the UK–EU relationship, pro-Brexit media outlets focus on narrating *domestic* divisions between politicians and the public. These different representations indicate a divergence in socio-political agendas in the media and government, with the former turning against the latter despite them both supporting Brexit.

In contrast to the pro-Brexit media, three of my Leave-voting interviewees *do* construct a global trading nation identity in their stories, such as Participant C's claim that Brexit will enable the UK to trade with any country again. Participants D and E, though more ambivalent about what Brexit means for the trading nation identity, state that Britain's influence in the past was a source of pride for them. Participant O also articulates a desire for British trading success when he argues that the country needs to 'roll up our sleeves and get into the fight' for a place in the world. The alignment between the governmental and Leave-voting citizen narratives suggests a future-oriented globalist national identity discourse has the potential to be convincing but has yet to be reified through foreign policy. In other words, Leave-voting participants find the internationalist vision appealing, but do not seem to think it reflects post-Brexit Britain at the time of interviewing. It is conceivable that if, long term, the UK does not achieve the promised global influence, these voters will feel cheated out of the Brexit they were promised (indeed, Browning (2018) suggests some already do). Whether this sentiment will translate into an increased sense of disillusion towards politicians and politics remains to be seen, but I suspect it is not unlikely given the current low levels of trust in politicians (Curtice et al., 2020).

Conceptualizations of Brexit

In addition to representations of Britain and Europe, the three data sets include discursive constructions of Brexit. In the pro-Brexit newspaper articles, Brexit is subtly framed as a panacea for British political ills. For instance, in Extract 1, Britain's EU membership is portrayed as causing uncontrollable levels of immigration that put pressure on public services. It follows from this representation that leaving the EU would reduce immigration levels and ease the pressure on the British health service, housing and schools. In Example 5, Theresa May frames post-Brexit Britain as 'stronger' than pre-Brexit Britain, which implies that membership of the EU led to national weakness. Although the newspapers remain committed to Brexit over the years, they discursively construct Theresa May's version of the Withdrawal Agreement as a national 'humiliation' on the scale of the Suez crisis. In this representation, a specific kind of Brexit is constructed as a national crisis (see Bennett, 2019; Krzyżanowski, 2019), but the idea of leaving the EU to solve British political problems remains present in the antagonistic representation of UK–EU relations.

As is the case with the media data, the UK government represents Brexit contradictorily. The government simultaneously envisions Brexit as a departure from an existing UK–EU relationship through the metaphor of onward movement, and as a continuation of existing relations in the verb 'stay' and the verb phrase 'carry on'. A further contradiction in the UK government's construction of Brexit is its representation as simultaneous progress ('race to the top') and a return to the past ('for the first time in more than forty years'). I argue that the inconsistent conceptualization of Brexit in the UK government documents renders unclear the institutional vision for post-Brexit Britain, which in turn could send the message to future international partners that Britain is unsure of its post-Brexit place in the world. The discursive tensions likely exist not by choice, but as a reflection of the competing pressures that the government faces to maintain a trading relationship with the EU while delivering on the Vote Leave rhetoric of becoming a global nation once again.

Much like the media and political data sets, there is no single conceptualization of Brexit among my interviewees. For Participant C, who voted Leave, Brexit is an opportunity to trade widely again. For Leave-voting Participants D and E, Brexit is unlikely to return Britain to its global trading past, but it remains the most attractive option for the UK. In contrast, for several Remain-voting participants, Brexit indicates that prejudice has prevailed in the country. For example, Participant H's ventriloquation (Bakhtin, 1981) of a Leave voter saying, 'it is our country again now', implies that the EU referendum was about defining what Britishness means and who can claim to be British. The Leave vote, the story implies, means that an ethnonationalist conceptualization of the UK has prevailed, which has alienated non-British white people and British minority ethnic people. For some of the Remain-supporting interviewees, post-Brexit Britain is a country that is 'on the precipice' and the solution is to leave the UK (Participants K and J). The multiple different representations of 'Brexit' suggest it is an empty signifier that can be used to mean different things according to different socio-political agendas. This emptiness is, of course, politically useful because it allows politicians like Theresa May to repeat 'Brexit means Brexit', seemingly confirming that whatever individuals understand Brexit to mean will be delivered.

A shared narrative?

As the above section indicates, there are important differences and contradictions within and between the data sets: the pro-Brexit media openly disparages the EU as an interfering bully while the UK government frames EU-rope as a friend, partner and ally. The press represents the UK as a victim, while government officials position it as an international powerhouse. Political officials homogenize Britain while citizens speak of multiple ways of being British. There are also shared ways of talking about Britain and Europe. Britain and Europe are positioned as distinct entities, often because Britain is framed as geographically and culturally separate from the continent. Journalists and politicians both talk about a British way of life, as the keyness of the Alive semantic domain in both data sets elucidates. What the diachronic analysis in the previous chapters reveals is a convergence between public, press and political constructions of Britishness in the later post-referendum years towards a narrative of widespread division. The image of Brexit Britain that emerges towards the end of the data collection period is of a politically, socio-economically and geographically divided nation.

I would argue that the representations of Britain as divided do not constitute a *shared* national identity narrative, but a complementary one. That is, the nature of the division is different in each of the data sets. In the media data, division is constructed between politicians and the public and between members of the public. In the government data, division is largely envisioned between the UK and the EU, or British political officials – there is understandably no talk of politicians viewing citizens with contempt, even though there is mention of the public having lost faith in political institutions. In the stories told by citizens, politicians and the higher-level entities of the UK and the EU seldom appear, but divisions between individuals are rife. Place the three data sets side by side and the images reinforce one another to construct a deeply fractured nation. This representation of Britain is not only a direct contradiction of the great global trading nation narrative that the Vote Leave campaigners – and later the UK government – promised, but it is also at odds with what one might expect given the purposes of the institutional texts. That is, even though the government and the pro-Brexit press seek to persuade Britons that Brexit is the best option for the nation, neither journalists nor politicians provide a *positive* national identity narrative to support their post-Brexit vision.

To be more explicit, the pro-Brexit media seeks to persuade readers that they should vote to leave the EU and remain committed to their vote amid calls for Scottish independence and a second referendum. Based on this purpose, one might expect journalists to construct Brexit Britain as unified and thriving outside of the EU. However, this optimism is limited to the early post-referendum years, generally before negotiations with the EU begin. The closer the UK gets to its withdrawal from the EU, the more pejorative and divided the national identity narrative becomes. This descent into division might well suggest that the reality of Brexit negotiations was different from what the pro-Brexit media outlets initially expected. That is, May's Withdrawal Agreement did not align with the Brexit the news outlets supported and constructing divisions between politicians and the public enabled the newspapers to persuade readers that May was not the ideal person to deliver Brexit. However, by undermining Britain's status as a parliamentary democracy – which is a cornerstone of the British identity narrative (Marcussen et al., 1999) – the newspapers threatened to destabilize a collective Britishness.

The same argument can be made about the UK government documents. These documents are prepared not only for national readers (whom the government hopes to convince of national stability) but also for European officials whom the government seeks to engage in trade and defence deals. In other words, like the pro-Brexit press, the government seeks to persuade its audiences that Brexit is a positive decision for all involved. Despite this goal, the later UK government documents discursively construct Britain as divided and (implicitly) distrustful of supposedly antagonistic EU negotiators. The result, I argue, is that the government, like the pro-Brexit media, fails to provide British readers and prospective international partners with an image of a strong and stable union. This failure threatens the government's reputation for 'competent governance' (UK in a Changing Europe, 2020a: 55) and negatively affects its international standing. A weakened international reputation is, of course, not helpful for a government that is trying to 'build relationships with old friends and new allies alike'. Nonetheless, the government's foreign policy approach since the publication of these documents – trying to renege on international agreements such as the Brexit Withdrawal Agreement with Northern Ireland (Walker, 2021) – is clearly a continuation of the counterintuitive discourse I identify in this book.

If there is truth in Theresa May's (2017: n.p.) claim that the 'strength and stability of our union will become even more important' after Brexit, then the complementary trajectory towards national division across the three data sets suggests that Brexit Britain is not what it was first envisioned to be. At the time of writing, trust in politicians is at a record low (Curtice et al., 2020), the English are feeling the need to reassert themselves amid anxieties over increasing devolution (Henderson and Wyn Jones, 2021) and *The Irish Times* reported in August 2022 that more than half of voters in Northern Ireland supported a united Ireland within the next fifteen to twenty years (McClements, 2022). The foreign aid budget has been cut, and politicians are now stating that an early trade deal with the United States is unlikely (BBC News, 2021b). As alluded to above, then prime minister Boris Johnson considered reneging on international agreements the UK signed at the time that it left the EU, leading to questions about the place of Northern Ireland in the new UK–EU relationship. These incidents support the narrative of national disarray and suggest that a global post-Brexit British identity is in crisis.

A new national identity narrative? Brexit as a destabilizing force

The foregoing discussion has revealed that the early political, media and public conceptualizations of Brexit Britain are largely interdiscursive continuations of existing discourses about Britain as a nation. In other words, as Maccaferri (2019: 390) puts it, early 'Brexit discourse was actually an ongoing recontextualisation of traditional historical narratives' in many ways. For instance, Theresa May's focus on civic British institutions such as 'Parliamentary democracy' is part of an existing Eurosceptic discourse that foregrounds British parliamentary history as a source of differentiation from continental Europe (Cap, 2019; Maccaferri, 2019). What is different about its use in my data is that the focus is on constructing British unity amid calls for a second Scottish independence vote, rather than solely undermining the relationship between the UK and the EU. Similarly, the narrative of post-imperial decline that underpins the discourse in the three data sets was initiated by the Suez crisis (Maccaferri, 2019; Peden, 2012), and so, although then Conservative MP Jo Johnson argues that May's Brexit humiliation could be 'on the scale of Suez', it is not the first time Britain has been said to be in decline. On the contrary, May's Brexit deal is framed as further evidence of an ongoing, historical decline. Meanwhile, the global trading nation discourse harkens back to the British Empire even if it is framed as a new post-Brexit opportunity (Zappettini, 2019; Eaton and Smith, 2020). Europe is positioned as a British Other, which has long been the case in Eurosceptic discourses (Spiering, 2014) and has been found in pro-Remain discourses (Wodak, 2018), as well as in this book. The linguistic and discursive strategies that underpin these identity narratives – deixis, metonymy, metaphor, collectivization (van Leeuwen, 1995) and so on – are also a continuation of existing discursive strategies used to construct Britishness (see, e.g., Wenzl, 2019). In other words, a new national identity narrative did not emerge for Britain in the early post-referendum years, as I originally hypothesized when I began this project.

Drawing on existing discourses provides a sense of timelessness to the early institutional British identity narratives, as though, as Wenzl (2019) puts it, there is a long-enduring, homogenous and stable Britishness. In other words, it shows an attempt by journalists and politicians – at least in the early post-referendum years – to foster a collective sense of belonging to Britain. After all, the repeated use of familiar frames for Britishness provides a stable sense of shared values and history which are important for building a collective identity (Henderson and McEwan, 2005). The emerging discourse of division in the later post-referendum years destabilizes this familiar, British national identity narrative. I do not wish to suggest that it is the intention of media outlets (or indeed the government, which relies on a construction of national unity in its vision of 'the public') to undermine a collective sense of national identity in the long term. It is more likely, I think, that the discursive construction of a divided Britain, particularly in the media, is strategic. That is, for pro-Brexit journalists – who have less investment in national unity than UK government officials – discursively constructing divisions helped to undermine Theresa May's Withdrawal Agreement and shift the balance of power towards a different type of Brexit. Editors and proprietors of newspapers would likely be invested in this different type of Brexit for commercial reasons (see Daddow (2012) for a consideration of 'the Rupert Murdoch effect' on Euroscepticism in the British press). For the UK government, the antagonizing approach to negotiations allows political officials to convince a national audience that the EU is to blame for a lack of progress. That the interview data reveals representations of individual, personal divisions between Leave and Remain voters, white and minority ethnic people, 'natives' and immigrants, however, suggests that the institutional narratives of division reinforce and exacerbate personal divisions and feelings of national crisis that people are experiencing in their lives. At the same time, the narratives continue a rhetoric of division found in other aspects of the British media (e.g. between workers and 'benefits scroungers', or between 'natives' and immigrants). While the intention might not have been to challenge the stability of existing discourses of Britishness, then, the emerging post-Brexit narrative of widespread division does just that.

Seemingly cognizant of the prevailing tensions and the fact that a nation cannot sustain a long-term narrative of division, politicians appear to have tried to heal divides. Within the last few years, measures for national unity include an albeit brief weekly national clap for NHS and key workers on a Thursday evening, a governmental call for 'distinctively British' shows to be aired on television (Kanter, 2021: n.p.) and a new national flagship to promote the 'best of British' trade and industry (BBC, 2021d: n.p.). These symbolic political gestures exist alongside an increasingly polarizing rhetoric about 'culture wars' (Duffy et al., 2021), which encapsulates divisions about free speech in academia and the moral status of statues of historical figures involved in the slave trade. The number of UK newspaper articles focusing on culture wars rose from twenty-one in 2015 to 534 in 2020 (Duffy et al., 2021) suggesting a substantial increase in discourses of cultural division in addition to the political and national tensions uncovered in this book. Whether the governmental efforts to instil pride in the UK's soft power will be sufficient to heal such a prolonged period of widespread division remains to be seen. However, if the present high level of distrust in political officials is anything to go by, it will be a profoundly difficult task for the UK government.

What are the possible effects of the practice of polarizing opinion? As Duffy (2021: n.p.) argues, there is always the possibility that an increased sense of division could lead to 'implacable conflict where compromise is extremely difficult to achieve' and distrust in people we perceive to be 'Others' is high. Focusing on affective polarization – 'an emotional attachment to in-group partisans and hostility towards out-group partisans' – Hobolt, Leeper and Tilly (2021: 1478) contend that there are similar consequences to this phenomenon, including impairing democratic dialogue and eroding trust in political institutions. If individuals are already experiencing personal divisions around Brexit, as my research suggests, then polarizing rhetoric in the media and politics – even if it is strategic – is only likely to amplify that sense of division. In fact, it could overstate the degree to which longer-term divisions exist while increasing the already high levels of distrust in politicians and journalists (Curtice and Montagu, 2020). If the public continues to be distrustful of politicians and journalists, this will, of course, have negative implications for democracy, alienating potential voters and making a reality Conservative MP Michael Gove's claim that the public has had enough of experts.

Methodological reflections

Having considered the similarities and differences between the data sets and the possible consequences of the narrative of division I have uncovered, I turn now to some methodological reflections. Through the corpus-assisted (critical) discourse analytical approaches, and the collation and analysis of three different data sets, this book has achieved greater holistic coverage than any existing study of national identity construction in the Brexit context (e.g. Wenzl, 2019, 2020). In other words, its findings are more wide ranging than previous studies because of the consideration of intertextuality between the texts produced by the three main social actors involved in Brexit: politicians, journalists and citizens. Considering the texts both separately and in relation to one another, over a period of three years, has produced a panoptic vision of how national identity discourses developed as the Brexit process extended. The innovative, top-down diachronic approach (Marchi, 2018) to media and political texts allowed for a close mapping between text and socio-political context, enabling a consideration of the social consequences of polarizing rhetoric. The corpus linguistic tool of key semantic domain analysis helped to identify both consistent and diverging discursive patterns that would have been unidentifiable through manual linguistic analysis. This book therefore contributes not only to the literature that attempts to make sense of Brexit as a socio-political phenomenon from a discursive perspective (e.g. Buckledee, 2018; Koller et al., 2019), but also work on corpus-assisted critical discourse analytical methods. Importantly, it also demonstrates the fruitfulness of applying CADS approaches to contemporary political crises and has provided the basis for a forthcoming edited collection on CADS approaches to polycrisis (Parnell, van Hout and del Fante, forthcoming). Ultimately, I hope that this book will provide inspiration for those interested in the contemporary political landscape from a variety of disciplines to consider the crucial role that language plays in constructing political and national identities.

An important methodological decision was to employ key semantic domain analysis instead of the more traditional corpus approaches of keyword and collocation analysis. This method enabled identification of semantic fields which were salient in the media and government data, but which were comprised of lexical items that were not used frequently enough to be considered key by themselves. Through this approach, I found semantic fields such as No Respect which I would not have intuitively associated with national identity, but which have been proven throughout this book to be central to the discursive construction of the state of the nation and its international relationships. A keyword comparison with the same reference corpus would not have identified the same discourses: 'humiliat*', 'deride', 'scorn' and 'disdain' are not keywords by themselves in any of the four subcorpora (although 'respect' is a keyword in the 2019 subcorpus). Undoubtedly, then, the key semantic domain analysis allowed me to access subtler discourses surrounding national identity than other corpus approaches. In combination with concordance analysis, the key semantic domain approach was successful in achieving breadth through diachronicity and depth through micro-linguistic analysis. The approach was novel: to my knowledge, existing linguistic studies of national identity discourse that employ semantic tagging, such as Prentice (2010), are not diachronic.

One of the biggest potential challenges to completing this project was the Covid-19 pandemic, which affected the interview design. Ethical approval was awarded in February 2020, just weeks before the first lockdown in the UK restricted travel. As a result, interview recruitment had to be conducted online. This proved difficult, partly because with a pandemic raging, people were less concerned about Brexit (Davies and Carter, 2021), and partly because it restricted the pool of available participants to those who had the socio-economic and technological privilege to use social media. This inevitably had a knock-on effect, as older participants were not only less likely to use social media but also unfamiliar with the video conferencing software through which the interviews were conducted. Consequently, there was a clear younger, Remain-voting self-selection bias and snowball sampling was required to reach older Leave voters. I also had to conduct some interviews via telephone rather than video conferencing software, to enable older people to participate. This restriction meant that I could not comment on paralinguistic features in most of the Leave-voting interviews, which was a loss in terms of the richness of the data in comparison to face-to-face interviews.

Despite these challenges, there were clear benefits to conducting interviews via video conferencing software. As Hanna and Mwale (2017: 260) argue, software such as Skype, which enables participants to be interviewed from their homes, 'provides a space for interviews that in some sense is both "public" and "private"' which can 'lessen feelings of intimidation for participants'. This consideration was especially important in my project as discourses about Brexit are highly emotive (Davies and Carter, 2021; Patel and Connelly, 2019) and some Leave-voting participants expressed concerns about the intentions of the project. Joining from their homes placed a degree of distance between the researcher and the interviewee that potentially helped participants to share 'controversial' opinions. I hope, then, that the final analytical chapter of this book demonstrates changing approaches in the face of unprecedented crisis does not have to be conceptualized only as a limitation.

Like Davies and Carter (2021), I decided to adopt as much of a 'value-free' position as possible during the interviews I conducted for this book. This means that I informed participants when seeking consent that I was interested in the language they used to talk about their national identity and that it did not matter how they voted or what their opinion of Brexit was. As a result of this commitment, there were moments, like those described by Davies and Carter (2021: 175), when I chose not to challenge particular views because 'the research [was] not actually on the interrogation of people's political views', but their language choices when talking about national identity. For instance, when Participant E worried that she had 'said something out of turn', I replied that 'this is about your own experiences and opinions so there is no sense of anything being not the right thing to say'. This approach was, at times, uncomfortable and challenged my identity as a liberal Remain voter. However, I found upon analysing the interviews that I tended to engage in more laughter and backchannels with Remain-voting participants than Leave-voting participants, so I was not as 'value-free' in my approach as I had intended to be. Future research might consider, reflexively, the performance of interviewers' political identities through questions, laughter and other paralinguistic features.

Despite the challenges inherent in gathering and analysing this study's third data set, I would not choose to forego the public opinion section of the book because the interviewing process was a lesson in tolerance for me. I voted to Remain in the 2016 referendum and wanted to understand why some members of my family so passionately voted to Leave, and why others were more likely to favour Scottish independence after the referendum. This personal investment in the subject matter, while crucial for sustaining my interest in the project over three years, meant that I had preconceptions about what constituted a Leave or Remain voter. It was through talking to people who voted differently from me that I was able to understand that there is more common ground between Leave and Remain voters than I had anticipated (see also Davies and Carter, 2021). CDA research that foregoes interviewing may well prevent analysts from this transformative research experience. It inevitably also relies solely on the perspective of the analyst which this book does not do. Talking to citizens forced me to acknowledge that the critical discourse analytical approach of identifying a sociological problem and deconstructing it becomes more nuanced when the researcher works with real people, whose motivations are often more complex than faceless media outlets with socio-political power.

Beyond this, Chapter 6 has carved a new methodological path in its analysis of stories to understand how individuals position themselves in relation to Brexit. While research into lay attitudes towards Brexit has been conducted previously, often the analysis has been thematically structured or has considered broader patterns in the data (e.g. Andreouli, 2020; Davies, 2021). This book has been the first to examine the phenomenon of Brexit-related national identity construction through a micro-linguistic analysis of stories. It has revealed the ways in which individual personal experiences interact with broader cultural narratives about Britain and about the political identities of 'Remainer' and 'Leaver'. By privileging the individual, it has problematized some of the homogenizing quantitative research findings about Brexit, such as the argument that Leave voters were often people who felt economically left behind or disadvantaged by globalization (Goodwin and Heath, 2016). Hopefully, then, future research can find a balance between more quantitative and qualitative approaches to political phenomena.

Avenues for future research

As any novel research does, this book encourages further questions. A natural follow-up study would examine how the recent media constructions of 'culture wars' depict the state of the nation and consider whether this divided representation damages emerging efforts by the UK government to construct a post-Brexit national identity narrative rooted in British soft power. Exploring how discourses about the Covid-19 pandemic intersected with representations of Brexit Britain, for example, would also be interesting. It could be, for instance, that the measures taken to instil national unity during the Covid-19 pandemic – such as the national clap for key workers on a Thursday, or the daily briefings given by cabinet ministers – led to a slightly ameliorated institutional narrative of Britishness in the media in 2021. It would be especially fruitful to consider within this the position of the National Health Service as an institution often cited as a symbol of British national identity (see Antosa and Demata (2021) for a study on NHS discourses in the context of Brexit and Covid-19). Similarly, it would be insightful to examine the political and media references made during the pandemic to the unity of the British public throughout the Second World War. It could be interesting to consider how Britain was discursively constructed by Britons on Twitter during the pandemic when citizens shared photos of empty supermarket shelves. Perhaps these top-down and bottom-up discourses could be compared. Finally, it would be fascinating to consider how more recent political developments, such as Boris Johnson's resignation and the installation of two other prime ministers without a general election, might have affected the national identity crisis I uncover in this book – particularly from the citizens' perspective.

Concluding remarks

At the end of Chapter 4, I mentioned Ashcroft and Bevir's (2021: 118) claim that 'attempting to unite our society around a common national identity is futile, as a singular vision of Britain – no matter how putatively inclusive – cannot accommodate the plural identities, narratives, and traditions that constitute our contested polity'. In many ways, this book provides empirical support for this claim: the identities constructed in the narratives demonstrate that Britishness has different meanings for the same person at different times, and different people at the same time. Although I have not addressed it in the analysis in Chapter 6 due to the focus on stories, the stimulus task in the interviews examined how participants responded to the discourses of division in the pro-Brexit press and the early discourses of national unity in the government documents. My analysis found that even participants who constructed division in their stories were at best ambivalent towards the constructions of division in the media; some participants accused the pro-Brexit press of 'handwringing'. At the same time, discourses of unity in Theresa May's speech were labelled as 'disingenuous' and untrue. It appears, then, that for most participants, the political and media constructions of Britain and Britishness miss the mark precisely because they do not account for the 'inherent pluralism' (Ashcroft and Bevir, 2021: 129) of Britishness, brought about by the loss of empire and increasing globalization. In the words of Kenny (2012: 158), who was talking of Englishness, the politics of *Britishness* is 'now defined by the struggles in which . . . contending accounts are engaged'.

Ashcroft and Bevir (2021) go on convincingly to argue that 'to prevent the permanent fracturing of the polity itself', we must 'decentre the imagined national community' and focus on the 'plethora of communities and identities that comprise it' (Ashcroft and Bevir, 2021: 130). Part of this challenge will be to find discourses capable of centering these multiple communities without falling into the trap of discourses of division and linguistic Othering of the kind identified in this book. After all, discourses of difference can be just as problematic as homogenizing discourses. This is where linguistic research can be of use; analyses of language, context and social ramifications can provide evidence of how identity is being construed and contested across different domains and can raise awareness of the power of discourses of national identity to simultaneously include and exclude. By demystifying the discourses of the imagined community of Brexit Britain, this book has tried to make readers aware of the exclusionary effects of the language of national identity and the effect that this can have on feelings of belonging.

Ultimately, the book has shown that the transition from pre- to post-Brexit Britain was a crucial period of destabilization for institutional and lay national identity narratives. At this point, it seems sensible to predict that the next few years are likely to be just as important – if not more so – as post-Brexit Britain defines its place in a world plagued by the intersecting crises of, inter alia, war, climate change and a rising cost of living. The question will be if, and how, the UK can step back from the 'precipice' envisioned by several participants in this study and move beyond the widespread narrative of national disunity to discourses which account for the complex, contested and multiple nature of (supra)national identities in the UK.

Notes

Chapter 1

1 'Brexit' is a blend of *Britain/British* and *exit*. It was first used in 2010 but increased in usage around 2016 when it was used to refer to Britain's withdrawal from the EU (Mair, 2019).
2 Harmsen and Spiering (2004: 16) argue that 'the most common British usages of the term "Eurosceptic"' imply 'an opposition to UK membership of the European Union and its antecedents, rather than a milder lack of enthusiasm for the project'. They posit that British Euroscepticism goes beyond opposition to European integration and is 'rooted in a deeper sense of a (Franco-German dominated) Continent as "the Other"' (2004: 16).
3 See Westlake (2017) for more on how the EU membership referendum of 2016 came to be. He argues that 'the 23 June 2016 referendum was not only "about" Cameron's 2013 decision, nor was it only about the Conservatives and nor, ultimately, was it only about the UK. The UK's mainstream parties had been toying with the idea since before the UK even joined the EEC in 1973 and had increasingly played with it after 1993' (2017: 14).
4 See Brusenbauch Meislová, Koller, Kopf et al. (2021) for an introduction to a special issue on representations of Brexit from outside of the UK.
5 In this book, ideology is interpreted as 'a socially and politically dominant set of values and beliefs which are not "out there" but are constructed in all texts especially through language' (Carter and Nash, 1990: 21). Within this conceptualization of ideology, the researcher explores how ideologies 'impregnate a society's modes of thinking, speaking, experiencing and behaving, are therefore a necessary "condition" for action and belief within a social formation and hence are crucial in the construction of personal identity' (Carter and Nash, 1990: 21). This definition is selected because it usefully highlights the roles that language plays in conveying ideologies and ideologies play in the construction of identities.
6 See Rone (2022) for an insight into the role of sovereignty in citizen campaigns and street protests about Brexit.

Chapter 2

1. Of course, newspapers and news websites are part of a media ecology that also includes social media. This book does not consider the role of social media in the discursive construction of national identities, but for those interested in social media research on Brexit, the following work is available: Angouri et al. (2018), Bennett (2019), Bossetta et al. (2018), Bouko and Garcia (2020) and Hansson and Page (2022).

Chapter 3

1. It is worth noting that, since all participants are from England, the representations of Britishness in these stories are Anglo-British. It is important for future research to consider constructions of Britishness among Scottish, Welsh and Northern Irish people.
2. For a detailed introduction to process types, see Thompson (2013).

Chapter 5

1. It is important to recognize that incongruity in British political conceptualizations of the UK–EU relationship is not new: David Cameron's position on UK–EU ties was also notoriously inconsistent (Brusenbauch Meislová, 2019b).
2. As I outline in Parnell (2022c: 400), 'The noun "friendship" has long appeared in international treaties as a boundary producing term that recognises the distinctiveness of the two parties' (see, e.g., Roshchin, 2011).

References

Acheson, D. (1962). Dean Acheson 1893–1971 American politician. In: Ractliffe, S. (ed.) *Oxford Essential Quotations*. Oxford: Oxford University Press. Available at: https://www-oxfordreference-com.nottingham.idm.oclc.org/view/10.1093/acref/9780191866692.001.0001/q-oro-ed6-00000015 (Accessed: 7 October 2023).

Adler-Nissen, R., Galpin, C. and Rosamond, B. (2017). Performing Brexit: How a post-Brexit world is imagined outside the United Kingdom. *The British Journal of Politics and International Relations*, 19(3): 573–591.

Adler, K. (2019). Jean-Claude Juncker: 'I've had enough Brexit', outgoing EU chief says. *BBC News*. Available at: https://www.bbc.co.uk/news/world-europe-50308647 (Accessed: 15 December 2021).

Agnisola, G., Weir, S. and Johnson, K. (2019). The voices that matter: A narrative approach to understanding Scottish Fishers' perspectives of Brexit. *Marine Policy*, 110, 103563.

Alkhammash, R. (2020). Discursive representation of the EU in Brexit-related British media. *GEMA Online® Journal of Language Studies*, 20(1): 77–91.

Allen, K. (2016). IMF says Brexit would trigger UK recession. *The Guardian*, 18 June. Available at: https://www.theguardian.com/business/2016/jun/18/imf-says-brexit-would-trigger-uk-recession-eu-referendum (Accessed: 15 December 2021).

Andersen, J. G. and Bjørklund, T. (1990). Structural changes and new cleavages: The progress parties in Denmark and Norway. *Acta Sociologica*, 33(3): 195–217.

Anderson, B. (2006). *Imagined Communities: Reflections on the Origin and Spread of Nationalism*. Rev ed. London: Verso.

Andreouli, E. (2020). Lay Rhetoric on Brexit. In: Demasi, M. A., Burke, S. and Tileaga, C. (eds.) *Political Communication*. Palgrave Studies in Discursive Psychology. Switzerland: Palgrave Macmillan, pp. 63–87.

Andreouli, E., Greenland, K. and Figgou, L. (2019). Lay discourses about Brexit and prejudice: 'Ideological creativity' and its limits in Brexit debates. *European Journal of Social Psychology*, 50(2): 309–322.

Angouri, J., Boukala, S. and Dimitrakopoulou, D. (2018). From Grexit to Brexit and back: Mediatisation of economy and the politics of fear in the Twitter discourses of the Prime Ministers of Greece and the UK. *Language@internet*, 16.

Anthias, F. (2008). Thinking through the lens of translocal positionality: An intersectionality frame for understanding identity and belonging. *Translocations: Migration and Social Change*, 4(1): 5–20.

Antosa, S. and Demata, M. (2021). Get Covid done: Discourses on the National Health Service (NHS) during Brexit and the coronavirus pandemic. *Textus*, 34(2): 47–65.

Arminen, I. (2004). Second stories: The salience of interpersonal communication for mutual help in alcoholics anonymous. *Journal of Pragmatics*, 36(2): 319–347.

Ashcroft, L. (2016). *How the United Kingdom Voted on Thursday... and Why*. Available at: https://lordashcroftpolls.com/2016/06/how-the-united-kingdom-voted-and-why/ (Accessed: 15 December 2021).

Ashcroft, R. and Bevir, M. (2016). Pluralism, national identity and citizenship: Britain after Brexit. *The Political Quarterly*, 87(3): 355–359.

Ashcroft, R. and Bevir, M. (2021). Brexit and the myth of British national identity. *British Politics*, 16: 117–132.

Atkins, J. (2022). Rhetoric and audience reception: An analysis of Theresa May's vision of Britain and Britishness after Brexit. *Politics*, 42(2): 216–230.

Aughey, A. (2007). *The politics of Englishness*. Manchester: Manchester University Press.

Baker, P. (2006). *Using Corpora in Discourse Analysis*. London: Continuum.

Baker, P., Gabrielatos, C., KhosraviNik, M., et al. (2008). A useful methodological synergy? Combining critical discourse analysis and corpus linguistics to examine discourses of refugees and asylum seekers in the UK press. *Discourse & Society*, 19(3): 273–306.

Bakhtin, M. (1981). *The Dialogic Imagination*. Austin: University of Texas Press.

BBC News. (2016a). Brexit vote: Nicola Sturgeon statement in full. 24 June. Available at: https://www.bbc.co.uk/news/uk-scotland-36620375 (Accessed: 21 June 2021).

BBC News. (2016b). Brexit: David Cameron to quit after UK votes to leave EU. 24 June. Available at: https://www.bbc.co.uk/news/uk-politics-36615028 (Accessed: 15 December 2021).

BBC News. (2016c). Reality Check: What role do unelected EU officials play? Available at: https://www.bbc.co.uk/news/uk-politics-eu-referendum-36429482 (Accessed: 15 December 2021).

BBC News. (2018a). Brexit secretary David Davis resigns. *BBC News*, 9 July. Available at: https://www.bbc.co.uk/news/uk-politics-44761056 (Accessed: 7 October 2023).

BBC News. (2018b). Juncker: 'Those who reject Brexit deal will be disappointed'. *BBC News*, 25 November. Available at: https://www.bbc.co.uk/news/av/uk-politics-46334316 (Accessed: 7 October 2023).

BBC News. (2019). MPs' fury at Boris Jonson's 'dangerous language'. Available at: https://www.bbc.co.uk/news/uk-politics-49833804 (Accessed: 2 August 2023).

BBC News. (2020). Brexit: What are problem issues in UK-EU trade talks? *BBC News*, 8 September 2020. Available at: https://www.bbc.co.uk/news/av/uk-politics-54073996 (Accessed: 28 April 2021).

BBC News. (2021a). EU referendum: The result in maps and charts. Available at: https://www.bbc.co.uk/news/uk-politics-36616028 (Accessed: 15 February 2022).

BBC News. (2021b). Covid: What is happening with the EU vaccine rollout? 27 April. Available at: https://www.bbc.co.uk/news/explainers-52380823 (Accessed: 28 April 2021).

BBC News. (2021c). Impact of Brexit on economy 'worse than Covid'. *BBC News*, 27 October. Available at: https://www.bbc.co.uk/news/business-59070020 (Accessed: 15 December 2021).

BBC News. (2021d). Joe Biden plays down chances of UK-US trade deal. *BBC News*, 22 September. Available at: https://www.bbc.co.uk/news/uk-politics-58646017 (Accessed: 7 October 2023).

Beaumont, P. (2017). Brexit, Retrotopia and the perils of post-colonial delusions, *Global Affairs*, 3(4–5): 379–390.

Bednarek, M. (2009). Corpora and discourse: A three-pronged approach to analyzing linguistic data. In: Haugh, M. (ed.) *Selected Proceedings of the 2008 HCSNet Workshop on Designing the Australian National Corpus.* Cascadilla Proceedings Project. Somerville, MA, pp. 19–24.

Bednarek, M. (2016). Voices and values in the news: News media talk, news values and attribution. *Discourse, Context and Media*, 11: 27–37.

Bednarek, M. and Caple, H. (2017). *The Discourse of News Values: How News Organizations Create Newsworthiness*. Oxford: Oxford University Press.

Bellucci, P., Sanders, D. and Serricchio, F. (2012). Explaining European identity. In: Sanders, D. Bellucci, P., Toka, G., et al. (eds.) *The Europeanisation of National Polities? Citizenship and Support in Post-Enlargement Union*. Oxford: Oxford University Press, pp. 61–90.

Benhabib, S. (1998). *Democracy and Difference: Contesting the Boundaries of the Political*. Princeton: Princeton University Press.

Bennett, S. (2018). *Constructions of Migrant Integration in British Public Discourse: Becoming British*. London: Bloomsbury.

Bennett, S. (2019). 'Crisis' as a discursive strategy in Brexit referendum campaigns. *Critical Discourse Studies*, 16(4): 449–464.

Bennett, S. (2022). Mythopoetic legitimation and the recontextualisation of Europe's foundational myth. *Journal of Language and Politics*, 21(2): 370–389.

Benson, M. and Lewis, C. (2019). Brexit, British people of colour in the EU-27 and everyday racism in Britain and Europe. *Ethnic and Racial Studies*, 42(13): 2211–2228.

Benwell, B. and Stokoe, E. (2006). *Discourse and Identity*. Edinburgh: Edinburgh University Press.

Bhambra, G. K. (2017). Brexit, Trump, and 'methodological whiteness': On the misrecognition of race and class. *The British Journal of Sociology*, 68(S1): 214–232.

Billig, M. (1995). *Banal Nationalism*. London: Sage.

Bland, A. (2016). How did the language of politics get so toxic? Available at: https://www.theguardian.com/politics/2016/jul/31/how-did-the-language-of-politics-get-so-toxic (Accessed: 2 August 2023).

Blommaert, J. (2005). *Discourse: A Critical Introduction*. New York: Cambridge University Press.

Blommaert, J. (2007). Sociolinguistics and discourse analysis: Orders of indexicality and polycentricity. *Journal of Multicultural Discourses*, 2(2): 115–130.

Blommaert, J. (2015). Chronotopes, scales, and complexity in the study of language in society. *Annual Review of Anthropology*, 44: 105–116.
BNC. (2008). BNC sampler: XML edition. Available at: http://www.natcorp.ox.ac.uk/corpus/sampler/sampler.pdf (Accessed: 12 January 2024).
Bogdanor, V. (2020). *Britain and Europe in a Troubled World*. New Haven: Yale University Press.
Bolt, M. (2022). Britain, Britishness, and exceptionalism within the rhetoric of David Cameron. *British Politics*, 18(1): 128–146.
Bond, R. and McCrone, D. (2004). The growth of English regionalism? Institutions and identity. *Regional & Federal Studies*, 14(1): 1–25.
Bossetta, M., Segesten, A. D. and Trenz, H.-J. (2018). Political participation on Facebook during Brexit: Does user engagement on media pages stimulate engagement with campaigns? *Journal of Language and Politics*, 17(2): 173–194.
Bouko, C. and Garcia, D. (2019). Citizens' reactions to Brexit on Twitter: A content and discourse analysis. In: Koller, V., Kopf, S. and Miglbauer, M. (eds.) *Discourses of Brexit*. London: Routledge, pp. 171–190.
Bouko, C. and Garcia, D. (2020). Patterns of emotional tweets: The case of Brexit after the referendum results. In: Bouvier, G. and Rosenbaum, J. (eds.) *Twitter, the Public Sphere, and the Chaos of Online Deliberation*. Cham: Palgrave Macmillan, pp. 175–203.
Bourdieu, P. (1991). *Language and Symbolic Power*. Cambridge, MA: Harvard University Press.
Breuilly, J. (1993). *Nationalism and the State*. Manchester: Manchester University Press.
Brezina, V. (2018). *Statistics in Corpus Linguistics*. Cambridge: Cambridge University Press.
Bromley-Davenport, H., MacLeavy, J. and Manley, D. (2018). Brexit in Sunderland: The production of difference and division in the UK referendum on European Union membership. *Environment and Planning C: Politics and Space*, 37(5): 795–812.
Brookes, G. and Baker, P. (2021). *Obesity in the News: Language and Representation in the Press*. Cambridge: Cambridge University Press.
Brown, K. and Mondon, A. (2021). Populism, the media, and the mainstreaming of the far right: The Guardian's coverage of populism as a case study. *Politics*, 41(3): 279–295.
Browne, I. (2017). Neo-liberalism, identity and Brexit. *Romanian Review of Political Sciences & International Relations*, 14(1): 89–110.
Browning, C. S. (2018). Brexit populism and fantasies of fulfilment. *Cambridge Review of International Affairs*, 32(3): 222–244.
Brusenbauch Meislová, M. (2019a). Brexit means Brexit---Or does it? The legacy of Theresa May's discursive treatment of Brexit. *The Political Quarterly*, 90(4): 681–689.

Brusenbauch Meislová, M. (2019b). All things to all people? Discursive patterns on UK–EU relationship in David Cameron's speeches. *British Politics*, 14: 681–689.

Brusenbauch Meislová, M. (2022). Discursive construction of affective polarization in Brexit Britain: Opinion-based identities and outgroup differentiation. In: Pérez-Escolar, M. and Noguera-Vivo, J. M. (eds.) *Hate Speech and Polarization in Participatory Society*. Abingdon and New York: Routledge, pp. 98–112.

Brusenbauch Meislová, M., Koller, V., Kopf, S., et al. (2021). Recontextualizing Brexit: Discursive Representations from outside the UK. *Critical Approaches to Discourse Analysis Across Disciplines*, 13(1): 1–11.

Bucholtz, M. and Hall, K. (2004). Language and identity. In: Duranti, A. (ed.) *A Companion to Linguistic Anthropology*. Oxford: Blackwell Publishing, pp. 369–394.

Bucholtz, M. and Hall, K. (2005). Identity and interaction: A sociocultural linguistic approach. *Discourse Studies*, 7(4–5): 585–614.

Bucholtz, M. and Hall, K. (2010). Locating identity in language. In: Llamas, C. and Watt, D. (eds.) *Language and Identities*. Edinburgh: Edinburgh University Press, pp. 18–28.

Buckledee, S. (2018). *The Language of Brexit: How Britain Talked Its Way Out of the European Union*. London: Bloomsbury.

Bucktin, C. (2013). 'Captain Hook' Abu Hamza pleas for transfer to softer jail in America as his stumps have become infected. *Daily Mirror*. Available at: https://www.mirror.co.uk/news/world-news/captain-hook-abu-hamza-pleas-2854750 (Accessed: 8 August 2023).

Burr, V. (2015). *An Introduction to Social Constructionism*. London: Routledge.

Cabinet Office. (2021). *Global Britain in a Competitive Age: The Integrated Review of Security, Defence, Development and Foreign Policy*. Available at: https://assets.publishing.service.gov.uk/government/uploads/system/uploads/attachment_data/file/975077/Global_Britain_in_a_Competitive_Age-_the_Integrated_Review_of_Security_ _Defence__Development_and_Foreign_Policy.pdf (Accessed: 15 December 2021).

Calhoun, C. (2017). Populism, nationalism and Brexit. In: Outhwaite, W. (ed.) *Brexit: Sociological Responses*. Cambridge: Cambridge University Press, pp. 55–76.

Cameron, D. (2013). *EU Speech at Bloomberg*. Available at: https://www.gov.uk/government/speeches/eu-speech-at-bloomberg (Accessed: 4 December 2019).

Cap, P. (2019). 'Britain is full to bursting point!': Immigration themes in the Brexit discourse of the UK Independence Party. In: Koller, V., Kopf, S. and Miglbauer, M. (eds.) *Discourses of Brexit*. Oxford: Routledge, pp. 69–85.

Capoccia, G. (2016). Critical junctures. In: Fioretos, O., Falleti, T. and Sheingate, A. (eds.) *The Oxford Handbook of Historical Institutionalism*. Oxford: Oxford University Press, pp. 89–106.

Carey, S. (2002). Undivided loyalties: Is national identity an Obstacle to European integration? *European Union Politics*, 3(4): 387–419.

Carl, N., Dennison, J. and Evans, G. (2019). European but not European enough: An explanation for Brexit. *European Union Politics*, 20(2): 282–304.

Carranza, I. (2015). Narrating and arguing: From plausibility to local moves. In: de Fina, A. and Georgakopoulou, A. (eds.) *The Handbook of Narrative Analysis*. New Jersey: Wiley Blackwell, pp. 57–75.

Carrell, S. (2019). Sturgeon demands Scottish independence referendum powers after SNP landslide. *The Guardian*, 13 December. Available at: https://www.theguardian.com/politics/2019/dec/13/nicola-sturgeon-to-demand-powers-for-scottish-independence-referendum (Accessed: 17 April 2020).

Carter, R. and Nash, W. (1990). *Seeing Through Language: A Guide to Styles of English Writing*. Oxford: Basil Blackwell.

Catenaccio, P. (2008). Press releases as a hybrid genre. *Pragmatics*, 18(1): 9–31.

Charles, C., Pecorari, D. and Hunston, S. (eds.) (2009). *Academic Writing: At the Interface of Corpus and Discourse*. London: Continuum.

Charteris-Black, J. (2019). *Metaphors of Brexit - No Cherries on the Cake?* Hampshire: Palgrave Macmillan.

Chernobrov, D. (2019). Who is the modern 'traitor'? 'Fifth column' accusations in US and UK politics and media. *Politics*, 39(3): 347–362.

Cinque, S., Nyberg, D. and Starkey, K. (2021). 'Living at the border of poverty': How theater actors maintain their calling through narrative identity work. *Human Relations*, 74(11): 1755–1780.

Clarke, J. and Newman, J. (2019). What's the subject? Brexit and politics as articulation. *Journal of Community & Applied Social Psychology*, 29(1): 67–77.

Cockburn, P. (2018). Brexit Britain is facing a deep crisis of self-confidence. It will only end in tears – And rising nationalism. *The Independent*, 7 December. Available at: https://www.independent.co.uk/voices/brexit-britain-nationalism-racism-class-religion-leave-remain-identity-a8672691.html (Accessed: 17 April 2020).

Colley, L. (1992). *Britons: Forging the Nation 1707–1837*. London: Yale University Press.

Conboy, M. (2006). *Tabloid Britain: Constructing a Community Through Language*. Oxford: Routledge.

Condor, S. (2000). Pride and prejudice: Identity management in English people's talk about 'this country'. *Discourse & Society*, 11(2): 175–205.

Cook, G. (2011). British applied linguistics: Impacts of and impacts on. *Applied Linguistics Review*, 3(1): 25–45.

Coupland, N. (2008). The delicate constitution of identity in face-to-face accommodation: A response to Trudgill. *Language in Society*, 37(2): 267–270.

Curtice, J., Hudson, N. and Montagu, I. (eds.). (2020). *British Social Attitudes: The 37th Report*. London: The National Centre for Social Research.

Daddow, O. (2006). Euroscepticism and the culture of the discipline of history. *Review of International Studies*, 32(2): 309–328.

Daddow, O. (2012). The UK media and 'Europe': From permissive consensus to destructive dissent. *International Affairs*, 88(6): 1219–1236.

Daddow, O. (2015). Interpreting the outsider tradition in British European policy speeches from Thatcher to Cameron. *Journal of Common Market Studies*, 53(1): 71–88.

Daily Express. (2016). We're out of the EU. *Daily Express*, 25 June.

Daily Mail. (2016). *Lies. Greedy Elites. Or a Great Future Outside a Broken, Dying Europe… If You Believe in Britain Vote Leave* . Available at: https://www.dailymail.co.uk/debate/article-3653385/Lies-greedy-elites-divided-dying-Europe-Britain-great-future-outside-broken-EU.html (Accessed: 13 January 2024).

Daily Star. (2016). *Cam Quits, BoJo Favourite for PM. Now Let's Make Britain Great Again*. Available at: https://www.pressreader.com/uk/daily-star/20160625/283132838125934 (Accessed: 13 January 2024).

Davies, K. (2021). Sticking together in 'Divided Britain': Talking Brexit in everyday family relationships. *Sociology*, 56(1): 97–113.

Davies, K. and Carter, A. (2021). Research relationalities and shifting sensitivities: Doing ethnographic research about Brexit and everyday family relationships. *Families, Relationships and Societies*, 10(1): 169–177.

Dearing, J. and Rogers, E. (1996). *Agenda-Setting*. London: Sage.

De Cillia, R., Reisigl, M. and Wodak, R. (1999). The discursive construction of national identities. *Discourse & Society*, 10(2): 149–173.

De Fina, A. (2003). *Identity in Narrative: A Study of Immigrant Discourse*. Amsterdam: John Benjamins.

De Fina, A. (2009). Narratives in interview. The case of accounts: For an interactional approach to narrative genres. *Narrative Inquiry*, 19(2): 233–358.

De Fina, A. (2015). Narrative and identities. In: De Fina, A. and Georgakopoulou A. (eds.) *The Handbook of Narrative Analysis*. Malden, MA: Wiley Blackwell, pp. 351–368.

De Fina, A. and Georgakopoulou, A. (2012). *Analyzing Narrative: Discourse and Sociolinguistic Perspectives*. Cambridge: Cambridge University Press.

Delanty, G. and Rumford, C. (2005). *Rethinking Europe: Social Theory and the Implications of Europeanization*. London: Routledge.

Demata, M. and Zummo, M. L. (2020). 'The war is over': Militarising the language and framing the nation in Post-Brexit discourse. In: Balirano, G. and Hughes, B. (eds.) *Homing in on Hate: Critical Discourse Studies of Hate Speech, Discrimination and Inequality in the Digital Age*. Napoli: Paolo Loffredo, pp. 169–189.

Department for International Trade. (2017). *Preparing for Our Future UK Trade Policy*. Available at: https://assets.publishing.service.gov.uk/government/uploads/system/uploads/attachment_data/file/654714/Preparing_for_our_future_UK_trade_policy_Report_Web_Accessible.pdf (Accessed: 5 December 2019).

Diez Medrano, J. (2003). *Framing Europe: Attitudes to European Integration in Germany, Spain, and the United Kingdom*. New Jersey: Princeton University Press.

Di Masso, A., Dixon, J. and Durrheim, K. (2013). Place attachment as discursive practice. In: Manzo, L. and Devine-Wright, P. (eds.). *Place Attachment: Advances in Theory, Methods and Applications*. London: Routledge, pp. 75–86.

Donoghue, M. and Kuisma, M. (2022). Taking back control of the welfare state: Brexit, rational-imaginaries and welfare chauvinism. *West European Politics*, 45(1): 177–199.

Drummond, R. and Schleef, E. (2016). Identity in variationist sociolinguistics. In: Preece, S. (ed.) *The Routledge Handbook of Language and Identity*. London: Routledge, pp. 50–65.

Du Bois, J. W. (2007). The stance triangle. In: Englebretson, R. (ed.) *Stancetaking in Discourse: Subjectivity, Evaluation, Interaction*. Philadelphia: John Benjamins, pp. 139–182.

Duchesne, S. and Frognier, A. (2008). National and European identifications: A dual relationship. *Comparative European Politics*, 6(2): 143–168.

Duffy, B. (2021). *UK's 'Culture War' Risks Leading to US-style Divisions – But We're Not There Yet*, 29 June. Available at: https://www.kcl.ac.uk/news/uks-culture-war-risks-leading-to-us-style-divisions-although-not-there-yet (Accessed: 8 August 2023).

Duffy, B., Hewlett, K., Murkin, G., et al. (2021). *'Culture Wars' in the UK*. Available at: https://www.kcl.ac.uk/policy-institute/assets/culture-wars-in-the-uk.pdf (Accessed: 8 August 2023).

Dugalès, N. and Tucker, G. (2012). Representations of representation: European institutions in the French and British press. In: Bayley, P. and Williams, G. (eds.) *European Identity: What the Media Say*. Oxford: Oxford University Press, pp. 21–54.

Eaton, M. and Smith, A. (2020). The use of historical analogy in the 2017 Parliamentary debates on the future of post-Brexit commonwealth trade. *Political Studies Review*, 18(4): 591–610.

Edgington, T. and Morris, C. (2021). Brexit: What's the Northern Ireland protocol? *BBC News*, 8 November. Available at: https://www.bbc.co.uk/news/explainers-53724381 (Accessed: 15 December 2021).

Eldridge, J., Kitzinger, J. and Williams, K. (1997). *The Mass Media and Power in Britain*. Oxford: Oxford University Press.

El-Enany, N. (2021). *Bordering Britain: Law, Race and Empire*. Manchester: Manchester University Press.

Elphicke, C. (2019). The ghost of project fear is back again, but Britain stands ready for Brexit. *BrexitCentral*, 8 July. Available at: https://brexitcentral.com/the-ghost-of-project-fear-is-back-again-but-britain-stands-ready-for-brexit/ (Accessed: 8 August 2020).

European Union. (2019). *EU citizenship*. Available at: https://europa.eu/european-union/about-eu/eu-citizenship_en (Accessed: 5 December 2019).

Eurostat. (2019). *Glossary: Extra-EU*. Available at: https://ec.europa.eu/eurostat/statistics-explained/index.php/Glossary:Extra-EU (Accessed: 5 December 2019).

Evans, C. (2019). Investigating 'care leaver' identity: A narrative analysis of personal experience stories. *Text & Talk*, 39(1): 25–45.

Express Online. (2019). Joy that turned to anger over big Brexit betrayal, express comment. *Express Online*, 30 March.

Fabbrini, S. (2019). Constructing and de-constructing the European political identity: The contradictory logic of the EU's institutional system. *Comparative European Politics*, 17(4): 477–490.

Fairclough, N. (1989). *Language and Power*. London: Longman.

Fairclough, N. (2003). *Analysing Discourse: Textual Analysis for Social Research*. London: Routledge.

Fairclough, N. (2010). *Critical Discourse Analysis: The Critical Study of Language*. London: Routledge.

Fairclough, N. (2011). Critical discourse analysis. In: Gee, J. P. and Handford, M. (eds.) *The Routledge Handbook of Discourse Analysis*. London: Routledge, pp. 9–20.

Fairclough, N. (2015). *Language and Power*. 3rd ed. Oxford: Routledge.

Farage, N. (2013). *Nigel Farage's Speech at the UKIP Conference--Full Text and Audio*. Available at: http://blogs.spectator.co.uk/coffeehouse/2013/09/nigel-farages-speech-full-text-and-audio (Accessed: 9 December 2019).

Filsinger, M., Wamsler, S., Erhardt, J., et al. (2021). National identity and populism: The relationship between conceptions of nationhood and populist attitudes. *Nations and Nationalism*, 27(3): 656–672.

Financial Times. (2016). *Britain Has Had Enough of Experts, Says Gove*. Available at: https://www.ft.com/content/3be49734-29cb-11e6-83e4-abc22d5d108c (Accessed: 31 March 2022).

Financial Times. (2021). *Labour Shortages Must Not Be Seen as Simple Case of Business vs Brexit*. Available at: https://www.ft.com/content/7c8bf648-dd0a-4558-9544-f77bde4798b2 (Accessed: 15 December 2021).

Friedland, L. A., Hove, T. and Rojas, H. (2006). The networked public sphere. *Javnost – the Public*, 13(4): 5–26.

Full Fact. (2017). *£350 Million EU Claim 'a Clear Misuse of Official Statistics.'* Available at: https://fullfact.org/europe/350-million-week-boris-johnson-statistics-authority-misuse/ (Accessed: 15 December 2021).

Gabrielatos, C. (2018). Keyness analysis: Nature, metrics and techniques. In: Taylor, C. and Marchi, A. (eds.) *Corpus Approaches to Discourse: A Critical Review*. Routledge: London, pp. 225–258.

Gabrielatos, C. and Baker, P. (2008). Fleeing, sneaking, flooding: A corpus analysis of discursive constructions of refugees and asylum seekers in the UK Press, 1996–2005. *Journal of English Linguistics*, 36(1): 5–38.

Garside, R. and Smith, N. (1997). A hybrid grammatical tagger: CLAWS4. In: Garside, R., Leech, G. and McEnery, A. (eds.) *Corpus Annotation: Linguistic Information from Computer Text Corpora*. London: Longman, pp. 179–193.

Garton-Ash, T. (2001). Is Britain European? *International Affairs*, 77 (1): 1–13.

Gaskarth, J. (2013). *British Foreign Policy: Crises, Conflicts and Future Challenges*. Cambridge: Polity.

Gaskarth, J. (2014). Strategizing Britain's role in the world. *International Affairs*, 90(3): 559–581.

Gaston, S. (2020). *UK Public Opinion on Foreign Policy and Global Affairs Annual Survey –2020*. London: British Foreign Policy Group.

Gawlewicz, A. (2020). 'Scotland's different': Narratives of Scotland's distinctiveness in the post-Brexit-vote era. *Scottish Affairs*, 29(3): 321–335.

Geddes, A. (2017). The referendum and Britain's broken immigration politics. In: Jackson, D., Thorsen, E. and Wring, D. (eds.) *EU Referendum Analysis 2016: Media, Voters and the Campaign*. Available at: http://www.meandeurope.co.uk/wp-content/uploads/EU-Referendum-Analysis-2016-Jackson-Thorsen-and-Wring-v2.pdf (Accessed: 28 April 2020).

Gee, J. P. (2001). *An Introduction to Discourse Analysis*. London: Routledge.

Georgakopoulou, A. (2007). *Small Stories, Interaction and Identities*. Amsterdam: Benjamins.

George, S. (1990). *An Awkward Partner: Britain in the European Community*. Oxford: Oxford University Press.

Gibbins, J. (2014). *Britain, Europe & National Identity: Self and Other in International Relations*. Hampshire: Palgrave Macmillan.

Gifford, C. (2016). Brexit: The destruction of a collective good. In: Jackson, D., Thorsen, E. and Wring, D. (eds.) *EU Referendum Analysis 2016: Media, Voters and the Campaign*. Poole: Bournemouth University, p. 15.

Gillings, M. and Mautner, G. (2023). Concordancing for CADS. Practical challenges and theoretical implications. *International Journal of Corpus Linguistics*. Online First.

Glencross, A. (2016). The great miscalculation: David Cameron's renegotiation and the EU referendum campaign. In: Jackson, D., Thorsen, E. and Wring, D. (eds.). *EU Referendum Analysis 2016: Media, Voters and the Campaign*. Poole: Bournemouth University, p. 19.

Goodman, S. and Speer, S. (2007). Category use in the construction of asylum seekers. *Discourse Studies*, 4(2): 165–185.

Goodwin, M. J. and Heath, O. (2016). The 2016 referendum, Brexit and the left behind: An aggregate-level analysis of the result. *The Political Quarterly*, 87(3): 323–332.

Government Digital Service. (2020). *Content Design: Planning, Writing and Managing Content*. Available at: https://www.gov.uk/guidance/content-design/content-types (Accessed: 15 December 2021).

Green, C. (2017). Mapping the Brexit vote. Available at: https://www.ox.ac.uk/news-and-events/oxford-and-brexit/brexit-analysis/mapping-brexit-vote (Accessed: 15 February 2022).

Greenfeld, L. and Eastwood, J. (2009). National identity. In: Boix, C. and Stokes, C. (eds.) *The Oxford Handbook of Comparative Politics*. Oxford: Oxford University Press, pp. 256–272.

Gumperz, J. J. and Cook-Gumperz, J. (1982). Introduction: Language and the communication of social identity. In: Gumperz, J. (ed.) *Language and Social Identity*. Cambridge: Cambridge University Press, pp. 1–21.

Habib, B. (2019). The success of Brexit Britain has left Project Fear on its deathbed. *Telegraph Online*, 20 September. Available at: https://www.telegraph.co.uk/politics/2019/09/20/success-brexit-britain-has-left-project-fear-deathbed/ (Accessed: 16 April 2020).

Hadfield, A. and Whitman, R. G. (2023). The diplomacy of 'Global Britain': Settling, safeguarding and seeking status. *International Politics*. Online First.

Hall, S. (1973). *Encoding and Decoding in the Television Discourse*. Centre for Contemporary Cultural Studies, University of Birmingham.

Hall, S. (1996). Introduction: Who needs 'identity'? In: Hall, S. and Du Gay, P. (eds.) *Questions of Cultural Identity*. London: Sage, pp. 1–17.

Halliday, M. A. K. (1985). *An Introduction to Functional Grammar*. London: Edward Arnold.

Halliday, M. A. K. and Matthiessen, C. (2004). *An Introduction to Functional Grammar*. 3rd ed. London: Hodder Arnold.

Hanna, P. and Mwale, S. (2017). 'I'm not with you, yet I Am . . .' virtual face-to-face interviews. In: Braun, V., Clarke, V. and Gray, D. (eds.) *Collecting Qualitative Data*. Cambridge: Cambridge University Press, pp. 235–255.

Hanel, P. H. and Wolf, L. J. (2020). Leavers and remainers after the Brexit referendum: More united than divided after all? *British Journal of Social Psychology*, 59(2): 470–493.

Hansard Society. (2019). *Audit of Political Engagement 16: The 2019 Report*. 16. London: Hansard Society. Available at: https://www.hansardsociety.org.uk/publications/reports/audit-of-political-engagement-16 (Accessed: 7 December 2020).

Hansson, S. and Page, R. (2022). Corpus-assisted analysis of legitimation strategies in government social media communication. *Discourse & Communication*, 16(5): 551–571.

Harcup, T. and O'Neill, D. (2017). What is News? News values revisited (again). *Journalism Studies*, 18(12): 1470–1488.

Hardman, R. (2017). ROBERT HARDMAN: Why the EU's hypocrite-in-chief is a prime example of the hubris that could tear it apart. *Daily Mail*, 3 January.

Hardt-Mautner, G. (1995). 'Only connect.' Critical discourse analysis and corpus linguistics. In: *UCREL Technical Paper 6*. Lancaster: Lancaster University.

Harmsen, R. and Spiering, M. (eds.) (2004). *Euroscepticism: Party Politics, National Identity and European Integration*. Amsterdam: Rodopi.

Hawkins, B. (2012). Nation, separation and threat: An analysis of British media discourses on the European Union treaty reform process. *Journal of Common Market Studies*, 50(4): 561–577.

Hayes, N. and Poole, R. (2022). A diachronic corpus-assisted semantic domain analysis of US presidential debates. *Corpora*, 17(3): 449–469.

Hearn, J. (2017). Vox Populi: Nationalism, globalisation and the balance of power in the making of Brexit. In: Outhwaite, W. (eds.) *Brexit: Sociological Responses*. London: Anthem Press, pp. 19–30.

Henderson, A., Jeffery, C., Liñeira, R., Scully, R., Wincott, D. and Wyn Jones, R. (2016). England, Englishness and Brexit. *The Political Quarterly*, 87(2): 187–199.

Henderson, A. and McEwen, N. (2005). Do shared values underpin national identity? Examining the role of values in national identity in Canada and the United Kingdom. *National Identities*, 7(2): 173–191.

Henderson, A. and Wyn Jones, R. (2021). *Englishness: The Political Force Transforming Britain*. Oxford: Oxford University Press.

Henkel, I. (2018). How the laughing, irreverent Briton trumped fact-checking: A textual analysis of fake news in British newspaper stories about the EU. *Journalism Education*, 6(3): 87–97.

Higgins, K. (2018). National belonging post-referendum: Britons living in other EU member states respond to 'Brexit'. *Area*, 51(2): 277–284.

HM Government. (2019). Global Britain in a competitive age. The Integrated Review of Security, Defence, Development and Foreign Policy. Available at: https://assets.publishing.service.gov.uk/government/uploads/system/uploads/attachment_data/file/975077/Global_Britain_in_a_Competitive_Age-_the_Integrated_Review_of_Security__Defence__Development_and_Foreign_Policy.pdf (Accessed: 3 August 2023).

HM Government. (2023). Integrated review refresh 2023: Responding to a more contested and volatile world. Available at: https://www.gov.uk/government/publications/integrated-review-refresh-023-respondingto-a-more-contested-and-volatile-world (Accessed: 3 August 2023).

Hobolt, S. B. (2016). The Brexit vote: A divided nation, a divided continent. *Journal of European Public Policy*, 23(9): 1259–1277.

Hobolt, S. B., Leeper, T. J. and Tilley, J. (2021). Divided by the vote: Affective polarization in the wake of the Brexit referendum. *British Journal of Political Science*, 51(4): 1476–1493.

Holmes, C. (1991). *A Tolerant Country? Immigrants, Refugees and Minorities in Britain*. London: Routledge.

Home Office. (2019). Hate crime, England and Wales, 2018/19. Available at: https://assets.publishing.service.gov.uk/media/5da47329ed915d17b9646841/hate-crime-1819-hosb2419.pdf (Accessed: 12 January 2024).

Hroch, M. (2019). The nation as the cradle of nationalism and patriotism. *Nations and Nationalism*, 26(1): 5–21.

Hug, A. (2020). *Finding Britain's Role in a Changing World: The Principles for Global Britain*. London: The Foreign Policy Centre. Available at: https://fpc.org.uk/publications/the-principles-for-global-britain/ (Accessed: 18 November 2020).

Hume, M. (2004). So Captain 'Hamza' Hook is a threat? Oh no he isn't! *The Times*. Available at: https://www.thetimes.co.uk/article/so-captain-hamza-hook-is-a-threat-oh-no-he-isnt-h2qjvh230cc (Accessed: 8 August 2023).

Hurst Media. (n.d.). Daily Express. Sensational stories that appeal to everyday people. Available at: https://www.hurstmediacompany.co.uk/daily-express-profile/ (Accessed: 30 July 2023).

Gaskell, J., Stoker, G., Jennings, W. and Devine, D. (2019). Will getting Brexit done restore political trust? Available at: https://ukandeu.ac.uk/wp-content/uploads/2020/09/Will-getting-Brexit-done-restore-political-trust.pdf (Accessed: 3 August 2023).

Ichijo, A. (2008). *The Balancing Act: National Identity and Sovereignty for Britain in Europe*. Exeter: Societas.

Ifversen, J. (2019). A guided tour into the question of Europe. In: Brolsma, M., Bruin, R. and Lok, M. (eds.) *Eurocentrism in European History and Memory*. Amsterdam: Amsterdam University Press, pp. 195–222.

Islentyeva, A. and Dunkel, D. (2022). National Myth in UK-EU representations by British conservative Prime Ministers from Churchill to Johnson. *Societies*, 12(14): 1–17.

ITV Central. (2020). People in the Midlands see themselves as more "English" than "British." *ITV Central*, 6 January. Available at: https://www.itv.com/news/central/2020-01-06/people-in-the-midlands-see-themselves-as-more-english-than-british/ (Accessed: 8 August 2023).

Jahedi, M., Abdullah, F. and Mukundan, J. (2014). An overview of focal approaches of critical discourse analysis. *International Journal of Education & Literary Studies*, 2(4): 28–35.

Jarvis, L., Marsden, L. and Atakav, E. (2020). Public conceptions and constructions of 'British values': A qualitative analysis. *The British Journal of Politics and International Relations*, 22(1): 85–101.

Jennings, W. and Stoker, G. (2016). The bifurcation of politics: Two Englands. *The Political Quarterly*, 87(3): 372–382.

Johnson, B. (2016). Please vote leave on Thursday, because we'll never get this chance again. *The Telegraph*, 19 June. Available at: https://www.telegraph.co.uk/news/2016/06/19/please-vote-leave-on-thursday-because-well-never-get-this-chance/ (Accessed: 18 May 2020).

Johnson, B. (2019). Boris Johnson: "Let's get Brexit done. Let's bring our country together." Full text of his conference speech. Available at: https://www.conservativehome.com/parliament/2019/10/boris-johnson-lets-get-brexit-done-lets-bring-our-country-together-full-text-of-his-conference-speech.html (Accessed: 28 April 2021).

Jones, R. H. (2020). (Inter)visibility: A rejoinder to 'Collecting qualitative data during a pandemic' by David Silverman. *Communication & Medicine*, 17(2): 187–190.

Joseph, G. G., Reddy, V. and Searle-Chatterjee, M. (1990). Eurocentrism in the social sciences. *Race & Class*, 31(4): 1–26.

Julios, C. (2008). *Contemporary British Identity. English Language, Migrants and Public Discourse*. Hampshire: Ashgate.

Jump, C. and Michell, J. (2021). *Educational Attainment Alone Can Correctly Classify Over 90% of Local Authorities by Voting Outcome in the EU Referendum*. Available at: https://blogs.lse.ac.uk/politicsandpolicy/educational-attainment-brexit/ (Accessed: 15 February 2022).

Kallis, A. (2013). 'Breaking taboos and 'mainstreaming the extreme': The debates on restricting Islamic symbols in contemporary Europe. In: Wodak, R., KhosraviNik, M. and Mral, B. (eds.) *Right-Wing Populism in Europe. Politics and Discourse*. London: Bloomsbury, pp. 55–70.

Kang, B. (2018). Collocation and word association. *International Journal of Corpus Linguistics*, 23(1): 85–113.

Kanter, J. (2021). We want more Britishness on TV, John Whittingdale tells broadcasters. *The Times*, 16 September.

Keith, J. (2019). 'Polish go home' – Racist messages appear in public areas in Dundee. *The Courier*, 14 March. Available at: https://www.thecourier.co.uk/fp/news/local/dundee/847130/polish-go-home-racist-messages-appear-in-public-areas-in-dundee/ (Accessed: 27 April 2020).

Kelley, N. (2019). *British Social Attitudes Survey: Britain's Shifting Identities and Attitudes*. 36. National Centre for Research.

Kennedy, C. R. (2022). Worthiness, unity, numbers and commitment: Strengthening qualitative corpus methods in the critical discourse analysis of protest press coverage. *Discourse & Society*, 33(5): 611–630.

Kennedy, C. R. (Forthcoming). Expressions of (de)legitimation in the UK press reporting of Brexit-related protests. In: Abdelhay, A., Gorski, C. and Makoni, S. (eds.) *Sociolinguistics of Protesting*. Berlin: De Gruyter.

Kenny, M. (2012). The many faces of Englishness. Identity, diversity and nationhood in England. *Public Policy Research*, 19(3): 152–159.

KhosraviNik, M. (2010). Actor descriptions, action attributions, and argumentation: Towards a systematization of CDA analytical categories in the representation of social groups. *Critical Discourse Studies*, 7(1): 55–72.

Koegler, C., Malreddy, P. K. and Tronicke, M. (2020). The colonial remains of Brexit: Empire nostalgia and narcissistic nationalism. *Journal of Postcolonial Writing*, 56(5): 585–592.

Koller, V., Kopf, S. and Miglbauer, M. (eds.) (2019). *Discourses of Brexit*. Oxford: Routledge.

Koller, V. and Ryan, J. (2019). A nation divided: Metaphors and scenarios in the media coverage of the 2016 British EU referendum. In: Hart, C. (ed.) *Cognitive Linguistic Approaches to Text and Discourse: From Poetics to Politics*. Edinburgh: Edinburgh University Press, pp. 131–156.

Kopf, S. (2019). 'Get your shyte together Britain': Wikipedians' treatment of Brexit. In: Koller, V., Kopf, S. and Miglbauer, M. (eds.) *Discourses of Brexit*. London: Routledge, pp. 155–170.

Krzyżanowski, M. (2010). *The Discursive Construction of European Identities: A Multilevel Approach to Discourse and Identity in the Transforming European Union*. Frankfurt am Main: Peter Lang.

Krzyżanowski, M. (2016). Recontextualisation of neoliberalism and the increasingly conceptual nature of discourse: Challenges for critical discourse studies. *Discourse & Society*, 27(3): 308–321.

Krzyżanowski, M. (2019). Brexit and the imaginary of 'crisis': A discourse-conceptual analysis of European news media. *Critical Discourse Studies*, 16(4): 465–490.

Kuhn, R. (2017). *Politics and the Media in Britain*. Hampshire: Palgrave Macmillan.

Labov, W. (1966). *The Social Stratification of English in New York City*. Washington, DC: Center for Applied Linguistics.

Labov, W. (1972). *Language in the Inner City: Studies in the Black English Vernacular*. Philadelphia: University of Pennsylvania Press.

Lakoff, G. and Johnson, M. (1980). *Metaphors We Live By*. Chicago: University of Chicago Press.

Law, A. (2001). Near and far: Banal national identity and the press in Scotland. *Media, Culture & Society*, 23(3): 299–317.

Lawler, S. (2002). Narrative in social research. In: May, T. (ed.) *Qualitative Research in Action*. London: Sage, pp. 242–258.

Leave, V. (2016). *Why Vote Leave*. Available at: http://www.voteleavetakecontrol.org/why_vote_leave.html (Accessed: 5 December 2019).

Le Bossé, M. (2021). Ethnonationalism. In: *Oxford Bibliographies*. Oxford: Oxford University Press.

Leith, M. S. and Sim, D. (2022). Indifference or hostility? Anti-Scottishness in a post-Brexit England. *Identities*, 30(4): 588–606..

Leith, M. S. and Soule, D. (2011). *Political Discourse and National Identity in Scotland*. Edinburgh: Edinburgh University Press.

Lennon, H. W. and Kilby, L. (2020). A multimodal discourse analysis of 'Brexit': Flagging the nation in political cartoons. In: Demasi, M. A., et al. (eds.) *Political Communication: Discursive Perspectives*. Switzerland: Palgrave Macmillan, pp. 115–146.

Levy, D., Aslan, B. and Bironzo, D. (2016). *UK Press Coverage of the EU Referendum*. Oxford: Reuters Institute for the Study of Journalism.

Linell, P. (2009). *Rethinking Language, Mind, and World Dialogically: Interactional and Contextual Theories of Human Sense-Making*. Charlotte, NC: Information Age Publishing.

Llamas, C., Watt, D. and Johnson, D. E. (2009). Linguistic accommodation and the salience of national identity markers in a border town. *Journal of Language and Social Psychology*, 28(4): 381–407.

Lutzky, U. and Kehoe, A. (2019). 'Friends don't let friends go Brexiting without a mandate': Changing discourses of Brexit in The Guardian. In: Koller, V., Kopf, S. and Miglbauer, M. (eds.) *Discourses of Brexit*. London: Routledge, pp. 104–120.

Maccaferri, M. (2019). Splendid isolation again? Brexit and the role of the press and online media in re-narrating the European discourse. *Critical Discourse Studies*, 16(4): 289–402.

Machin, D. and Mayr, A. (2012). *How to Do Critical Discourse Analysis: A Multimodal Introduction*. London: Sage.

Macnab, S. (2019). Nicola Sturgeon to talk up independent Scotland's EU status in Brussels visit. *The Scotsman*, 11 June. Available at: https://www.scotsman.com/news/politics/scottish-independence/nicola-sturgeon-to-talk-up-independent-scotland-s-eu-status-in-brussels-visit-1-4944888 (Accessed: 4 December 2019).

Mair, C. (2019). Brexitness: The Ebbs and flows of British Eurosceptic rhetoric since 1945. *Open Library of Humanities*, 5(1): 1–26.

Malkki, L. (1992). National geographic: The rooting of peoples and the territorialization of national identity among scholars and refugees. *Cultural Anthropology*, 7(1): 24–44.

Mann, R. and Fenton, S. (2017). *Nation, Class and Resentment: The Politics of National Identity in England, Scotland and Wales*. London: Palgrave Macmillan.

Manners, I. (2018). Political psychology of European integration: The (re)production of identity and difference in the Brexit debate. *Political Psychology*, 39(6): 1213–1232.

Marchi, A. (2018). Dividing up the data: Epistemological, methodological and practical impact of diachronic segmentation. In: Marchi, A. and Taylor, C. (eds.) *Corpus Approaches to Discourse: A Critical Review*. London: Routledge, pp. 174–196.

Marchi, A. and Partington, A. (2012). Does "Europe" have a common historical identity? In: Bayley, P. and Williams, G. (eds.) *European Identity: What the Media Say*. Oxford: Oxford University Press, pp. 118–148.

Marcussen, M., Risse, T., Engelmann-Martin, D., et al. (1999). Constructing Europe? The evolution of French, British and German nation state identities. *Journal of European Public Policy*, 6(4): 614–633.

Marquand, D. (1995). After Whig imperialism: Can there be a new British identity? *Journal of Ethnic and Migration Studies*, 21(2): 183–193.

Marshall, P. J. (1996). *Cambridge Illustrated History: British Empire*. Cambridge: Cambridge University Press.

Martin, J. and Rose, D. (2008). *Genre Relations: Mapping Culture*. London: Equinox.

Martin, J. R. and Plum, G. (1997). Construing experience: Some story genres. *Journal of Narrative and Life History*, 7(1–4): 299–308.

Mautner, G. (2001). British national identity in the European Context. In: Musolff, A. Good, C., Points, P., et al. (eds.) *Attitudes Towards Europe: Language in the Unification Process*. Aldershot: Ashgate, pp. 3–22.

May, T. (2017). *The Government's Negotiating Objectives for Exiting the EU: PM Speech*. Available at: https://www.gov.uk/government/speeches/the-governments-negotiating-objectives-for-exiting-the-eu-pm-speech (Accessed: 28 April 2021).

McClements, F. (2022). NI survey shows half of voters support a united Ireland within 15–20 years. Available at: https://www.irishtimes.com/ireland/2022/08/21/ni-survey-shows-half-of-voters-support-a-united-ireland-within-15-20-years/ (Accessed: 24 October 2022).

McCrone, D. (1997). Unmasking Britannia: The rise and fall of British national identity. *Nations and Nationalism*, 3(4): 579–596.

McCrone, D. and Kiely, R. (2000). Nationalism and citizenship. *Sociology*, 34(1): 19–34.

Meredith, J. and Richardson, E. (2019). The use of the political categories of Brexiter and Remainer in online comments about the EU referendum. *Journal of Community & Applied Social Psychology*, 29(1): 43–55.

Miglbauer, M. and Koller, V. (2019). 'The British people have spoken': Voter motivations and identities in vox pops on the British EU referendum. In: Koller, V., Kopf, S. and Miglbauer, M. (eds.) *Discourses of Brexit*. London: Routledge, pp. 86–103.

Mintchev, N. (2021). The cultural politics of racism in the Brexit conjuncture. *International Journal of Cultural Studies*, 24(1): 123–140.

Moffitt, B. (2016). *The Global Rise of Populism: Performance, Political Style, and Representation*. Redwood City, CA: Stanford University Press.

Moffitt, B. and Tormey, S. (2014). Rethinking populism: Politics, mediatisation and political style. *Political Studies*, 62: 381–397.

Morris, D. (2021). *Skilled Worker Visa*. Available at: https://www.davidsonmorris.com/skilled-worker-visa/ (Accessed: 15 December 2021).

Morrison, J. (2019). *Essential Public Affairs for Journalists*. 6th ed. Oxford: Oxford University Press.

Morton, G. (2001). National identity: The Victorian and Edwardian era. In: Lynch, M. (ed.) *The Oxford Companion to Scottish History*. Oxford: Oxford University Press. Available at: https://www.oxfordreference.com/view/10.1093/acref/9780199234820.001.0001/acref-9780199234820-e-215 (Accessed: 8 October 2023).

Mulderrig, J. (2011). Manufacturing Consent: A corpus-based critical discourse analysis of New Labour's educational governance. *Educational Philosophy and Theory*, 43(6): 562–578.

Murray, I., Plagnol, A. and Corr, P. (2017). 'When things go wrong and people are afraid': An evaluation of group polarisation in the UK post Brexit. Available at SSRN 3041846: http://www.philipcorr.net/uploads/downloads/429.pdf (Accessed: 1 August 2023).

Musolff, A. (2017). Truths, lies and figurative scenarios: Metaphors at the heart of Brexit. *Journal of Language and Politics*, 16(5): 641–657.

Mycock, A. and Hayton, R. (2012). The party politics of Englishness. *The British Journal of Politics and International Relations*, 16(2): 251–272.

Nortio, E., Jasinskaja-Lahti, I., Hämäläinen, M., et al. (2022). Fear of the Russian bear? Negotiating Finnish national identity online. *Nations and Nationalism*, 28(3): 861–876..

O'Doherty, K. and Le Couteur, A. (2007). "Asylum seekers", "boat people" and "illegal immigrants": Social categorisation in the media. *Australian Journal of Psychology*, 59(1): 1–12.

O'Keeffe, A. (2012). Media and discourse analysis. In: Gee, J. and Handford, M. (eds.) *The Routledge Handbook of Discourse Analysis*. London: Routledge, pp. 441–454.

Oberhuber, F., Barenreuter, C., Krzyżanowski, M., et al. (2005). Debating the European constitution: On representations of Europe/the EU in the press. *Journal of Language and Politics*, 4(2): 227–271.

Ochs, E. (1992). Indexing gender. In: Duranti, A. and Goodwin, G. (eds.) *Rethinking Context: Language as an Interactive Phenomenon*. Cambridge: Cambridge University Press, pp. 335–358.

Ochs, E. and Capps, L. (2001). *Living Narrative: Creating Lives in Everyday Storytelling*. Cambridge, MA: Harvard University Press.

Oelsner, A. and Koschut, S. (2014). A framework for the study of international friendship. In: Koschut, S. and Oelsner, A. (eds.) *Friendship and International Relations*. Hampshire: Palgrave Macmillan, pp. 3–33.

Ofcom. (2017). *News Consumption in the UK: 2016*. Ofcom. Available at: https://www.ofcom.org.uk/__data/assets/pdf_file/0016/103570/news-consumption-uk-2016.pdf (Accessed: 15 December 2021).

Ofcom. (2021). *Section Five: Due impartiality and Due Accuracy*. Available at: https://www.ofcom.org.uk/tv-radio-and-on-demand/broadcast-codes/broadcast-code/section-five-due-impartiality-accuracy (Accessed: 13 May 2021).

Office for National Statistics. (2011). *2011 Census. Who We Are. How We Live. What We Do*. Available at: https://webarchive.nationalarchives.gov.uk/ukgwa/20160129062745/http://www.ons.gov.uk/ons/guide-method/census/2011/index.html (Accessed: 15 December 2021).

Office for National Statistics. (2015). *Migration Statistics Quarterly Report: November 2015*. ONS. Available at: https://www.ons.gov.uk/peoplepopulationandcommunity/populationandmigration/internationalmigration/bulletins/migrationstatisticsquarterlyreport/november2015 (Accessed: 28 April 2020).

Opinium. (2021, June 25). The political report. Available at: https://www.opinium.com/wp-content/uploads/2021/06/Opinium-Political-Report-25th-June-2021.pdf (Accessed: 12 January 2024).

Parekh, B. (2009). Defining British national identity. *The Political Quarterly*, 80(1): 251–262.

Parnell, T. (2021). Humiliating and dividing the nation in the British pro-Brexit press: A corpus-assisted analysis. *Critical Discourse Studies*, 20(1): 53–69.

Parnell, T. (2022a). 'Tinpot revolutionary agitation': Framing Brexit-related demonstrations in the British pro-Brexit press. *Critical Approaches to Discourse Analysis Across Disciplines*, 14(1): 45–62.

Parnell, T. (2022b). The representation of migrant identities in UK Government documents about Brexit. A corpus-assisted analysis. *Journal of Language and Politics*, 22(1): 46–65.

Parnell, T. (2022c). Unravelling the Global Britain vision? International relationships and national identity in UK government documents about Brexit, 2016–2019. *Discourse & Society*, 33(3): 391–410.

Parnell, T. (2023). 'A tide of homeless, drug-addicted and mentally ill people': Representing homeless people in MailOnline content. *Journal of Corpora and Discourse Studies*, 6: 1–24.

Parnell, T. (Forthcoming). '"Don't let 'em hear us speaking English": Constructing national and Brexit-related identities in oral interviews. In: Tyler, K., Banducci, S. and Degnen, C. (eds.) *Reflections on Polarisation and Inequalities in Brexit Pandemic Times*. London: Routledge.

Parnell, T., van Hout, T. and Del Fante, D. (eds.) (Forthcoming). *Critical Approaches to Polycrisis: Discourses of Conflict, Migration, Risk and Finance*. London: Palgrave Macmillan.

Partington, A., Duguid, A. and Taylor, C. (2013). *Patterns and Meaning in Discourse: Theory and Practice in Corpus-Assisted Discourse Studies (CADS)*. Studies in Corpus Linguistics 55. Amsterdam: John Benjamins.

Patel, T. G. and Connelley, L. (2019). "Post-race" racisms in the narratives of "Brexit" voters. *The Sociological Review*, 67(5): 968–984.

Peden, G. C. (2012). Suez and Britain's decline as a world power. *The Historical Journal*, 55(4): 1073–1096.

Pérez-Paredes, P., Aguado Jiménez, P. and Sánchez Hernández, S. (2016). Constructing immigrants in UK legislation and Administration informative texts: A corpus-driven study (2007–2011). *Discourse & Society*, 28(1): 81–103.

Pojanapunya, P. and Watson Todd, R. (2018). Log-likelihood and odds ratio: Keyness statistics for different purposes of keyword analysis. *Corpus Linguistics and Linguistic Theory*, 14(1): 133–167.

Potts, A. (2015). Filtering the flood: Semantic tagging as a method of identifying salient discourse topics in a large corpus of Hurricane Katrina reportage. In: Baker, P. and McEnery, T. (eds.) *Corpora and Discourse Studies - Integrating Discourse and Corpora*. Hampshire: Palgrave Macmillan, pp. 285–304.

Preece, S. (2016). Introduction: Language and identity in applied linguistics. In: Preece, S. (ed.) *The Routledge Handbook of Language and Identity*. London: Routledge, pp. 1–16.

Prentice, S. (2010). Using automated semantic tagging in critical discourse analysis: A case study on Scottish independence from a Scottish nationalist perspective. *Discourse & Society*, 21(4): 405–437.

Pritchard, A. E. (2016). Brexit vote is about the supremacy of Parliament and nothing else. *The Telegraph*, 13 June. Available at: https://www.telegraph.co.uk/business/2016/06/12/brexit-vote-is-about-the-supremacy-of-parliament-and-nothing-els/ (Accessed: 18 May 2020).

Raab, D. (2019). *A Truly Global Future Awaits Us After Brexit: Article by Dominic Raab*. Available at: https://www.gov.uk/government/speeches/a-truly-global-future-awaits-us-after-brexit-dominic-raab (Accessed: 15 December 2021).

Radziwinowiczówna, A. and Galasińska, A. (2021). 'The Vile Eastern European': Ideology of deportability in the Brexit media discourse. *Central and Eastern European Migration Review*, 10(1): 75–93.

Räikkönen, J. (2022). Are 'we' European? We and us in British EU-related newspaper articles in 1975–2015. *Journal of Corpora and Discourse Studies*, 5(1): 1–25.

Rayson, P. (2008). From key words to key semantic domains. *International Journal of Corpus Linguistics*, 13(4): 519–549.

Rayson, P., Archer, D., Piao, S., et al. (2004). The UCREL semantic analysis system. In *Proceedings of the Workshop on Beyond Named Entity Recognition Semantic labelling for NLP Tasks in Association with 4th International Conference on Language Resources and Evaluation (LREC 2004)*, pp. 7–12.

Richards, L. and Heath, A. (2023). How divided is Britain? Symbolic boundaries and social cohesion in post-Brexit Britain. *PS: Political Science & Politics, First View*, 56(4): 553–559.

Richards, L., Heath, A. and Elgenius, G. (2020). Remainers are nostalgic too: An exploration of attitudes towards the past and Brexit preferences. *The British Journal of Sociology*, 71(1): 74–80.

Riessman, C. K. (2008). *Narrative Methods for the Human Sciences*. London: Sage.

Ringeisen-Biardeaud, J. (2017). "Let's take back control": Brexit and the debate on sovereignty. *French Journal of British Studies*, 22(2): 1–17.

Risse, T. (2004). European institutions and identity change: What have we learned? In: Herrmann, R., Brewer, M. and Risse, T. (eds.) *Identities in Europe and the Institutions of the European Union*. Lanham: Rowman & Littlefield, pp. 247–272.

Roberts, A. (2018). *With Europe, But Not of It*. 17 February. Available at: https://www.spectator.co.uk/article/with-europe-but-not-of-it (Accessed: 31 August 2021).

Rone, J. (2022). Instrumentalising sovereignty claims in British pro- and anti-Brexit mobilisations. *The British Journal of Politics and International Relations*, 25(3): 444–461..

Roshchin, E. (2011). Friendship of the enemies: Twentieth century treaties of the United Kingdom and the USSR. *International Politics*, 48(1): 71–91.

Rowinski, P. (2017). *Evolving Euroscepticisms in the British and Italian Press: Selling the Public Short*. Switzerland: Palgrave Macmillan.

Saunders, R. (2020). Brexit and Empire: 'Global Britain' and the myth of imperial nostalgia. *The Journal of Imperial and Commonwealth History*, 48(6): 1140–1174.

Saurugger, S. (2013). Constructivism and public policy approaches in the EU: from ideas to power games. *Journal of European Public Policy*, 20(6): 888–906.

Schlesinger, P. (1991). Media, the political order and national identity. *Media, Culture & Society*, 13(3): 297–308.

Schrøder, K. C. (2018). Audience reception research in a post-broadcasting digital age. *Television & New Media*, 20(2): 155–169.

Scott, M. (1999). *WordSmith Tools Help Manual*. Oxford: Mike Scott and Oxford University Press.

Scottish Government. (2017). *Scotland Must Have Choice Over Future*. Available at: https://news.gov.scot/news/scotland-must-have-choice-over-future (Accessed: 6 July 2020).

Searle, J. R. (1979). *Expression and Meaning: Studies in the Theory of Speech Acts*. Cambridge: Cambridge University Press.

Semino, E., Deignan, A. and Littlemore, J. (2013). Metaphor, genre, and recontextualization. *Metaphor and Symbol*, 28(1): 41–59.

Shackleton, M. (2016). Britain in Brussels after the Referendum: Insider or outsider? *Journal of Contemporary European Research*, 12(4): 816–823.

Shoemaker, P., Lee, J. H., Han, G. and Cohen, A. A. (2007). Proximity and scope as news values. In: Devereux, E. (ed.) *Media Studies: Key Issues and Debates*. London: Sage, pp. 231–248.

Siles-Brügge, G. (2019). Bound by gravity or living in a "post geography trading world"? Expert knowledge and affective spatial imaginaries in the construction of the UK's post-Brexit trade policy. *New Political Economy*, 24(3): 422–439.

Skey, M. (2011). 'Sod them, I'm English': The changing status of the 'majority' English in post-devolution Britain. *Ethnicities*, 12(1): 106–125.

Smith, A. (1991). *National Identity*. Reno: University of Nevada Press.

Smith, A. (1992). National identity and the idea of European unity. *International Affairs*, 68(1): 55–76.

Smith, F. (2016). Britishness and Brexit. In: Jackson, D. and Thorsen, E. (eds.) *EU Referendum Analysis 2016: Media, Voters and the Campaign. Early Reflections from Leading UK Academics*. Bournemouth: Bournemouth University, p. 64.

Sobolewska, M. and Robert, F. (2020). *Brexitland*. Cambridge: Cambridge University Press.

Spiering, M. (2014). *A Cultural History of British Euroscepticism*. Hampshire: Palgrave Macmillan.

Stubbs, M. (2001). British traditions in text analysis: From Firth to Sinclair. In: Baker, M., Francis, F. and Tognini-Bonelli, T. (eds.) *Text and Technology: In Honour of John Sinclair*. Amsterdam: John Benjamins, pp. 1–36.

Sumner, W. G. (1906). *Folkways: A Study of the Sociological Importance of Usages, Manners, Customs, Mores, and Morals*. Boston, MA: Ginn and Company.

Swales, K. (2016). Understanding the leave vote. London: NatCen Social Research.

Sykes, O. (2018). Post-geography worlds, new dominions, left behind regions, and 'other' places: Unpacking some spatial imaginaries of the UK's 'Brexit' debate. *Space & Polity*, 22(2): 137–161.

Tabachnik, M. (2019). Untangling liberal democracy from territoriality: from ethnic/civic to ethnic/territorial nationalism. *Nations and Nationalism*, 25(1): 191–207.

Taylor, C. (2018). Representing the Windrush generation: Metaphor I discourses then and now. *Critical Discourse Studies*, 17(1): 1–21.

Teubert, W. (2001). A province of a federal superstate, ruled by an unelected bureaucracy - Keywords on the Euro-sceptic discourse in Britain. In: Musolff, A., Good, C., Points, P., et al. (eds.) *Attitudes Towards Europe: Language in the Unification Process*. Aldershot: Ashgate, pp. 45–86.

Thatcher, M. (1988). *Speech to the College of Europe ("The Bruges Speech")*. Available at: https://www.margaretthatcher.org/document/107332 (Accessed: 15 December 2021).

The Sun. (2016). It's The Sun wot swung it. Our paper led the fight against the EU and had the strongest influence on people voting for Leave. Available at: https://www.thesun.co.uk/news/1338543/our-paper-led-the-fight-against-the-eu-and-had-the-strongest-influence-on-people-voting-for-leave/ (Accessed: 13 January 2024).

The Telegraph. (2016). If this Thursday's referendum is a choice between fear and hope, then we choose hope. Available at: https://www.telegraph.co.uk/opinion/2016/05/27/the-eu-bureaucrats-cannot-cope-with-democracy/ (Accessed: 13 January 2024).

The Telegraph. (2016). The EU bureaucrats cannot cope with democracy. *The Telegraph*, 27 May. Available at: https://www.telegraph.co.uk/opinion/2016/05/27/the-eu-bureaucrats-cannot-cope-with-democracy/ (Accessed: 18 May 2020).

Thommessen, L. S. (2017). "Othering" the "left behind"? A critical discourse analysis of the representation of leave voters in British broadsheet coverage of the EU referendum. In: Cammaerts, B., Anstead, N. and Stupart, R. (eds.) Media@LSE Working Paper Series. London: London School of Economics and Political Science, n.p.

Thomas, R. J. and Antony, M. G. (2015). Competing constructions of British national identity: British newspaper comment on the 2012 Olympics opening ceremony. *Media, Culture & Society*, 37(3): 493–503.

Thompson, G. (2013). *Introducing Functional Grammar*. 3rd ed. Routledge.

Thornborrow, J., Haarman, L. and Duguid, A. (2012). Discourses of European identity in British, Italian, and French TV news. In: Bayley, P. and Williams, G. (eds.) *European Identity: What the Media Say*. Oxford: Oxford University Press, pp. 84–116.

Toynbee, P. and Walker, D. (2020). *The Lost Decade: 2010–2020, and What Lies Ahead for Britain*. London: Guardian Books.

Tranter, B. and Donoghue, J. (2021). Embodying Britishness: National identity in the United Kingdom. *Nations and Nationalism*, 27(4): 992–1008.

Trentmann, F. (2008). *Free Trade Nation: Commerce, Consumption and Civil Society in Modern Britain*. Oxford: Oxford University Press.

Triandafyllidou, A. (1998). National identity and the "other." *Ethnic and Racial Studies*, 21(4): 593–612.

Trudgill, P. (1974). *The Social Differentiation of English in Norwich*. Cambridge: Cambridge University Press.

Tyler, K., Degnan, C. and Blamire, J. (2022). Leavers and remainers as 'kinds of people': Accusations of racism amidst Brexit. *Ethnos*, 1–18.

UCL. (2021). *Brexit Driven by Cultural Values and National Identity More Than Social Class*. Available at: https://www.ucl.ac.uk/ioe/news/2021/feb/brexit-driven-cultural-values-and-national-identity-more-social-class (Accessed: 11 December 2021).

UCREL. (1998). *The British National Corpus Sampler Corpus: Explanatory Documentation*. Available at: http://ucrel.lancs.ac.uk/bnc2sampler/sampler.htm (Accessed: 28 April 2021).

UK in a Changing Europe. (2020a). *What Would No Deal Mean?* London: King's College London. Available at: https://ukandeu.ac.uk/wp-content/uploads/2020/09/UKICE-What-would-no-deal-mean.pdf (Accessed: 16 November 2020).

UK in a Changing Europe. (2020b). *What Is a Hard Brexit?* Available at: https://ukandeu.ac.uk/the-facts/what-is-hard-brexit/ (Accessed: 16 May 2022).

UK Government. (2019). Global Britain: Delivering on our international ambition. Available at: https://www.gov.uk/government/collections/global-britain-delivering-on-our-international-ambition (Accessed: 12 January 2024).

UK Parliament. (2018). The 'meaningful vote': A user's guide. Available at: https://commonslibrary.parliament.uk/the-meaningful-vote-a-users-guide/#:~:text=In%20its%20narrow%20sense%2C%20the,Government%20and%20the%20EU%27s%20negotiators (Accessed: 10 January 2024).

UK Parliament. (2022). The 'meaningful vote': A user's guide. Available at: https://commonslibrary.parliament.uk/the-meaningful-vote-a-users-guide/ (Accessed: 2 May 2022).

UNESCO. (n.d.). The soft power of culture. Available at: http://www.unesco.org/culture/culture-sector-knowledge-management-tools/11_Info%20Sheet_Soft%20Power.pdf (Accessed: 22 November 2022).

Valluvan, S. (2019). *The Clamour of Nationalism. Race and Nation in Twenty-First-Century Britain*. Manchester: Manchester University Press.

Van De Mieroop, D. (2021). The Narrative Dimensions Model and an exploration of various narrative genres. *Narrative Inquiry*, 31(1): 4–27.

van Dijk, T. (1992). Discourse and the denial of racism. *Discourse & Society*, 3(1): 87–118.

van Dijk, T. (1997). What is political discourse analysis? *Political Linguistics*, 11: 11–52.

van Dijk, T. (2010). Political identities in parliamentary debates. In: Ilie, C. (ed.) *European Parliaments Under Scrutiny. Discourse Strategies and Interaction Practices*. Amsterdam: John Benjamins, n.p.

van Dijk, T. (2015). Critical discourse analysis. In: Tannen, D., Hamilton, H. and Schiffrin, D. (eds.) *The Handbook of Discourse Analysis.* 2nd ed. John Wiley & Sons, pp. 466–485.

van Leeuwen, T. (1995). The representation of social actors. In: Caldas-Coulthard, C. R. and Coulthard, M. (eds.) *Texts and Practices: Readings in Critical Discourse Analysis.* London: Routledge, pp. 32–70.

van Leeuwen, T. (2007). Legitimation in discourse and communication. *Discourse & Communication,* 1(1): 91–112.

van Leeuwen, T. (2008). *Discourse and Practice: New Tools for Critical Discourse Analysis.* Oxford: Oxford University Press.

van Leeuwen, T. and Wodak, R. (1999). Legitimizing immigration control: A discourse-historical analysis. *Discourse Studies,* 1(1): 83–118.

Virdee, S. and McGeever, B. (2023). *Britain in Fragments. Why Things Are Falling Apart.* Manchester: Manchester University Press.

Vote Leave. (2016). *Why Should I Vote Leave.* Available at: http://www.voteleaveta kecontrol.org/why_vote_leave.html (Accessed: 23 July 2021).

Wahl-Jorgensen, K. (2018). Toward a typology of mediated anger: Routine coverage of protest and political emotion. *International Journal of Communication,* 12: 2071–2087.

Walker, N. (2021). *Brexit Timeline: Events Leading to the UK's Exit from the European Union.* 7960. London: House of Commons Library.

Walker, P. (2020). *Reneging on Brexit Deal Would strengthen Case for Breaking up UK, Government Told.* 7 September. Available at: https://www.theguardian.com/politics/2020/sep/07/reneging-on-brexit-deal-would-strengthen-case-for-breaking-up-uk-government-told (Accessed: 14 December 2021).

Watkins, J. (2015). Spatial imaginaries research in geography: Synergies, tensions and new directions. *Geography Compass,* 9(9): 508–522.

Wellings, B. (2010). Losing the peace: Euroscepticism and the foundations of contemporary English nationalism. *Nations and Nationalism,* 16(3): 488–505.

Wenzl, N. (2019). "This is about the kind of Britain we are": National identities as constructed in parliamentary debates about EU membership. In: Koller, V., Kopf, S. and Miglbauer, M. (eds.) *Discourses of Brexit.* London: Routledge, pp. 32–47.

Wenzl, N. (2020). "There is a wonderfully contrary spirit among the British people": Conservative MPs' (un)successful branding of the British nation in the Brexit debate. In: Theodoropoulou, I. and Tovar, J. (eds.) *Research Companion to Language and Country Branding.* Taylor & Francis, pp. 72–89.

Westlake, M. (2017). The increasing inevitability of that referendum. In: Outhwaite, W. (ed.) *Brexit: Sociological Responses.* London: Anthem Press.

Whigham, S. (2019). Nationalism, party political discourse and Scottish independence: Comparing discursive visions of Scotland's constitutional status. *Nations and Nationalism,* 25(4): 1212–1237.

Wikström, P. (2016). No one is 'pro-politically correct: Positive construals of political correctness in Twitter conversations. *Nordic Journal of English Studies*, 15(2): 159–170.

Wilkinson, M. (2019). 'Bisexual oysters': A diachronic corpus-based critical discourse analysis of bisexual people in *The Times* between 1957 and 2017. *Discourse & Communication*, 13(2): 249–267.

Williams, G. and Piazza, R. (2012). Nation and supernation: A tale of three Europes. In: Bayley, P. and Williams, G. (eds.) *European Identity: What the Media Say*. Oxford: Oxford University Press, pp. 55–83.

Wincott, D. (2019). Brexit and the state of the United Kingdom. In: Diamond, P., Nedergaard, P. and Rosamond, B. (eds.) *The Routledge Handbook of the Politics of Brexit*. London: Routledge, pp. 15–26.

Winder, R. (2018). After Brexit, England will have to rethink its identity. *The Guardian*, 8 January. Available at: https://www.theguardian.com/commentisfree/2018/jan/08/brexit-england-rethink-identity-nation (Accessed: 17 April 2020).

Wodak, R. (2001a). The discourse historical approach. In: Wodak, R. and Meyer, M. (eds.) *Methods of Critical Discourse Analysis*. London: Sage, pp. 63–94.

Wodak, R. (2018). 'We have the character of an island nation': A discourse-historical approach to David Cameron's 'Bloomberg speech' on the European Union. In: Kranert, M. and Horan, G. (eds.) *Doing Politics: Discursivity, Performativity and Mediation in Political Discourse*. Netherlands: John Benjamins, pp. 27–58.

Wodak, R., De Cillia, R., Reisigl, M., et al. (2009). *The Discursive Construction of National Identity*. 2nd ed. Edinburgh: Edinburgh University Press.

Woollen, C. (2022). The space between leave and remain: Archetypal positions of British parliamentarians on Brexit. *British Politics*, 17: 97–116.

Wortham, S. (2001). *Narrative in Action – A Strategy for Research and Analysis*. London: Teachers College, Columbia University.

Yang, K. Y. (2018). A comparative analysis of the two different framing strategies of Brexit: Exemplified by the speeches of David Cameron and Theresa May. *Open Journal of Modern Linguistics*, 8: 71–86.

YouGov. (2016). *How Britain Voted at the EU Referendum*. Available at: https://yougov.co.uk/topics/politics/articles-reports/2016/06/27/how-britain-voted (Accessed: 8 August 2023).

YouGov. (2018). *Which Do You Feel Is the Greater Threat to the West?* Available at: https://yougov.co.uk/topics/politics/survey-results/daily/2018/02/23/2ba80/1 (Accessed: 8 August 2023).

Zappettini, F. (2018). *European Identities in Discourse: A Transnational Citizens' Perspective*. London: Bloomsbury.

Zappettini, F. (2019). The official vision for 'global Britain': Brexit as rupture and continuity between free trade, liberal internationalism and 'values'. In: Koller, V., Kopf, S. and Miglbauer, M. (eds.) *Discourses of Brexit*. London: Routledge, pp. 140–154.

Zappettini, F. (2021). The UK as victim and heroin the Sun's coverage of the Brexit 'humiliation'. *Russian Journal of Linguistics*, 25(3): 645–662.

Zappettini, F. and Krzyżanowski, M. (2019). The critical juncture of Brexit in media & political discourses: From national-populist imaginary to cross-national social and political crisis. *Critical Discourse Studies*, 16(4): 381–388.

Zappettini, F. and Unerman, J. (2016). 'Mixing' and 'Bending': The recontextualisation of discourses of sustainability in integrated reporting. *Discourse & Communication*, 10(5): 521–542.

Zürn, M. and de Wilde, P. (2016). Debating globalization: Cosmopolitanism and communitarianism as political ideologies. *Journal of Political Ideologies*, 21(3): 280–301.

Appendix A

Media Corpora Composition

Table A.1 Composition of overall media corpus

Publication	Number of Articles	Percentage of Media Corpus
Express Online	2,883	43.05
Telegraph Online	1,353	20.21
MailOnline	893	13.34
Daily Telegraph	555	8.29
The Sun	260	3.9
Daily Mail	265	4.0
The Sun Online	238	3.55
The Express	165	2.47
Daily Star Online	74	1.11
Daily Star	12	0.18

Table A.2 Composition of media corpus

Publication	No. of Articles (2016)	Percentage of 2016 Corpus	No. of Articles (2017)	Percentage of 2017 Corpus	No. of Articles (2018)	Percentage of 2018 Corpus	No. of Articles (2019)	Percentage of 2019 Corpus
Express Online	262	35.74	204	49.51	135	38.03	136	38.86
Telegraph Online	166	22.65	74	17.96	55	15.49	72	20.57
MailOnline	124	16.92	61	14.81	50	14.08	48	13.71
Daily Telegraph	65	8.87	27	6.55	33	9.3	24	6.86
The Sun	38	5.18	17	4.13	16	4.51	18	5.14
Daily Mail	27	3.68	16	3.88	19	5.35	16	4.57
The Sun Online	0	0	0	0	36	10.14	22	6.29
The Express	17	2.32	5	1.21	9	2.54	8	2.29
Daily Star Online	31	4.23	8	1.94	2	0.56	4	1.14
Daily Star	2	0.27	0	0	0	0	2	0.52

Appendix B

Interview Plan

Personal section

This section involves questions about the person's relationship with the local/national community – have they always lived here? Have they ever lived abroad? Are they part of any local community groups or national online groups? This section is about identifying potential influences on later responses (e.g. having lived in Europe might strengthen/weaken ties to European identity). It is also about relaxing the interviewee and helping them to feel settled before later questions.

Tell me about yourself and your relationship to the area you're currently living in. Did you always live here, or have you moved here recently?

Are you part of any face-to-face or online groups through which you interact with people in your area?

Would you say you feel a connection to the area in which you live?

Have you ever lived abroad for an extended period of time (either to study, work or for retirement)? If so, where did you live? If not, is this something you would consider?

Can you tell me which way you voted in the EU referendum?

Have you come across any other people who voted like you in Nottingham?

What about people who voted differently from you – have you had any encounters with people who voted to Leave?

Nottinghamshire voted in the majority to Leave the EU. Do you have any thoughts about why this might be?

National identity

This section will be about the person's conceptualization of national identity, what it means to them, what characteristics they associate with their national identity and how much of a role national identity plays in their daily interactions.

What nationality or nationalities do you feel that you belong to?

What do you think makes you this nationality? Are there any things about you that make you X?

Are there any events or experiences you've had that have shaped the way you feel about your national identity? (Prompt: any times where you've felt particularly more X?)

Do you feel attached or connected to this identity emotionally?

Where, if anywhere, do you feel your attachment most strongly – your regional identity in Nottingham, England, Britain?

Would your national identity figure in how you define yourself as a person?

Do you think there are any characteristics of being a British national?

Do you think these characteristics are unique to your nation or do you think they are likely to be characteristics of other nationalities too?

Have you become more aware of your national identity since the EU referendum or is this something you haven't thought about?

What kind of attitudes towards national identity have you experienced in Nottingham?

European identity

This section will be about European identity, attitudes towards Europe and the EU and what has potentially shaped those attitudes.

What does 'Europe' mean to you?

Do you think of Europe as different to the EU?

Do you identify/have you ever on any level as European?

What is your attitude towards Europe as a geographical place?

Is that attitude different to or the same as your attitude towards the EU?

Are there any particular events or experiences you've had that you think have shaped your view of Europe and the EU?

What kinds of attitudes towards Europe have you experienced in Nottingham?

The EU membership referendum (for British/Irish/Commonwealth respondents)

This section will investigate the relationship between the vote cast by the respondent and their conceptualizations of national and European identity. It considers potential sources of information about the referendum that may have contributed to the vote, and about the extent to which 'Brexit' and national identity have become part of participants' daily interactions since the EU referendum.

You voted to X: to what extent did national identity play a part in how you decided to vote?

How did you make your decision to vote X? Did you consult any materials about the referendum?

Do you think the referendum made you think more about your national identity, European identities and other international identities than before?

Is the referendum/Brexit something you have talked to friends and family about? (If so, what kind of discussions have you had? Have they been positive or negative? If not, why not?)

What about national identity – have you talked to your friends and family about that?

What kind of ideas or arguments were important to you during the referendum campaign?

Here's an extract from a government document talking about British and European identities and the relationship between them. Take as long as you need to read it.

This section will involve asking the participant to read and respond to conceptualizations of national identity in government discourse. It asks them to reflect on the extent to which their own attitudes align with or diverge from those expressed by the government.

What are your thoughts on the way that Theresa May describes Britain?

Does this seem similar to the way you see Britain, or does it seem different?

Have these kinds of ideas of Britishness come up in your conversations with people you know/people you've met?

Do you think they're quite common or not very common attitudes based on your experience?

What are your thoughts on the way that the government represents Europe?

Does this seem similar to the way you see Europe, or does it seem different?

Have these kinds of ideas of Europeanness come up in your conversations with people you know/people you've met?

Do you think they're quite common or not very common attitudes based on your experience?

Here's an extract from an article published by *The Telegraph* newspaper, talking about British and European identities and the relationship between them. Take as long as you need to read it.

This section will involve asking the participant to read and respond to conceptualizations of national identity in media discourse. It asks them to reflect on the extent to which their own attitudes align or diverge from those expressed by the pro-Brexit press.

What are your thoughts on the way that this newspaper represents British national identity?

Does this seem similar to the way you see Britain, or does it seem different?

Have these kinds of ideas of Britishness come up in your conversations with people you know/people you've met?

Do you think they're quite common or not very common attitudes based on your experience?

What are your thoughts on the way that this newspaper represents European identity?

Does this seem similar to the way you see Europe, or does it seem different?

Have these kinds of ideas of Europeanness come up in your conversations with people you know/people you've met?

Do you think they're quite common or not very common attitudes based on your experience?

Index

anecdote 64–6, 152, 154

Brexiteer 17, 91, 98–100, 104, 105
British
   exceptionalism
      in Cameron's speeches 31
      definitions 30
      in government documents 112, 117, 168, 176
      in the pro-Brexit press 82, 83, 87
   history
      in government documents 110–12, 118
      in oral interviews 135–9
      in politics 28–30
      in press 31–2
      in the pro-Brexit press 77–9
      in public narratives 27
      in public opinion 32
   values
      in government documents 113, 117
      in oral interviews 146
      in press and politics 31–2
      in the pro-Brexit press 79–84
      in public narratives 27, 29, 30
      in public opinion 32
Britishness 26–8
   in press, politics, and public opinion 28–33
bureaucracy
   allegations that the EU is bureaucratic 19, 31, 36, 37
   in citizen discourse 39
   in the pro-Brexit press 71, 74, 75, 93, 173, 174

Cameron, David
   Bloomberg speech 27, 28, 37, 168
   other speeches 31, 38
   in the pro-Brexit press 92
   role in Brexit 2, 3, 157
   talking about the nation 79

Cap, P.
   on British history 29
   on discourses of difference 167
   on the Leave campaign 83
   on Parliamentary discourse 182
   quoting Farage 28, 38, 91
collocation 9–10, 44, 58, 59
critical discourse analysis 7–9

Daddow, O. 31, 107, 112, 114, 131, 183
Daily Express
   corpus composition 46, 49
   in the EU referendum 42, 43
   in the pro-Brexit press 71, 75, 76, 81, 87–9, 91, 95–7, 99, 101, 102, 104, 167, 169, 175, 219, 220
Daily Mail
   corpus composition 46–9, 219–20
   euromyths in 31
   in the pro-Brexit press 71–2, 75–6, 81, 86, 92–4, 175
   readers of 56
   role in Brexit 43–4
Daily Star 44, 48, 219, 220
Daily Telegraph
   corpus composition 44, 46–7, 49, 219–20
   in the pro-Brexit press 80–2, 87, 89, 94–6, 99–101, 168–9
   readers of 56
   role in Brexit 44
Davis, David
   quotations from 108–9, 115–16, 118–19, 124–7
   resignation 3, 47
de Fina, A. 11, 66, 67
discourse 6–8
   and identities 12–14
   and nation 14–15
division
   in the Conservative party 2
   in government documents 116, 117, 128–31

in oral interviews   150–1, 161
in the pro-Brexit press   98–105
as a theme   169–72, 177, 180–4, 188

ethics   54–5
Euroscepticism
   in British politics   2, 27–33, 53
   in government documents   118, 128
   in oral interviews   135, 150
   in the press   36–7
   in the pro-Brexit press   73, 74, 79, 88, 91
exemplum
   definition   64–5
   in oral interviews   136, 139, 140, 143, 145, 157–8

Farage, Nigel   28, 91, 93–4

global Britain
   constructed by government   27, 107
   constructed by Raab   16
   in government documents   114, 117, 120, 123, 128–31
   for Leave voters   169, 172
   spatial imaginary   138
The Guardian   35, 36, 42, 56, 97, 102

identities   12–13
   and Brexit   16–20
   Brexit-related   33–5
   British   26–8 (*see also* Britishness)
   European   25, 35–9
   and narratives   11–12
immigration
   anti-immigration   142, 145, 146, 148
   in the EU referendum campaign   18–19
   Farage's representations of   37–8
   illegal   114, 120
   in Nottingham   155–6
   and Remainers   90–1
   securitization of   73
   as a threat   110
indexicality   12, 13, 67–8, 137, 140, 145

Johnson, Boris
   colonial rhetoric   29
   dangerous language   97
   in government documents   115, 116, 124–9

metaphor   38
   as prime minister   181, 188
   role in EU referendum   3, 5, 19, 43, 45, 47
Juncker, Jean-Claude   92–3, 127

key semantic domain analysis   57–62
keywords   9–10, 36, 58

Leaver
   in oral interviews   143, 146, 151, 164
   as a political identity   3, 17, 20, 33–4
   in the pro-Brexit press   82, 84, 98–102, 105
log ratio   60–1, 69, 80, 85, 108, 121
log-likelihood   60, 70, 80, 85, 108, 121

Maccaferri, M.   27, 31, 42–3, 95, 168, 182
May, Theresa
   in government documents   109–12, 115, 118–19, 124–5, 168
   in oral interviews   135, 143, 189
   in the pro-Brexit press   75–8, 94–6, 104, 169
   role in the Brexit process   3–4
metaphor
   broaden horizons   128
   Brussels machine   88
   conceptual   82, 94, 99, 120
   cross-pollination   116
   David Davis's   118–19
   definition of discourse   6
   family   121
   international relationships   38–9
   onward movement   131

narrative
   analysis of   133–66
   definitions   10–12
   story genres   64–8
nation   14–16
   British Island   27, 28, 112, 168
   global trading   29, 107
   in government documents   116, 119–21, 129, 131, 132, 169
   invaded   30, 72, 74–5, 102, 173
   in oral interviews   135, 138, 169
   sovereign   30
   as a theme   177–9
nationalism   14–15

observation   64–6, 136–7, 142–5

Raab, Dominic
   as Brexit secretary   4, 47
   global Britain   16
   in government documents   118–20, 126–8
recontextualization
   definitions   7–8, 24
   examples of   29
   in oral interviews   144, 146
   in the pro-Brexit press   72, 90, 92, 94, 100
recount   64–6, 138, 152, 161
Remainer
   in oral interviews   133, 141, 142, 146, 151, 176, 187
   political identity   3, 17, 20, 33–4
   in the pro-Brexit press   69, 80, 82, 84, 90, 91, 98–101, 104, 105, 171
Retrotopian   77, 136, 139, 163, 169

Scotland
   and Britishness   26–8, 175
   and division   150, 157
   EU referendum vote   3
   fishers   11
   independence   6, 16, 23, 71, 75–8, 80, 84, 180, 182, 187
   and nationalism   32, 59, 103
sovereignty
   in the British press   27–31, 36, 37
   definition   18–19
   in government documents   112, 114
   in the pro-Brexit press   71
Sturgeon, Nicola   3, 6, 75–7
Suez
   and decline   168–9, 182
   and history   174
   and Jo Johnson   95–6
   in narratives of Britishness   27
The Sun
   corpus composition   48–9, 219–20
   gangsterism   92

Leave campaign   43
   in oral interviews   142
   quotations from   96, 97
   readers of   56

tolerance
   as a British value   31, 79
   as an EU value   35, 80, 82, 84
   for interviewer   187
   and Leavers   143, 144, 146, 170

van Leeuwen, T.   7, 9, 63, 67
   association   90
   authorization   102
   collectivization   142, 144, 153, 182
   functionalization   92
   mythopoesis   135
   naturalization   116
   suppression   113, 146, 164
ventriloquation   67, 143, 160, 179
Vote Leave
   and Boris Johnson   43
   campaign   2–3
   and global Britain   169, 179, 180
   and immigration   18
   and metaphor   38
   sign new deals   119
   and sovereignty   19
   Take Back Control   114, 146

Wenzl, N.   19, 20, 29, 37
Wmatrix   57–60

Zappettini. F.
   on Britain Stronger in Europe   2
   on the Department of International Trade   29, 30, 177
   on the European Commission   37
   on Europeanness   25
   on Euroscepticism   150
   on gangsterism   92
   on identity   163, 167, 176
   on internationalist Britain   128
   on migrants   73
   on recontexualization   8

www.ingramcontent.com/pod-product-compliance
Lightning Source LLC
Chambersburg PA
CBHW071829300426
44116CB00009B/1485